SCHWEITZER

Books by George Marshall

CHURCH OF THE PILGRIM FATHERS
AN UNDERSTANDING OF ALBERT SCHWEITZER
CHALLENGE OF A LIBERAL FAITH

By David Poling

THE LAST YEARS OF THE CHURCH

44

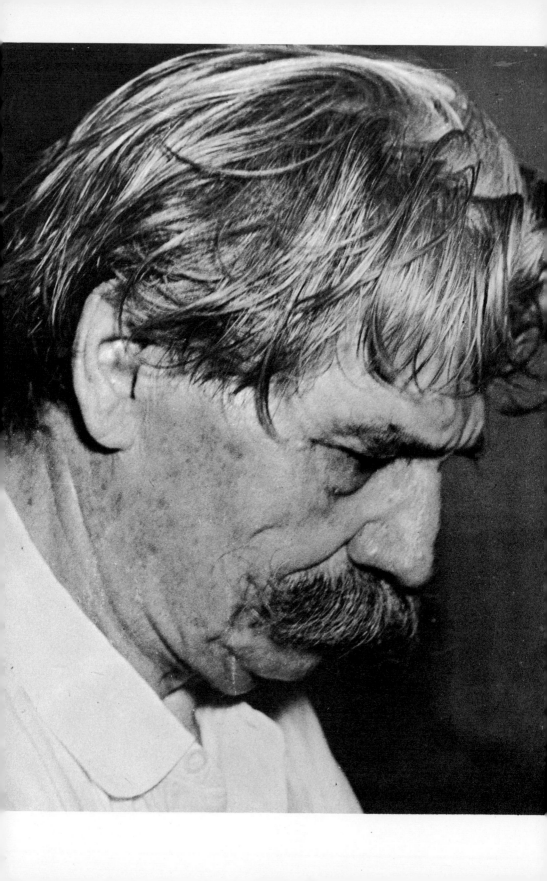

SCHWEITZER

A BIOGRAPHY BY GEORGE MARSHALL
AND DAVID POLING

DOUBLEDAY & COMPANY, INC., GARDEN CITY, NEW YORK

921 (Schweitzer)

To Our Favorite Young People—
Charles and Peggy Marshall
John, Lesley, Andrew and Charles Poling

PHOTO CREDITS

Copyright Erica Anderson, Albert Schweitzer
Friendship House, Great Barrington, Massachusetts:
frontispiece and photos 1–9, 12–22, and 24–26
Hans Steiner: photo 23

Library of Congress Catalog Card Number 71–130888

Acknowledgments

Grateful acknowledgment is made to those who have given permission to reproduce the following material:

Excerpts from *Goethe: Five Studies* by Albert Schweitzer and *Indian Thought And Its Development* by Albert Schweitzer. Reprinted by permission of Beacon Press;

Excerpt from *The Words* by Jean-Paul Sartre, translated from the French by Bernard Frechtman. Copyright © 1964 by Editions Gallimards. English translation copyright © 1964 by George Braziller, Inc. Reprinted by permission of George Braziller, Inc., and Hamish Hamilton, London;

Excerpt from *The Hospital At Lambaréné During The War Years* by Albert Schweitzer, Letter from Mrs. Helene Schweitzer to Magnus Ratter, Two letters from Albert Schweitzer to Albert Einstein, Letter from Albert Schweitzer to Einstein's niece, Letter from Albert Schweitzer to George Marshall (February 15, 1965), Letter from Albert Schweitzer to Dr. A. A. Roback (February, 1965). Reprinted by permission of Rhena Eckert-Schweitzer;

Excerpt from two letters to Dr. Albert Schweitzer from Albert Einstein. Reprinted by permission of the Estate of Albert Einstein;

Excerpt from *Men of Dialogue: Martin Buber and Albrecht Goes*, edited by E. Williams Rollins and Harry Zohn. Published by Funk & Wagnalls;

Excerpt from preface of *The Deputy* by Rolf Hochhuth, translated by Richard and Clara Winston. Copyright © 1964 by Grove Press, Inc. Reprinted by permission of Grove Press, Inc.;

Excerpt from *The Schweitzer Album* by Erica Anderson. Reprinted by permission of Harper & Row, Publishers and Roslyn Targ Literary Agency; Excerpts from *Dr. Schweitzer of Lambaréné* by Norman Cousins with Clara Urquhart. Reprinted by permission of Harper & Row, Publishers; Excerpts from *No Rusty Swords* by Dietrich Bonhoeffer and *Teilhard de Chardin Album*. Reprinted by permission of Harper & Row, Publishers and William Collins Sons & Co., Ltd.

© Philip Wayne. Reprinted by permission of Philip Wayne and Penguin Books, Ltd.;

Excerpt from *An Understanding of Albert Schweitzer* by George N. Marshall. Reprinted by permission of The Philosophical Library, Inc.;

Excerpt from Dr. Albert Schweitzer, quoted by Fulton Oursler in "Your Second Job," *Reader's Digest*, October 1949, Copyright 1949 by the Estate of Fulton Oursler. Reprinted by permission of The Reader's Digest;

Excerpt from a letter to the London *Observer*. Reprinted by permission of the Estate of Bertrand Russell;

Excerpts from *The Albert Schweitzer Jubilee Book*, edited by A. A. Roback, 1945, taken from an article by Henry Clark; *The Albert Schweitzer Jubilee Book*, edited by A. A. Roback, 1955, taken from an article by W. E. B. Dubois, "The Black Man and Albert Schweitzer;" *In Albert Schweitzer's Realms*, edited by A. A. Roback, 1962. Published by Sci-Art publishers;

Excerpt from *The Kingdom of God and Primitive Christianity* by Albert Schweitzer. Copyright © 1967 by Rhena Eckert-Schweitzer. Reprinted by permission of The Seabury Press;

Excerpt from introduction by Kimon Friar which appeared in *The Odyssey: A Modern Sequel* by Nikos Kazantzakis. Copyright © 1958 by Simon & Schuster. Reprinted by permission of Simon & Schuster and Kimon Friar;

Excerpt taken from the article "*Laughter in Lambaréné*" by Homer Jack, January 1965. Reprinted by permission of Unitarian Universalist Associates;

Excerpt from the article "Words to Live By," *This Week Magazine*, November 29, 1959.

Contents

Contents

List of Illustrations

Frontispiece–Portrait of Albert Schweitzer

Following page 102

1. Günsbach, Alsace, home town of Schweitzer family
2. Schweitzer home
3. Pastor Louis Schweitzer, Albert's father
4. Albert Schweitzer's mother
5. Albert Schweitzer, age five
6. Black African. Sculpture by Bartholdi at Colmar
7. Albert Schweitzer, age eighteen
8. Albert, the young pastor
9. Albert Schweitzer and Helene Bresslau
10. Schweitzer at Lambaréné, 1913
11. Native African living quarters
12. Schweitzer with his daughter, 1923

Following page 222

13. Albert Schweitzer, musician
14. Schweitzer as physician
15. Albert's study at Lambaréné
16. Christmas service at Lambaréné
17. The doctor as construction engineer
18. Schweitzer the traveler
19. Schweitzer with wife and family
20. Visiting former elementary school
21. At the African school, Lambaréné
22. Albert Schweitzer and Bertrand Russell

Prologue

The drums echoed the sad message from village to village. Half a century earlier the drummers of Gabon had transmitted the news: "Oganga—the White Fetishman—has come among us." Now they tolled the dirge: "*Papa Pour Nous* is dead."

Black families began to fill the trails to Lambaréné. Farther away, natives with transistor radios strapped over their shoulders heard in French accents from Radio Gabon the accomplishments of the doctor who had created a hospital in the jungle. From distant points in the republic they gathered to mourn at Albert Schweitzer's grave. There in Lambaréné many who expressed their grief in song and dance had been born. In the doctor's hospital some had been healed of leprosy, ulcers and tumors, others had been treated for injuries from the giant saws and cranes of the country's mushrooming new industries. Now the man who had known brotherhood with all who experienced pain, le Grand Docteur, was dead.[1]

Foreword

It is now five years since my father died. He was a man who had decided to make his life his argument and as a consequence had chosen to work for more than fifty years in an African jungle hospital.

During his lifetime Albert Schweitzer was a man surrounded by controversy, in Europe as well as Africa, in America as well as in Asia. He developed and lived for ideas in many fields which were revolutionary and much misunderstood in his time. Until the end of his life he fought for better understanding between all men and peace on this earth. This was of course a utopian struggle and one in which he could not succeed, though he managed to make of his hospital in Lambaréné a kind of island of peace in which people of different nationalities, races and backgrounds could live in harmony with each other and with nature. At his death, he was almost universally mourned.

Albert Schweitzer's thoughts are as vital as ever. He spoke of the interrelatedness of all living beings and the importance of reverence for life, when these notions were of little meaning to the general public. They have now become among our most urgent concerns. My father went to Africa and gave his skill as a physician, builder and administrator, when it was still "the dark continent" and when help for developing countries was limited to that provided by the mission societies. He spoke out against the dangers of nuclear tests and weapons, when the world was ecstatic about its technical progress and unconcerned about its consequences. Man today is faced in a much more pressing way with the problems which determined the course of my father's life. The methods of solution have changed, but the fundamental issues with which he was concerned remain the same and with the passage of time increase in urgency.

Five years is a span of time in which memories remain clear, in which people still remember, but long enough to allow an objective appraisal of a man and his life. This is the aim of this biography. George Marshall has known my father and his hospital personally and has studied his thoughts extensively. David Poling has brought further vision to this work.

I value this book for several reasons. It is the first biography that gives an account of the last years of my father's life. It helps to explain and dissipate some of the false ideas about his relationship to the Africans. Finally, it is of special significance because it shows the full development of my father's thought and its practical realization in his life's commitments in general and at the Lambaréné hospital in particular.

                                                    Rhena Schweitzer

Introduction

Schweitzer. He is one of the personalities of this century who has become almost a myth. His sacrificial work in Africa, the natural outlet for his vital, practical philosophy of life, established him as a saint in the minds of millions. His compassion for the animal kingdom, his creation of a jungle hospital, his plea for international understanding amid a global arms race—all seemed to set him apart from common humanity.

Others recognized his musical genius, as one who not only performed with brilliance and gained critical acclaim as an interpreter of Bach, but also had the mechanical skills to repair pipe organs with his own hands. In the academic world of philosophy and religion he became more than an excellent student—he was to make major contributions to philosophy through his theme of "reverence for life" and to shatter the rigid crusts of theology with his biblical studies in the life of Jesus. Orthodoxy found in him a full-time opponent.

He was a healer. Following his medical studies he went immediately into Africa, performing thousands of operations, delivering babies and treating victims of every tropical malady including leprosy.

For many people Schweitzer has become an unbelievable figure. He appears as one floating several feet above the ground, lifted by heavenly force, complete with halo, lambs, and laughing children. Unreal, unknowable, unreachable except through legends and African communal fantasies. But if these are to stand as the final summary of his life, the last judgment on his work in this world, a more unsatisfactory and unfair appraisal would be hard to imagine.

In the face of such spiritual beatification, this conferred sainthood by acclamation (if not investigation), his critics have surfaced. Many hailed him as a mere "celebrity" during the last decade of his life. With pith helmet, baggy trousers and hesitant comments about the future of African self-determination, Schweitzer became a sharp profile in the blurred cultural and sociopolitical landscape. Black militants doubted his political sagacity and denigrated his motivations for service in French Equatorial Africa. European journalists visited his Lambaréné operations and faulted open sewers and wandering livestock in a medical compound. Americans who made a pilgrimage to the West African outpost wondered aloud about Schweitzer's authoritarian style and his commitment to "old ways" in medicine for modern Africa.

The Church and religious establishment made negative remarks about his theology and biblical commentary. The orthodox had always been angered by his conclusions about the New Testament, and now the liberals were puzzled by his independence and "straying" into what they considered a vague humanitarianism. The seminaries were unsure: one theologian told a divinity student that he had "Schweitzeritis" when he expressed an interest in overseas work. To others Schweitzer became sacred enough to mock: Mike Nichols, the humorist, began calling him "Al" in his dialogue skits with Elaine May.

A great man attracts critics, large and small. Schweitzer did not avoid combat, for he was a born critic of his culture, his church, his country, his civilization. In this book we hope to present a broad examination of Schweitzer. For his friends, we hope to provide new information and insights that explain the man and his work. For his critics some new faults, perhaps to be forgiven, for this is not an anthem to his greatness but an examination of his excellence and of his eccentricities. In Schweitzer's life one finds contrast, disappointment, frustration, anger, defeat, and fame.

Our hope, especially for those finding in this book their first introduction to the full life of Albert Schweitzer, is to overcome the popular, almost overwhelming image of an old man famous for his long stay in the wilds of Africa. The Schweitzer saga has dwelt so much on his latter years, the grand-old-man theme, that one can ignore the stirring drama of his student days, the incredible achievement of his work in theology and music, the almost hidden days of his physical collapse following World War I. Schweitzer made so many contributions to the life of civilization that the greatest obstacle which his biographers must face is the length of his life, and especially the danger of losing the brilliance of his middle years in the tenacity of his old age. He was more than a man for all seasons—he was a participant, at all times in, and a forerunner of every major social and humanitarian movement for a century.

Looking into his life one continues to marvel at a man who could set himself against the culture that had created the very environment of his early life. He observed the warfare culture of Western civilization. He sensed the decaying forms of its religious life, especially in the state churches of Europe. He was ashamed at the white man's colonialistic ravaging of primitive societies and believed in personal reparations to the innocent victims of preindustrial cultures. He attempted payment for some of these wrongs with the commitment of his life. With faint scoldings from his family and reactions of disappointment and chagrin from his wide circle of friends, he set out. He was often alone but never lonely, for he shared an unacknowledged fellowship with others caught up in the same spirit.

He corresponded and met briefly with Albert Einstein. Like Schweitzer, this most famous of physicists found that much of his life was spent opposing the currents and persuasions of society. Einstein shared many of the same concepts enunciated by Schweitzer: alarm at the use of creative force for destructive military machinery; the rigid attitudes of the Church; the repressive measures of the modern state; the inhumanity of man toward the animal kingdom.

The spirit that bound these two is also present in the lives of other great men that have influenced this century. Their lives have a place in this biography, for their attitudes and ethics, their philosophies and world-views constantly intersect and merge with those of Schweitzer. There is Martin Buber, the distinguished Jewish philosopher and theologian, who has done so much to influence the Christian family as well as the Jewish community. Buber was, like Schweitzer, to live out his last days away from his home and family. Also like Schweitzer, he was often forced to challenge the people he most dearly loved. Buber lived in Jerusalem and was the chief proponent of a spiritual Zionism—a relationship for *all* people. He fought political orthodoxy and religious fanaticism.

There is Dietrich Bonhoeffer, the brilliant young German pastor who defied Hitler, established an underground seminary, conspired to overthrow the Nazi regime, and was hanged by the Gestapo for his involvement. His commitments to preaching, teaching and simple hope have brought excitement to the present generation of young people who look for courage within the Church and honesty within the State. Bonhoeffer died pursuing both ends, and his ways were not foreign to the work of Schweitzer.

There is as well, Pierre Teilhard de Chardin, the French Jesuit, who as scientist and theologian, combined similar talents that were prominent in Schweitzer's career. His journeys to China and Mongolia were in the field of paleontology. His observations about evolution and religion brought censure and enforced silence from the Catholic Church. Like Schweitzer, he spent much of his life away from family and familiar surroundings. His findings and philosophy created conflict and tension with the accepted tenets of Church and society. His work was as a pioneer; his goal nothing less than the advance beyond Church and creed of man's awareness of God in the world. His similarity to Schweitzer provides additional points of punctuation to this volume.

In a time when the young and the concerned are trying to reclaim the loveliness of the world and the sacredness of all the living in creation, it is proper that we discover afresh the contributions of Albert Schweitzer. His thoughts on philosophy and religion found practical expression in commitment to the betterment of man and the concern for all that lives. In a world torn with conflict and competition, ringed with armaments and military threats, it is heartening to trace the life of one who both rejected these traditional roads to mass destruction and pointed to alternate paths of service and caring. In a materialistic climate where cold cash awaits the talented few for their success in the arts, in literary achievement, and technical prowess, it is nothing less than inspirational to follow the footsteps of a genius who spent his life among those who could never appreciate his inordinate talents but simply blessed this healer who could respond to a child's cry, a young mother's fear or an old man's dread.

So many young people today speak wistfully of dropping out of their society today to "do their own thing," to establish a life-style that is neither programmed nor monitored by a computer-business culture. They may find in this book one who made the ultimate protest with a creative burst of assistance and affection for the sick and forgotten and lost.

Schweitzer. The strong-willed, often downright obstinate. He had the ability to anger his closest associates by his unwillingness to change, an anger that in retrospect often turned to delightful recollection. He built *his* hospital; he made *his* decisions; he acted *his* way—and there was no question of doing it some other way.

He may be far beyond the accomplishments and abilities of all of us. His single-minded determination and his incredible resources of energy may nearly anger us. But surely they do not justify the construction of myths and unreal legends about this gentle man.

For we have been unfair to him if the humanity of Albert Schweitzer does not appear stronger, more real, more intense in what we report here. If you have ever been in debt and had to scrounge, borrow, plead for funds, you will feel close to

Schweitzer and his hospital. If you have suffered some shocking sorrow, a totally unjustified personal grief, you are in the circle of Schweitzer, who having suffered confinement as a prisoner of war, returned to bury his mother after she was trampled to death by German cavalry in World War I. If you have been a prisoner of war, a political refugee, a displaced person, you are in the company of one who was interned by the French. And if you have wandered in that dark kingdom of mental depression groping, praying, pleading for recovery and release, you will find a closeness to Schweitzer, who struggled for not months but years to regain his balance and perspective, indeed, to truly live again.

Schweitzer. Not a myth but a man.

George Marshall
David Poling

September 1970

Childhood and Youth: Toward the Light

On a bleak January 14, 1875, Albert Schweitzer was born in the little village of Kaysersberg, Alsace, in the borderland between Germany and France. It is a confusing question as to whether the towns, customs and people of Alsace are really German or French; actually, they exhibit some aspects of both countries.

At the close of the nineteenth century, Alsace was a district of farms and vineyards. Townspeople purchased their food directly from the farmers who had brought it to the local markets. Peddlers sold clothing and knickknacks from door to door. Life was similar in many ways to life in England or America at that time—except for the presence of tremendous local tensions.

Pastor Louis Schweitzer raised his son Albert in the frugal life-style customary in small Protestant parishes. The times were economically difficult and politically unstable. Three and a half years before Albert Schweitzer's birth, the provinces of Alsace and Lorraine had been taken from France as part of the settlement of the Franco-Prussian War. Bismarck believed that the French would quickly forget the loss of their Eastern provinces, and that the Alsatians would accept Germanization without question, once the region's integrity as a separate, independent province became clear. The people of Alsace demanded a plebiscite to allow them a chance to vote on the disposition of their land (and hence on their nationality). Bismarck would not hear of such a proposal, for he knew that the French-oriented Alsatians would likely vote for French rule.

But there were economic factors which made Bismarck and

the Kaiser sure that Germanization of these two provinces was good not only for Germany but for the Alsatians as well. The textile mills and the mines of Alsace, linked to the German economy, would provide markets for Alsatian goods and bring greater prosperity to everyone. Besides, through Alsace flowed the great German rivers, the Rhine, the Moselle and the Saar, all leading to the sea. German military and economic policy made it imperative that these rivers be German-controlled.

Furthermore, Germany could offer Alsace and Lorraine something France could not: independence. Germany was a federation of separate principalities whose local legislatures had considerable self-governing authority. Since France was a centralized state without regional governments and was ruled from Paris, Germany could offer the Alsatians a much greater measure of self-rule. (Actually, it was not until 1910, when Albert Schweitzer was already a doctor, that Alsace-Lorraine was permitted to organize its own government.)

Then there was the matter of religion. Under Catholic France the Alsatian Protestants were a helpless minority. United with Germany, they would be accepted by a Protestant government whose religious sympathies went back to the same Reformation that had produced the sturdy Protestant peasants of the borderland. From Germany's standpoint there were thus many reasons why Alsace should happily accept German rule.

France and Germany had long been using Alsace-Lorraine as the prize in their perpetual tug of war. When Alsace fell to Germany in Albert Schweitzer's youth, many Germans with strong loyalties to the Fatherland were settled there; but just as many French citizens had been brought in previously. After a few generations, however, the residents became Alsatians, loyal first of all to their new homeland and resisting the two giant powers on both sides. The Alsatians were among the first peoples of Europe to become truly international in viewpoint and hopeful of the breakdown of provocative boundaries. They had to be bilingual, to be at ease with both German and French. The native language of a family depended upon which government was in power when a given generation was growing up.

Since young Schweitzer's family was Protestant, and his father was a minister, Alsatian absorption by Germany seemed to offer some benefits. No longer would the Protestant Church be a persecuted minority, even though there was in truth little French intolerance. The seeming advantages were superficial, however, for the type of Protestant making up the State Church in Germany was different from the type in Alsace. The German Protestants were the spiritual descendants of Luther and the mainstream of the Reformation. The Alsatian Protestants, on the other hand, had descended from Zwingli and the radical wing of the Reformation, the Free Church movement. They did not subscribe to the Augsburg Confession of the Lutherans until 1530 when they were coerced to accept it by Charles V. They were then given standing in the German Empire. The protection of the Empire was extended only to those churches which signed the Treaty of Augsburg—those who would not accept the Confession were declared heretical. The political events of 1871 brought the Alsatians again into closer relationship with the German Lutheran State Church. And since 1871, the absorption of the Alsatian Church into the Lutheran movement has been greatly advanced. But the liberal, Free Church strains have continued, true to the independent Alsatian heritage.

Louis Schweitzer was a strong, articulate preacher who prided himself on being a liberal Protestant, and who looked upon religious liberalism as the main fruit of the Christian heritage. A devout, faithful, conscientious pastor, he was a true shepherd of his flock, a guide his people knew was strong and reliable.

Albert Schweitzer spent most of his boyhood in the small Alsatian village of Günsbach, and many incidents that occurred there left a permanent mark on his character.

One day, as a young child, he saw two men leading an old,

sickly horse through the narrow streets. The boy knew it was
bound for the local glue factory. One man kept yanking
cruelly at the animal's bridle in a relentless attempt to keep it
in motion. The other cursed and pushed from behind, striking the horse's bony haunches and sagging ribs with sharp
blows from a switch. It was obvious to young Schweitzer that
the feeble horse was simply not capable of moving more than
another step or two without at least a brief rest to gather
strength for another step. But oblivious to the agony of the
faltering animal, the men seemed intent only on getting it to
its destination before it collapsed. Their cruel disregard of
the horse's suffering made an indelible impression on Albert
Schweitzer.[1]

The boy had a dog named Phylax. Like thousands of other
dogs, Phylax was aroused by uniforms and often charged at
the postman. Albert was given the duty of keeping the dog in
rein during the postman's daily visit. In later years Schweitzer
recalled the thrill he experienced as he restrained the dog
with a switch. He also remembered the pangs of guilt he felt
afterward when his beloved Phylax wagged his tail and snug-
gled close to him. He knew he could easily have held Phylax
back with only a hand on his collar and a gentle stroking of
his head, yet he could not resist the impulse to use his power
over the animal. Later in life he found it impossible to enjoy
the performance of trained animals at the circus, for he knew
the suffering and punishment the stock had undergone to
learn these tricks.[2]

A friend named Henry Brasch once asked young Schweitzer
to go with him to shoot birds, and with homemade slingshots
the two set out. They climbed a hill, crouched, and waited
for the birds to appear. Just at the moment of attack, a distant bell began to ring. It was the warning bell that always
preceded the bell ringing of Lent, and for Albert it seemed to
represent a divine warning. He jumped to his feet, shouting
and waving his arms to startle the birds out of their dangerous
location, and ran home. Years later he wrote:

. . . ever since, when the Passiontide bells ring out to the leafless trees and the sunshine, I reflect with a rush of grateful emotion how on that day their music drove deep into my heart the commandment: "Thou shalt not kill."

From that day onward I took courage to emancipate myself from the fear of men, and whenever my inner convictions were at stake I let other people's opinions weigh less with me than they had done previously. I tried also to unlearn my former dread of being laughed at by my schoolfellows. *This early influence upon me of the commandment not to kill or to torture other creatures is the great experience of my childhood and youth.** By the side of that all others are insignificant.[3]

Schweitzer was taught bedtime prayers by his mother. It disturbed him that prayers were always said for *people,* and revolved mostly around one's own interests. He thought of the creatures who had no one to pray for them, and so after his mother had left he would add a prayer of his own: "Bless and protect all things that have breath, guard them from evil, and let them sleep in peace."[4]

This early devotion to compassion and concern for all life was the first great watershed in Albert Schweitzer's moral and intellectual development. Many years later he told a friend of his shock when, as a young student of the theologies and philosophies of civilization, he was forced to face the facts that man's ethics end with man, that man's concern is centered on man, and that man's unselfishness ends with man. It remained for Schweitzer to proclaim that man's ethics must go *beyond* man, that he must expand his loyalty and concern to include all living creatures.

This sensitivity for life (which was to remain lifelong and was recalled again and again in Schweitzer's old age) was also a shaping force in the boyhood of Martin Buber. This eminent Jewish philosopher, who would share correspondence and so many ideas with Schweitzer, wrote:

"When I was eleven years of age, spending the summer on my grandparents' estate, I used, as often as I could do it unobserved,

* Author's italics

to steal into the stable and gently stroke the neck of my darling, a broad dapple-gray horse. It was not a casual delight but a great, certainly friendly, but also deeply stirring happening. If I am to explain it now, beginning from the still fresh memory of my hand, I must say that what I experienced in touch with the animal was the Other, the immense otherness of the Other, which, however, did not remain strange like the otherness of the ox and the ram, but rather let me draw near and touch it. When I stroked the mighty mane, sometimes marvellously smooth-combed, at other times astonishingly wild, and felt the life beneath my hand, it was as though the element of vitality itself bordered on my skin, something that was not I, was certainly not skin to me, the other, not just another, really the Other itself; and yet it let me approach, confided itself to me, placed itself elementally in the relation of Thou and Thou with me."[5]

Occasionally Günsbach was visited by a Jewish peddler from a neighboring town. Since there were no Jews in Günsbach, Mäusche the peddler was both an oddity and an object lesson. The town's young boys, having heard lurid stories about the Jewish people, projected all their learned animosity upon Mäusche; to the boys, the peddler was the perfect prototype of the enemies of Christ. When Mäusche drove into town, the boys would run after his donkey cart, jeering, shouting his name and chanting invectives. Their shouting would follow the peddler all the way through town. One day young Schweitzer joined the other boys. Running close to the peddler's cart, he noticed that the man drove on, seemingly unperturbed, his freckled face wearing a patient expression except when he turned around and looked at the boys with an embarrassed but good-natured smile. It was almost as though Mäusche were sorry for them. "This smile overpowered me," Schweitzer recalled later. "From Mäusche I learned what it meant to keep silent under persecution, and this was a most valuable lesson."[6]

During one of the periods when Alsace was occupied by the French, every village with seven or more families was required to have its Protestant church reconsecrated and used by both the Catholics and Protestants. Eventually all churches became Catholic-Protestant churches, served at different hours by the respective pastors who learned to work together in the face of common hardships. To young Schweitzer this situation was a symbol of the co-operation possible between different faiths. As the boy's sympathies and loyalties expanded, he developed the private theory that in time understanding would increase until "the differences which separate churches today are destined to disappear." Later he reminisced, "When I was still merely a child, I felt it to be something beautiful that in our village Catholics and Protestants worshiped in the same building."[7]

This freedom from religious prejudice was a hallmark of Albert Schweitzer's mature life.

In one respect it also brought him great personal fulfillment. When he was a university student at Strasbourg, he had no prejudices to block his meeting and sharing ideas with the pretty daughter of one of the professors of history, Helene Bresslau. In time she would become his wife. The fact that her family origins were Jewish and his were Gentile was no obstacle to either.

A third youthful impression also broadened Albert Schweitzer's outlook permanently. Like many young people, Albert could be moved by heroic beauty. Often he was stirred by things which many adults passed without a second glance. One of these was a statue by the great Alsatian sculptor Frederic Auguste Bartholdi which had been placed in the Champ de Mars in his native town, Colmar. Americans know the force of Bartholdi's work from the Statue of Liberty. The Colmar statue was another of those colossal works for which Bartholdi is famous. Clustered around the central figure of Admiral Bruat were four figures, one of which never ceased to interest the boy. It depicted the stooped figure of an African native. His powerful muscles, sensitive features and melancholy spirit held a deep fascination for Schweitzer.

Whenever he visited his grandparents, who lived near the square where the great statue stood, Albert went to gaze at Bartholdi's creation.

The poignant figure with its portrait of a colonial people's bondage and despair haunted the boy. To him it carried one message: "Let my people go." It may well have had a profound effect on his later decision to help release Africans from their bondage to suffering.[8]

Albert Schweitzer learned to speak both French and German with fluency (and later wrote in both languages); in his university days he would be at home in Berlin and Paris, as well as in Strasbourg. He was to grow up as a man with no country, with two countries, with all the world as his country. Perhaps more than any other man of his time he was to become a citizen of the world. When he was asked late in life what country he considered his homeland, he replied, "I am just an old man who has lived most of his life in Africa."

Schweitzer, the relatively frail child, developed into a robust, husky young man. Yet he became ashamed that he was so strong in a country where there were so many impoverished youngsters, weak from lack of nourishment. In contemporary America, a hungry child feels ashamed that he has no lunch money; Schweitzer was mortified because he had better food than his classmates.

He passionately loved music, also deeply admired by his pastor-father, and he never doubted that the ecclesiastical life was meant for him as well. But until mid-adolescence he protected his sensitive spirit by what he later described as a "shell of reserve." When he was fourteen he suddenly found his tongue and intruded into every conversation with a zealot's compulsion to set straight anyone whose viewpoint seemed to diverge from what was obviously the correct one.

Many adolescents go through a similar syndrome, but for a young boy to argue with grown-ups in Prussian Germany was shocking; an aunt told Albert he was insolent, and his father made him promise to stop his "stupid behavior."[9] Looking back, the mature Schweitzer regretted his intolerable adolescent manners, but reflected that he had been impelled not by egotism but by the spirit of his grandfather Schillinger, who had in his life constantly sought with passion for truth and light. And the boy never lost the yearning to think things through, to base opinion on logical analysis, to find "the true and serviceable."

"I am, therefore," he wrote, "essentially as intolerable as ever, only I try as well as I can to reconcile that disposition with the claims of conventional manners, so as not to annoy other people. Bowing to these claims, I force myself to take part in conversations which are merely conversations, and to listen to empty, unthinking chatter without rebelling against them. My innate reserve has in this matter helped me to adopt as my own this usual behaviour of the well-bred.

"But how often do I inwardly rebel! How much I suffer from the way we spend too much of our time uselessly instead of talking in serious-wise about serious things, and getting to know each other well as hoping and believing, striving and suffering mortals! I often feel it to be absolutely wrong to sit like that with a mask on, so to say. Many a time I ask myself how far we can carry this good breeding without harm to our veracity.

"If I meet people to whom it is possible to open oneself out as a man who thinks, I feel as passionate enjoyment in their society as if I were as young as ever, and if I stumble on a young man who is ready for serious discussion, I give myself up to a joyous exchange of cut and thrust which makes the difference between our ages, whether for good or ill, a thing of no account."[10]

But here is an example of another kind of thoughtfulness reflected from Schweitzer's youth:

"When I look back upon my early days I am stirred by the thought of the number of people whom I have to thank for what they gave me or for what they were to me. At the same time I am haunted by an oppressive consciousness of the little gratitude I really showed them while I was young. How

many of them have said farewell to life without my having
made clear to them what it meant to me to receive from them
so much kindness or so much care! Many a time have I, with
a feeling of shame, said quietly to myself over a grave the
words which my mouth ought to have spoken to the departed,
while he was still in the flesh.

"For all that, I think I can say with truth that I am not
ungrateful, I did occasionally wake up out of that youthful
thoughtlessness which accepted as a matter of course all the
care and kindness that I experienced from others, and I believe I became sensitive to my duty in this matter just as early
as I did to the prevalence of suffering in the world. But down
to my twentieth year, and even later still, I did not exert myself sufficiently to express the gratitude which was really in
my heart. I valued too low the pleasure felt at receiving real
proofs of gratitude. Often, too, shyness prevented me from
expressing the gratitude that I really felt.

"As a result of this experience with myself I refuse to think
that there is as much ingratitude in the world as is commonly
maintained: I have never interpreted the parable of the Ten
Lepers to mean that only one was grateful, but nine of them
hurried home first, so as to greet their friends and attend to
their business as soon as possible, intending to go to Jesus
soon afterwards and thank him. But things turned out otherwise; they were kept at home longer than they meant to be,
and in the meanwhile Jesus was put to death. One of them,
however, had a disposition which made him act at once as his
feelings bade him; he sought out the person who had helped
him, and refreshed his soul with the assurances of his gratitude.

"In the same way we ought all to make an effort to act on
our first thoughts and let our unspoken gratitude find expression. Then there will be more sunshine in the world, and
more power to work for what is good. But as concerns ourselves we must all of us take care not to adopt as part of our
theory of life all people's bitter sayings about the ingratitude
in the world. A great deal of water is flowing underground

which never comes up as a spring. In that thought we may find comfort. But we ourselves must try to be the water which does find its way up; we must become a spring at which men can quench their thirst for gratitude."[11]

This attitude had much to do with determining the future life of Albert Schweitzer. It shows the depth of his mind, the loyalties that rose above nationalism, the religious perspective that could not be contained in narrow sectarian walls, and yet the hope that within the Church an ideal could be found to which he could remain true.

This same kind of universal mind that could grow and find hope within the Church revealed itself also in Teilhard de Chardin. As geologist, paleontologist, explorer, traveler, Jesuit and scientist, Pierre Teilhard de Chardin sang about Creation as often as he studied it. This Frenchman could look upon the evolutionary process as yet another manifestation of the life force of God. In a profession that produced fragments of truth and only bits and pieces of scientific research, he greeted discovery with prayer, accomplishment like Holy Communion. Indeed, when on the "roof of the world" following the animal paths in Mongolia he sent to friends a copy of the "Mass of the World":

Since once again, Lord—though this time not in the forests of the Aisne but the steppes of Asia—I have neither bread, nor wine, nor water, I will raise myself beyond these symbols, up to the pure majesty of the real itself; I, your priest, will make the whole earth my altar and on it will offer you all the labours and sufferings of the world.[12]

And then, very much in the vein of the mature Schweitzer, who never forgot his helpers and loved ones, he wrote:

One by one, Lord, I see and I love all those whom you have given me to sustain and charm my life. One by one also I number all those who make up that other beloved family which has gradually surrounded me, its unity fashioned out of the most disparate elements, with affinities of the heart, of scientific research and of thought. And again one by one—more vaguely it is true yet all-inclusively—call before me the whole vast anonymous army of living humanity; those who surround me and support me though I do not know them; those who come, and those who go; above all, those who in office, laboratory and factory, through their vision of truth or despite their effort, truly believe in the progress of earthly reality and who today will take up again their impassioned pursuit of the light.[13]

Albert Schweitzer was seeking the light, but at times he was to follow more than one star. For his sky was filled with many.

2

Early Commitments

From his youth, it was clear that Albert Schweitzer was preparing for two careers: music and the Church. As he grew older, these careers became more clearly defined. Organ playing, organ building, and interpretation of the life and music of Johann Sebastian Bach emerged as one great vocation. Schweitzer's interest in theology and philosophy led him into the roles of preacher, teacher and writer as the second vocation.

The youth's budding intellectual life was evident during his early years at school when he met a visiting supervisor, a Mr. Steinert, who was also an author. Albert regarded him with awe, because "for the first time I was actually setting eyes on a man who had written a book! It was his name—Steinert—which was on the title page . . . and now I had in bodily presence before me the author of these two books . . . It was to me then incomprehensible that the Schoolmaster and Schoolmistress could be talking with him just as they would any ordinary mortal."[1] This early idolization of an author indicates how important books were to the growing boy, and may reveal as well a secret desire he had even then to become a writer.

He had begun school at home, but when he was ten he was sent to live with his Uncle Louis and Aunt Sophia in Mülhausen.[2] His uncle was director of the elementary schools in Mülhausen, and there Schweitzer would have the opportunity of an excellent education. The aunt and uncle, with no children of their own, wanted very much to further the boy's education. Uncle Louis was a methodical schoolmaster who worked on a rigid schedule. Albert's life with him was organized as though he were at a military school. Meals, chores, school, homework, piano, with more piano if there was any extra time from his schoolwork—this was the daily routine in the new home. On Sundays there was the inevitable church service, not nearly so exciting as the comfortable and pleasant services in his father's church. Most difficult for the young Schweitzer was adjusting to the lack of freedom: he now had no time to run and play with classmates and friends. These were lonely years.

Albert was a quick, eager student, and most of all a conscientious one. His apparent academic difficulties lay in languages and mathematics, and he thus worked all the harder at these subjects. The intense power of concentration and thoroughness of approach he developed from this work served him well later on when he carried a heavy load of study, preaching, teaching and organ concert work.

He had begun playing the piano at the age of five.[3] His quick ear and ability to improvise almost instantly assured his family that it was well worth the sacrifice necessary to provide him with lessons. Once, when Albert was nine, the organist of his father's church became ill and there was need for a substitute at a moment's notice. With legs that barely reached the pedals of the massive organ, the small boy played for the service.

At Mülhausen he studied the organ under Eugene Münch, a master organ teacher who had just come from Berlin. Herr Münch reportedly complained, "Albert Schweitzer is the thorn in my flesh," for this student would not spend the long hours of practicing prescribed by his teacher. Instead he spent hours playing all the music he could find, and then went on to endless hours of his own improvisation. In the meantime, the lessons which Herr Münch wanted him to learn properly and correctly were ignored.[4]

As a result, when the formidable teacher required him to demonstrate his proficiency with the assigned exercises, he fumbled through them. And he dared not display his natural spirit before this stern and exacting master, who consequently developed the opinion that Schweitzer had absolutely no feeling for music. One day in exasperation Herr Münch thrust a copy of Mendelssohn's "Song Without Words" at the boy, exclaiming, "Really, you don't deserve to have such beautiful music given you to play. You'll come and spoil this "Lied ohne Worte" just like everything else. If a boy has no feeling, I certainly can't give him any!"

"Ah," thought Albert, "I'll show you whether I have any feeling or not."[5] To surprise his teacher, he practiced furiously for the whole week. Actually, he knew the piece very well, but during that week he worked out the best fingering for it, adding notations above the score to guide him. At the next lesson when he played the piece, Herr Münch sat stunned. The teacher said little, but then assigned a work by Beethoven, and after a few lessons made it known that he deemed the boy worthy of beginning on Bach. The teacher said little about his change of attitude, but he had come to recognize the talent of his young pupil. He carried the boy further and faster along than anyone had anticipated possible, never for a moment allowing him to become self-satisfied. But Schweitzer knew he had entered a select circle of qualified students of whom more and more was expected, and he was eager for the challenge and grateful for the master's confidence which lay beneath his strict regimen.

Then he was told that after his confirmation he would be allowed to take lessons on the beautiful organ at St. Stephen's Church. This rare opportunity was to be the fulfillment of a long-cherished secret dream.

Albert's maternal grandfather, Pastor Schillinger of Mühlbach, had been deeply interested in organs and organ building, and the first thing he did in any town he visited was to inspect the organs in its churches. When, for example, the famous organ at the Collegiate Church in Lucerne was being built, he spent whole days in the chancel, observing and studying it.[6] Albert's father also had this deep interest. It was only natural, then, that Albert, too, would be greatly interested in the whole art and science of the organ. When he was sixteen, he took the place of Eugene Münch at the organ of St. Stephen's for services, a recognition of his high accomplishments. Shortly thereafter, he gave his first organ concert. His teacher entrusted him with playing the accompaniment for Brahms's *Requiem*. Then for the first time he felt the joy "of letting the organ send the flood of its special tones to mingle with the crescendoing music of choir and orchestra."[7]

The organ was the national instrument of Germany. The skilled playing of it brought to its performer incredible esteem and appreciation. The organ was not merely an instrument, but *the* instrument among instruments.

In Mülhausen, Schweitzer's confirmation was to take place under the stern, colorless, pedantic tutelage of Pastor Wennagel. While Albert had great respect for the pastor, he could not relate to him personally. Albert learned the confirmation required answers, but he could not discuss troubling religious questions with Pastor Wennagel.

There were two compelling reasons why Albert had to be confirmed, quite beyond its necessity in the cultural heritage of Alsace. The first was his consuming desire to play the organ at St. Stephen's. The second was his wish to please his father. The youth had a very great admiration and respect for his father, whom he so dearly loved and missed. Pastor Schweitzer was making a sacrifice for the good of Albert's future in making it possible for him to live and study away from home. Nothing would hurt his father more than for Albert to fail his confirmation examinations, and nothing would bind the man and youth together more deeply than this additional tie of a common faith. Accordingly, the boy entered the confirmation classes of Pastor Wennagel resolutely determined to pass and receive confirmation.[8]

Like his father, Albert was inclined toward the liberal wing of the State Church, a minority group represented by old-line German intellectuals and Alsatian Free Church members. The younger generation was for the most part moving back to a more orthodox position, as the theological pendulum swung from a more liberal Protestantism toward an evangelical faith. And Pastor Wennagel and the confirmation classes were representative of the now dominant evangelical renaissance in the German Church.

Schweitzer was the product of a parsonage which represented the rationalism, intellectualism and liberalism then under attack. His father represented the position that Christianity was a religion which men could understand with their minds and could then affirm with their hearts. Out of the life of the mind came the life of the spirit.

Pastor Wennagel was apparently a thorough teacher who was able to explain, clarify, and present in a logical order the principles of faith, the history and policy of the Church, and so give a good foundation to his students. Schweitzer learned much from him. The pastor was well versed in the positions and reasoning advanced by the dominant evangelical school of German Protestantism, and Albert was always to remain grateful for this thorough introduction to the Church. It gave him a counterpoint to the liberal position and ideas of intellectual self-respect which his father personified. Thus, Schweitzer was developing the two great wings of Protestant thought—liberal and orthodox—which later were to make possible his own flights into the realms of theology and philosophy.

At the time of the confirmation classes Albert's mind was teeming with ideas. The literal truth of the Bible troubled him: What if there had been no flood? What if the flood was a great storm, or the melting of snows of the glaciers? Would a just God really condemn all animals except two of each species? Would a loving Father God destroy all mankind with the exception of one family, rather than reason with man and show him the errors of his way? Albert had hundreds of questions he would have liked to ask about the Bible, and about the creeds and beliefs of the Church.

Pastor Wennagel had one set of answers to all such questions: "You must accept it on faith. Do not question Divine Wisdom. Wiser heads than ours have agreed that the Bible must be accepted as the Truth, as the Word of God." It was

useless to try to involve the pastor in a discussion of the likelihood, possibilities or probabilities of faith. There is a platform of beliefs, he said, which are accepted by the Church.
Never question this platform, and your faith will remain in-
tact. Faith takes precedence over reason.

With this tenet Albert could not agree, although he realized he had to keep his personal opinions "tightly shut up"
within himself. He wrote, "He (Pastor Wennagel) wanted to
make us understand that in submission to faith all reasoning
must be silenced. But I was convinced—and I am so still—that
the fundamental principles of Christianity have to be proved
true by reasoning, and by no other method. Reason, I said
to myself, has been given us that we may bring everything
within the range of its action, even the most exalted ideas of
religion. And this certainly filled me with joy."[9]

As the day of confirmation approached, Pastor Wennagel
held private interviews with each boy. Schweitzer watched
the others take their turns to remain after class as requested,
and dreaded his own impending meeting and discussion with
the pastor. He inquired of his friends what was said during
the private meetings, and learned something about their
nature.

Finally, the day arrived when Schweitzer remained after
class to meet with Pastor Wennagel. The meeting was to the
point. Did he know the creeds? Yes. He could recite them,
and so demonstrated. Did he know the lessons from the Bible?
Yes. He gave the correct answers. He recited the memory portions well. Did he wish to be confirmed? Indeed he did. For
what reasons? There was his family and his love for the
Church. What about his own call? Was he born anew in the
Spirit? Confirmation was a great mystery, to be approached
with awe, reverence and due regard for its effect upon life:
What experience was he going through in this holy time?
Schweitzer recalled that at this point he hesitated; his answer
must have seemed evasive. It was impossible for him to open
his heart, to tell this man of his questions, of his doubts, of
his hopes and beliefs. The formidable teacher, he saw, was
a kindly man, and wanted to help him, wanted to share with

him this experience, and wanted to guide him properly in "the true faith." But Schweitzer knew he could not share his innermost thoughts with the pastor because he would not understand them. As a result, the meeting ended with awkward pauses, the pastor felt that Albert was not sufficiently involved in the "decision for the Church," and coolly dismissed him. Later, the pastor told Schweitzer's Aunt Sophia that he was one of the difficult students who were indifferent to matters of faith, having it in their minds but not in their hearts, and that confirmation would be only a formality.

Schweitzer, however, felt quite differently about it. He was strongly and strangely moved by the time of religious study through which he was proceeding. He wrestled privately and deeply with the great spiritual questions involving his integrity, the truth of religion, the role of the Church, and his total commitment to service in the Church. With Palm Sunday came one of the greatest moments of his life. He wished his father could have been present in church to greet him when he marched forward with the other youths to be confirmed.[10]

His revered organ teacher, Herr Münch, was at the console of the massive organ, and when the words, the music, and the formalities were over, and he played the majestic strains from Handel's *Messiah*, "Lift Up Your Heads," as the recessional, Albert felt in perfect harmony with the words, the music and spirit of the occasion. He experienced a deep love for the Church, its stirring music, its opportunities and its great truths that could lead to the meaning of life.

The pastor's fifteen-year-old son was confirmed in many ways—in his music, in his studies and in his quest for service through the Church. He was also confirmed in his faith, in his respect for the power of reason, in dedication to humanity, and all these things would lead him away from the Church to a distant jungle. He would never be satisfied with half answers, with less than the best, whether in music, scholarship or human service. He was confirmed to be himself, not what Herr Münch wanted, not what Uncle Louis wanted, not what Pastor Wennagel believed. There was simply to be no mold into which Albert Schweitzer could be poured.

The Scholar Emerges

Strasbourg was one of the old university towns of Europe. Students gathered in the evenings to sing, smoke, drink beer and talk endlessly of their hopes for the future. The ancient university buildings held memories of the great doctors, justices, professors, theologians and men of affairs who had once lived and studied there.

As a student caught up in the spirit of the Enlightenment, Albert Schweitzer gloried in Strasbourg's history. The city reflected the heritage of Western man. Here one of the decisive battles of the Roman Empire was fought when Julian turned back the barbarians in a bloody battle in 357 A.D. In 1261 Strasbourg won its right to be a free city; in the fourteenth century an internal revolution led to the establishment of guilds. Later, Strasbourg was a center of the reform movement of the Free Spirits, the left-wing group of the Reformation. Following Zwingli and the Anabaptists, the city remembered the witness of the early Christian martyrs against the State (Rome), and proclaimed its opposition to a Church-State relationship. It capitulated reluctantly to Charles V in accepting the Trinitarian Confession which Zwingli refused to sign. Strasbourg was also the seat of the Roman Catholic bishop. One of the city's grandest buildings was the Episcopal Palace, the Palais de Rohan, which was used for university classes during the years Schweitzer was a student.

The University of Strasbourg was one of the older European schools. Established in 1566, with a long heritage of liberal traditions, it epitomized the free spirit characteristic of this free imperial city. Schweitzer was at home in the university. This was his father's school, and over the generations his family had studied here. As he attended the same lecture halls and thumbed through the same worn texts in the dim and cluttered library, the youth felt that this was what he was meant for: he was destined to be a scholar.

The university was surrounded by an air of expectancy. Its ancient traditions were suddenly ignited by a spirit of inquiry on the part of its energetic faculty of scholars. Reverting along with Alsace from French to German control, the school had acquired new teachers infused with the spirit of German rationalism, motivated by such German philosophers as Hegel, Kant and Schopenhauer, inspired by the German giants of theology—Troeltsch, Baur, Weber, Müller, Harnack. Germany was then the intellectual center of the world. The spirit of the Enlightenment from the previous century, led by such intellects as Lessing, Mendelssohn and Reimarus, still glowed. To these men, rationalism, natural order and reason constituted the methodology of free inquiry. Inductive logic was encouraged, and the free mind was viewed as the highest achievement of intellectual authority.

Schweitzer enrolled at Strasbourg University in October 1893. It was at its height of fame, and it was the most liberal European university of that time. The students were urged to carry on independent research and study, and to make their own judgments and findings in a critical, though constructive, spirit. The new faculty felt itself unhampered by tradition regarding subject matter, rules and regulations. Most of the faculty were young men, and students and teachers alike strove to create the ideal modern university. "A fresh breeze of youthfulness penetrated everywhere," Schweitzer said later. This accelerated atmosphere challenged Schweitzer to move forward with fresh bold steps of intellectual investigation. During part of his university days he lived in the same house on the Old Fish Pier—No. 36—where Goethe had lived as a student.[1] And Goethe became an outstanding example to young Schweitzer.

Schweitzer's major subjects were theology, in which he studied the doctrines of the Church, and philosophy, in which he pursued the intellectual systems that enable thinking men to make sense of the world. In his emphasis on theology Schweitzer was under the tutorial guidance of Heinrich Julius Holtzmann, regarded as a leading New Testament scholar. Holtzmann's important scholarly studies established the basis for recognizing that the oldest of the four Gospels is that of Mark—a theory his pupil was to develop thoroughly.

In philosophy, Schweitzer's tutors were two renowned scholars: Wilhelm Windelband and Theobald Zeigler. These outstanding men stimulated him to develop original work even as a young man.

In the midst of his college course Schweitzer was drafted. This period taken from his studies might have been a tragedy, but it was, instead, a creative experience. The young draftee took with him a newly discovered Greek New Testament, spending many hours in tents, on hills, in garrison halls or dirt trenches, thumbing through its pages, reading in Greek the earliest record of the words of Jesus and meditating upon their meaning.

Throughout his service, his mind was churning with the problems and meanings of the Greek gospels, the difficulties of biblical exegesis. He was reconstructing the historical life of Jesus, sharply departing from what the creeds and confirmation lessons had revealed. And this modern historical criticism was a passport to a bright, fresh intellectual arena, offering salvation to Schweitzer during the weariness of months given over to drills and maneuvers. He was to return to the university as a more mature scholar.

On May 6, 1898, Schweitzer completed the first stage of his study in theology, passing the government test to qualify for his degree. He immediately turned to the study of philosophy. As a result of his high standing in the theological examination, he was awarded the Goll Scholarship Fund which provided a generous annual stipend for a period up to six years. But the scholarship contained one proviso: if at the end of six years, he had not earned his doctorate of theology, the money had to be refunded.

One rainy day Schweitzer met Professor Zeigler on the steps of the university. In the downpour, scholar and student shared the same umbrella as the young man's plans for the future were discussed.[2]

Zeigler wanted him to work for his doctorate of philosophy immediately rather than his doctorate of theology. It was considered the essential advanced degree for outstanding scholars and Zeigler felt that it would be well employed in his theological studies later. Schweitzer had done brilliant work already under Zeigler in his initial pursuit of the philosophy of Kant. Now he could specialize in the religious philosophy of Kant, a course that would strengthen his theological dissertation later on. After this discussion on the library steps, Schweitzer agreed to this change in plans. But it meant also a change in universities.

Schweitzer went to Paris to continue his studies in philosophy at the Sorbonne. Here was the pride of French intellectual achievement, one of the world's finest seats of learning. Schweitzer's credentials were in order and well prepared. He was launching on a career of international scholarship, moving up from a regional university to a distinguished international community of learning. He approached the Sorbonne with near reverence. With surprise and dismay he discovered that entrance was a mere formality. Anyone could study there: the true test in the Sorbonne came in the examinations. No one was concerned with Schweitzer's studies or his background or his aspirations. The leading professors carried on their studies independently and appeared on schedule for class, strode in, gave the lecture, and walked out. A relationship between scholar and student was nonexistent. There was no Holtzmann here to challenge one to say what one thought concerning the chronological order of the Gospels. Nor was there a Zeigler to stop one on the library steps in the rain to inquire about next term's program of study. The impersonality of this sprawling institution required a different type of academic discipline of Schweitzer.

Pierre Curie, the physicist who discovered radium, taught

at the Sorbonne until his death in 1906. His widow, Marie Curie, was a recognized physicist and took over her husband's lectures following his death. The day after his funeral, the students rose respectfully as she walked into the amphitheatre where he had taught. As they sat down, she opened Pierre's notes and began: "Pierre Curie was saying at the end of the last lecture . . ." She continued the lecture from the middle of the sentence where her husband had stopped on the stroke of the bell.[3]

This was the tradition of scholastic integrity at the Sorbonne, of pure rationalism in the classroom minus any show of emotion. The tradition stressed ideas, not people. In the mind of Madame Curie and her pupils, the highest honor they could render to the esteemed physicist was to remain faithful to his thought and to science. This type of rationalism has a high and lofty sentiment, and is deeply emotional in its own way. But after the warm personal academic atmosphere at Strasbourg, it was not what Schweitzer had expected. Later he wrote about great teachers such as Louis Auguste Sabitier and Louis Eugène Ménégoz, saying only "I felt great esteem for them both."[4]

The most exciting aspect of Schweitzer's stay in Paris was his studying the organ and piano. His teachers were Marie Jaell-Trautmann, J. Phillip, and Charles-Marie Widor. Schweitzer had studied under Widor previously for a short time. The eminent organist was so impressed with Schweitzer's talent that he offered him free lessons. The young man was to make many friends in the Parisian world of music and the performing arts.[5]

In March 1899, Albert Schweitzer returned to Strasbourg to pass his oral examination in philosophy. The following summer he began to study at the renowned University of Berlin. There he attended lectures by such scholars as Otto Pfleiderer, the noted New Testament critic, Friedrich Paulsen, the philosopher-educationalist who had defined the soul as "will to live," and Adolf von Harnack. The latter also taught Karl Barth, the prominent Swiss theologian. Harnack believed that Christian dogma was a reflection more of the Greek philosophers than of Jesus, and emphasized brotherhood above theology. Harnack and Schweitzer were to become life-long friends and two of Harnack's last messages were written to Schweitzer.[6]

The intellectual life of Berlin impressed Schweitzer much more than the Paris community. Berlin struck him as "a large provincial town," yet he found within the university a rallying point for its intellectual life. Paris had of course been much more sophisticated, and Schweitzer looked forward to the period in Berlin for undistracted study. At the end of July 1899, he returned to Strasbourg to take his examination for the degree of doctor of philosophy. His thesis was the treatise, *The Religious Philosophy of Kant from the Critique of Pure Reason to Religion Within the Limits of Reason Alone.*

Immanuel Kant was then to philosophy what Einstein was to twentieth-century physics. His ideas had overthrown the established foundations of ethics and apologetics, but had laid the foundation for making religion compatible with modern knowledge. Kant's statement, "Two things fill the human mind with awe: the starry heavens above and the moral law within," has become the basis of religious faith for many people. His philosophy marks a line dividing the biblical Reformation heritage of previous eras from our modern confrontation with the whole secular world of contemporary ideas and concerns.

Young Schweitzer decided to tackle a problem that had baffled the intellectual giants of the nineteenth century; the attempt to synthesize or clarify the disparate elements in Kant's works. The volumes already written on the problem were jealously guarded in the Bibliothèque Nationale—so jealously that, fortunately, Schweitzer decided to bypass them and spend his time on Kant's works themselves. A thrilling discovery emerged: certain terms were indeed in conflict with others. Making a careful count of key words, together with variations in the meaning, he came to the conclusion that *The Critique of Pure Reason* contained an earlier paper of

Kant's which he had added to it merely as an introduction, although it did not harmonize with the philosopher's mature reflections.[7]

Schweitzer also puzzled over Kant's treatment of the three fundamental concepts of God, freedom and immortality; they were not developed by Kant as one might have expected, and were finally abandoned by him. Schweitzer concluded that there was a basic antagonism between Kant's critical idealism and his ethics, producing a religious philosophy "in a state of constant flux." But it flowed toward the moral, the purely ethical. The culmination of Kant's thought, Schweitzer felt, was to view both God and mankind primarily in terms of morality.

One question that arose out of this study of Kant was this: What is religious genius? Schweitzer commented:

Therefore, the nature of every religious genius is shown in that he constructs a unity by working over the wreckage of a religion destroyed either deliberately or unconsciously as the exigencies of his religious personality dictate it without concern as to whether, for the average person, the broken pieces fit together into a structure or not. The genius seizes what is only in the light of his own convergence into a unified image—and the rest becomes blurred in the shade. Thus for Jesus of Nazareth, only that exists in the Old Testament which proves to be in harmony with his religious talent. It is from here that light is shed: "On these two hang all the law and the prophets." In this manner Augustine unites the contradictions of a Neoplatonic world-view and Catholicized Christianity into one whole; he established the higher unity of both without feeling the contradictions. Thus Luther, being the religious genius that he was, fits together the most contradictory portions of medieval dogma because he brings a unified principle to bear on it; he voiced contradictions but he never felt them. In every religious genius, progress toward the principle of unity is documented just as in the esthetic genius. Because progress cannot be achieved on the basis of the customary or the habitual, it is especially the religiously interested masses who sense the new structure not as religion but as appearance—that is, a conglomerate of religious pronouncements—and the religious genius becomes a deluded heretic.[8]

With these words, Schweitzer the graduate student may unwittingly have spoken both his own glory and doom—his destiny.

He now turned his attention to obtaining his doctor of theology degree. In the meantime, he accepted the post of preacher in the Church of St. Nicholai in Strasbourg. He felt it wonderful to be "allowed to address a congregation every Sunday about the deepest questions of life."[9] Today, there are still a few people in Alsace who tell of the joy of listening each Sunday to Albert Schweitzer speaking. These people are not only proud he was their pastor, but many of them were the Schweitzer Hospital's loyal supporters until he died.

Dr. Schweitzer preached there with deep satisfaction. But no pastor ever comes out of theological school a perfect shepherd for his flock, and Albert was no exception. Every minister, no doubt, recalls some of the humorous lessons learned in his first church, where he dealt with people rather than textbooks, and preached to a live congregation instead of a practice session of classmates. Inexperienced young ministers are often guided by an advisor or counselor. In St. Nicholai's Church, Albert Schweitzer was under the guidance of a Mr. Knittel who one day reported to Schweitzer that some of the older members of the congregation were complaining about the brevity of the sermons. Most ministers are told their sermons are too long. Mr. Knittel was very embarrassed about this charge, knowing that often there are members of a congregation who have to find something to criticize. He added, however, "I will have to tell them how you answered me; what can I say?"

Albert replied: "Tell them I am only a poor curate who hasn't learned much yet, and I stop speaking when I have nothing more to say."[10]

On July 15, 1900, Albert was examined for the doctor of theology degree. Elderly clerics were invited to join in the examination. The candidate was asked, among other questions, the name of the author of a particular hymn. He replied that he considered the hymn too insignificant to have noticed the name of its composer. The examiners were a little startled and embarrassed by this remark since the son of the composer, Karl Spitta, was among them that day.[11] Schweitzer only overcame this gaffe by a brilliant display of both his theological prowess and careful preparation for the larger questions that were asked. For the degree he had studied in detail the history of the Last Supper. This led to his great theological work, which when developed further was published in 1906, entitled *The Quest of the Historical Jesus.*

He had taken this examination only two years after being awarded the Goll Scholarship Fund. He could have postponed the examination for another four years, under its terms, and could have had sufficient funds for travel and study during that time.[12] However, Schweitzer knew there were other students who needed financial aid, and even though he had planned to study in Cambridge, England, he gave up that opportunity to help another student. This was simply his way: conscience always made him sacrifice his own good for the good of others.

At this point, Dr. Schweitzer might have said that he was prepared for his lifework. However, no one was aware of the direction his life was yet to take. Theology and philosophy were to be for him brilliant, but short-lived, careers.

Organist and Organ Builder

Albert Schweitzer was also a concert virtuoso. He was now a professor with doctor's degrees in both theology and philosophy, but to many people he remained primarily a great musician.

Charles Münch, the noted musician who was conductor of the Boston Symphony Orchestra longer than any other man, and whose sister was the wife of Albert Schweitzer's brother, Paul, wrote of his early remembrance of Schweitzer:

"The name of Albert Schweitzer is linked with my childhood. It brings back recollections of wonderful evenings, when I heard him passionately discussing with my father every little detail in a score by Bach, after they had worked together performing it. At that time Albert Schweitzer played the organ for the concerts my father conducted . . . He had studied previously with my uncle, Eugene Münch.

"Schweitzer had also studied with the great French organist, Charles-Marie Widor. At that time Widor was very much perplexed by some of the Bach movements, and Schweitzer who knew the texts of the old German chorales by heart, showed Widor how the words explained the music. Then they played through the chorale preludes . . . and a new Bach, that Widor had never known, was revealed to him. At Widor's suggestion Schweitzer undertook to write a book on Bach. That book, which was begun in 1899, took him six years to complete, and brought forth a new interpretation of Bach's music, and of art in general.

"Schweitzer's capacity for work is incredible. I have often seen him, after a full and strenuous day of activity, sit down with students and take the time to correct their work and to guide them through new problems. His talents and abilities are manifold. Through his great professional knowledge he has made an enormous contribution to the art of organ construction in France."[1]

Each spring Schweitzer returned to Paris to study for a few weeks with Widor. Widor had by now convinced Schweitzer that he should write something about Bach.[2] He began a pamphlet with the hope of having it ready in the fall for use in the classes at the Paris Conservatory. The few months Schweitzer proposed for the pamphlet's presentation extended into six years. The University of Strasbourg had multitudinous volumes with the complete scores and works of Bach at his disposal, but since Schweitzer's work as minister, professor and teacher took so much time, he could study Bach only at night, and too often the library was closed by the time he was able to study. Then one day a bookstore manager told Schweitzer that a woman from a neighboring area had subscribed to the Paris Bach Society's fund when they were raising money and had purchased an entire set of Bach's works. The books had arrived and had been placed on her shelves, but were seldom used by her, since her interest in Bach and his works was primarily that of a patron. Indeed, she wished to redecorate her parlor and the long rows of large gray volumes did not fit the proposed new décor. The bookseller had declined to purchase them. Schweitzer obtained her address and bicycled out to see her. She was delighted to find someone enthusiastic about the volumes and able to make use of them. Accordingly, she sold them for a ridiculously low sum, less than twenty-five dollars. Now Schweitzer had the volumes to use in his room, where he could study and work on the completed works of Bach whenever he wished. This purchase had been good luck indeed, and Schweitzer felt it augured success for the project.[3]

He enjoyed this work. "This was a task that attracted me because it gave me an opportunity of expressing thoughts at which I had arrived in the course of close study of Bach, both theoretical and practical. . . ." Before he was finished,

Schweitzer had written a six-hundred-page book in French and later rewrote it entirely as an even longer work in German. In these books he studied and interpreted the great master organist-composer whose cantatas, chorales and fugues gave him standing as perhaps the first modern musician. However, the style of writing and scoring music had changed considerably since Bach's day, and music had moved from the cathedral to the concert hall. As a result, much of the greatness of Bach was being lost through secularization. Albert Schweitzer felt he understood Bach. He comprehended what Bach was trying to say and do with his music and thus was able to reach into Bach's life and spirit. He was able to interpret Bach, to show his music's many meanings, to rescore his medieval arias for the present day. In Schweitzer's work, the full depth, richness and beauty of Bach's music came alive in the twentieth century. Schweitzer and Bach became as one. One cannot fully understand Bach without Schweitzer, nor in fact Schweitzer without Bach. For here was the artist, the musician, the philosopher, sensitive to beauty, expressing life's meaning in the sensuous joy of sound, a harmonious whole, helping to create the Renaissance man, Albert Schweitzer.

Schweitzer could be wholly absorbed in Bach, lose himself completely in the master's music. Professor Archibald T. Davidson, musical director at Harvard University, gave this picture of Dr. Schweitzer conducting a Bach concert:

"Turning his back squarely upon both orchestra and chorus, one hand thrust in his trouser pocket, his head back, staring up into the dark of the Salle Gaveau, his arm moving in awkward sweeps and unorthodox directions, it was quite obvious that if he gave himself a thought—which I doubt—it was only to consider himself the agent who should bring the music to life . . . Above all, there was complete detachment: entire absorption in the sound of the music. To this day I can remember the intense admiration I felt for Schweitzer's indifference to externals."[4]

The inner harmony and the simplicity to which music can bring one were deeply felt and noted by Schweitzer. In

Bach he found pure emotion and simplicity in music.

Schweitzer made notable contributions to the field of music as a writer: his French and German biographies of Bach are well known. In conjunction with Widor, he began the collection of *The Complete Organ Works of J. S. Bach*,[5] published in the United States by Schirmer. Widor died in 1937, unfortunately, with only five of the volumes published, and Schweitzer constantly hoped through the years to find a way to finish the series. In 1949, while in the United States on a lecture tour, he visited his old friend and pupil, Dr. Edouard Nies-Berger, an Alsatian who had become a noted American church organist. Together one day they toured the great churches of New York City, playing the organs which fascinated Dr. Schweitzer. He found there a whole new world of modern instruments. Then Dr. Schweitzer suddenly said, "We must go to see my music publishers, Schirmer." They called the office and made hasty arrangements for an appointment.

Mr. Schirmer, after they had talked a few moments, said he had always hoped Schweitzer would finish the *Organ Works*.

Dr. Schweitzer replied, "It is impossible without Charles Widor. It is out of the question for me to do it alone, unless . . . this man" and with a roguish smile on his face he pointed a long finger at Nies-Berger, "would help me."

Thus, it was agreed that Nies-Berger would become Dr. Schweitzer's collaborator for the concluding volumes of *The Complete Organ Works of J. S. Bach*. A few years later in the early 1950s, the long awaited sixth volume was issued. In the summer of 1962 when George Marshall was at Lambaréné, Dr. Nies-Berger was there also. "I have the final two volumes ready for publication," he told Marshall. "All I need is Dr. Schweitzer's approval."

Later, after Dr. Schweitzer and Dr. Nies-Berger had spent several afternoons together going over the music, and Marshall had heard them picking out the scores on the old piano, Marshall asked Dr. Nies-Berger as he was leaving Lambaréné, if they were finished.

He exploded, "No, the old man is a perfectionist. He is not satisfied. We'll probably have to do much of it over again." Thus, in 1962 the seventh and eighth volumes were nearing completion, but were not yet ready in Schweitzer's eyes to be released to the public. More work remained to produce the flawless pieces deserved by Bach and insisted upon by Schweitzer. Thus, Dr. Schweitzer, well along in his eighties, still had as a major preoccupation this first love—music, and the desire to finish *The Complete Organ Works of J. S. Bach,* but only if they met the highest standards of his critical judgment.

Dr. Schweitzer recorded some of his own organ music for the public, and it is a privilege to be able to hear the recording of his master hand, playing the works of Bach, and to experience the interpretative devotion he brings to the rendition of great music. Unfortunately, they are not recorded on stereo and the living impact of the great organ is therefore lost.

Dr. Schweitzer's further musical contribution was in the realm of organ building.[6] Like his maternal grandfather, Pastor Schillinger, who spent whole days watching a new organ being assembled and climbing around among the pipes of the newly built organ, Schweitzer felt one could not really be an organist without knowing how an organ was built, what materials were in the specific instrument and what the combinations of tones, pipes, pedals, stops and keys were. It was necessary to know how the instrument was placed in the particular hall where it stood, so as to be able to assess the acoustics and determine how one would play a particular instrument. Organ playing is not a standardized discipline in which the same performance is given on all keyboards. Each instrument has individuality. To be really accomplished one must know all details of the particular instrument to be played.

Albert Schweitzer studied each organ as a unique work of art. The story is told of an organ recital Dr. Schweitzer gave in a neighboring Alsatian town. The minister of the church had invited him to dinner preceding the concert, to meet influential persons of the community. Dr. Schweitzer did not arrive in the afternoon. He did not arrive in time for dinner. Host and guests went out and looked for him, but in vain. He never did arrive at the parsonage at all. The guests went to the church convinced that some emergency had arisen and that the great organist would not appear. No one at the church had seen him arrive either. The minister went into the chancel. Suddenly, his attention was attracted to the organ pipes—Dr. Schweitzer was descending them. He had arrived as scheduled, early that afternoon, and gone to the church to try out the organ he was to perform on that evening. It was not correctly synchronized, out of balance, and he could not perform adequately on it. Therefore, he had removed his coat and tie, climbed back into the organ, and had begun to make the necessary changes, first tuning it, then rearranging the stops and pipes, and adjusting the mechanism so that it would perform the way it was meant to. That night he gave a great concert on an instrument that sounded so much better than anyone had expected.

The old organs of the early craftsmen are fast disappearing. In Europe and America it is fashionable to scrap the old instruments and put in new, streamlined, "modern design" organs, often chosen because they look stylish or fit the modern décor better. Often electronic organs without pipes, reproducing sounds through vacuum tubes, or transistors such as those used in radios, have replaced the old organs. These new instruments imitate the sounds of a great organ played by a master organist but they lack the versatility that is present in the organ whose sound is "captured" in the tube, or even the versatility of a much smaller pipe organ.

Often, to have more stops and more pipes is considered a step toward progress and greater music, and small organs with fine tone, good sound and the valued flexibility of a superior instrument are discarded. This is a great tragedy, for the modern mass-reproduced, factory organ, fine as it may be, is seldom equal to the old instrument of the skilled craftsman.

But even large "organ factories" now realize that it is a mistake to simply put out a few models from which to make a selection, and thus "organ architects" design a specific instrument for the discerning buyer. Building committees sometimes become impatient when they sign a contract, only to discover that the new organ will not be ready for two or three years. But this is the price in time that must be paid for getting an instrument which is "tailor-made" rather than "ready-made" for their church. That there is today this opportunity to get organs structured for specific auditoriums is part of the music lover's debt to Albert Schweitzer. Almost single-handedly he stopped the movement toward mass production of standardized organs for churches and concert halls. He wrote two books on the subject: *Organ Building and Organ Playing in Germany and France;* and the very important volume, *International Regulations for Organ Building,* which was adopted as the official regulation by the Congress of the International Music Society held in Vienna in 1909. These regulations had a profound effect on organ manufacturers, musicians and architects both in Europe and in the United States.

With clarity and conviction, Albert Schweitzer made organ construction a cause. He alerted the world of music lovers to the great danger that truly fine organ creation was in jeopardy.

But as he saw the decline taking place in organ building he wrote not merely of the waste and loss, but offered suggestions that were helpful in doing something about it. He wrote:

"Today has come the desire to work our way out of this decline. Those who have so long been considered backward because they were prejudiced against the modern factory organ, now find listeners. The old, beautiful organs that remain are again valued; though, unfortunately, there are now left only poor remnants of the splendor that was still there a generation ago.

"The program for the future is simple: that we should

again build with artistic principles, starting once more with the fine traditions of the earlier organists.

"A prerequisite for this is that when an order is given for an organ, our concern should be not just for the number of its stops, but for its quality. This basic principle must become axiomatic to congregations and church authorities. Until this happens organ building will not improve.

"But when we shall have accomplished this, everything else will come of itself. No witchcraft is required to build a good organ. When we cease demanding of our organ builders more stops than excellent and artistic workmanship can furnish for the designated sum, and when we allow them the necessary time to build, they will again become genuine organ builders."[7]

Dr. Schweitzer was not someone trying to stop mass production, or the industrial revolution. He was, however, a champion of application of human values and human intelligence to problems. The conflict between the commercial and the artistic, in his view, called for adaptations to the factory method that would save the individual features of hand-tooled craftsmanship. He summed it up this way:

"But even if we had had artistic insight, so that the mounting possibility of wind pressure would not have tempted us in the wrong direction, nonetheless our organ building would have been forced along this road. It is all a financial question. Our organ builders found themselves in the embarrassing position of having to accept those inventions which made possible a reduction in prices, and therefore success in competition. Everything else, the purely artistic, was compelled to stand aside. The past forty years, the age of invention in organ building, will not appear some day on the pages of history as the great years of artistic progress, as many among us believe, but rather will they be described in this way: 'Battle between the commercial and the artistic; victory of the commercial over the artistic.'

"Any concern that placed the artistic above the commercial was from the beginning lost. The invention intoxication that gripped us organists in this period demanded external, epoch-making, cost-reducing discoveries. Our organ builders had to bow to this spirit; many of them, as I know, inwardly furious.

"So we have come to the factory organ—the good old factory organ. For what is artistic in it we are indebted to the sacrificial spirit of our organ builders, who even for these reduced prices still did the best work they could, and were satisfied if generally they could 'get by.' In the righteous judgment of history they will some day be honored, in spite of the fact that their organs are only good factory instruments; but we, who decided what organs should be built, and supposed that art could profit from this undercutting competition, shall be dishonored, because we did not sufficiently comprehend that an organ builder can be an artist only when he is engaged as an artist by an artist. If this support is lacking, then circumstances force him to become a dealer in objects of art."[8]

Dr. Schweitzer became one of the world's great organists. At the age of twenty-eight, he became the organist of the Paris Bach Society, and served its annual concerts as organist-accompanist until he went to Africa. The Society, in grateful appreciation, presented him with a zinc-lined piano equipped with organ pedals so that he could continue playing, and practicing, in the humid African jungle where no normal organ could survive.[9]

Later, when the French interned him as a prisoner of war in World War I, he would practice the key and foot movements of an organ on a dining table. It is reported that fellow prisoners would watch him by the hour as he pantomimed a great chorale or fugue on the table top, his fingers, in his mind's eye traveling the giant keyboards of some great organ, his feet restlessly working the organ pedals. The musical scores of all the great organ compositions were written on his mind. Practice kept his fingers agile, his feet in motion, and maintained his ability as thoroughly as if he had had the use of an organ.[10]

After the war, when his tropical hospital had been reclaimed by the jungle growth and vegetation, and he needed funds with which to rebuild it, his organ recitals were a major means of raising the necessary funds.

His organ-building knowledge was also needed. Many churches and public buildings had been bombed, and many great old organs were in need of repair. It is difficult to determine exactly how many organs he rebuilt, assisted or advised on their restoration. He reported, slyly, that a friend introduced him at a public meeting with these words: "In Africa he saves old natives; in Europe he saves old organs." In simple parish churches and in great medieval cathedrals today there are old organs functioning because of his interest following the demolition of war.[11]

Thus, even the artist, he learned, cannot be a recluse in a cloister, and cannot practice his art unconcerned with its technical aspects and the general technical direction of civilization. Mass production could unthinkingly destroy his art, as surely as war could. To the extent that there is good music today in churches and good organ music at concerts, we are greatly indebted to Schweitzer.

5

The Academic Life

Now thirty years of age, in 1905, Schweitzer was well known primarily for his theological pioneering. Ministers, pastors, students, philosophers began to look upon him as a provocative yet sound thinker. Scholars with books and published articles to their credit found that their positions were incomplete without some consideration of Schweitzer's writings in philosophy and religion.

Schweitzer worked exactingly on every detail of his studies. His published works took no assumptions for granted, left no argument to chance, ignored no available source or reference material.

Today, after half a century, his work is still acclaimed for its solid scholarship. For example, dozens of important books on the nature of Jesus written by eminent professors and scholars within recent years have paid tribute to *The Quest of the Historical Jesus*. This masterwork is a reference point, and authors point out either how their scholarship agrees with Dr. Schweitzer's position or to what extent it differs from it.

One such author is Martin Buber, who as a scholar, translator, theologian and interpreter distinguished himself as one of the great personalities of this century. He knew the Old Testament as well as most Jews and the New Testament better than many Christians. Near in spirit to the Christian faith, he spoke of Jesus in phrases such as, "Jesus is my great brother."

Buber was to share friendships with many Christian theologians and scholars and receive many invitations to lecture and speak on their writings. As he prepared his own studies of the New Testament, he turned again and again to the writings of Albert Schweitzer[1] and especially to the *Quest of the Historical Jesus.*

Buber believed that the real contrast between Judaism and Christianity was to be seen in the passage from Mark 8:27–30. Here Jesus and his disciples are in the region of Caesarea Philippi. In response to Jesus' question, "Whom do men say that I am," Peter replies, "Thou art the Christ." This phrase or name Christ has become a name. Buber maintains that it originally was a title and that Jesus' existence did not alone offer eternal redemption. Christos is the Greek word. The Hebrew translation is mashiach or king. Buber points out that this title belonged, over the centuries in Jewish thought to the one man who would fulfill and complete God's work on earth.

With this as background, Buber points out the difference between Christian and Jewish understanding of the event or claim:

I believe something was said in Caesarea Philippi that was well and truly intended, and yet was not true, and the fact that it has been repeated down the centuries still does not make it true. I believe that God reveals himself not in people but through them. I believe that the Mashiach (king) does not come at a particular moment in history; his coming can only be the end of history. I believe that the world's redemption did not become a fact nineteen centuries ago. We are still living in a world that is not redeemed; we are still looking forward to the redemption—and each of us is called to do his part in the work of redeeming the world.[2]

It remains clear that today significant scholarship must reckon with Schweitzer's position before presenting its own. For instance, in 1962, Professor Amos Wilder, then the department head in New Testament Literature at Harvard University, wrote a paper on "Albert Schweitzer and the New Testament" in which he said: "A lot of water has passed under the bridge since Schweitzer first published his views of Jesus and the Gospels. No informed scholarship since has been able to undercut the major contribution here, namely, that Jesus, an alien to our modern ideas and rooted in his own time and place, saw history and the world in terms of the late Jewish apocalyptic eschatology of his background, though he gave this outlook his own creative interpretation. Schweitzer's thought here made a new epoch in our understanding of Christian origins."[3]

If Dr. Schweitzer had stayed in the university atmosphere of Europe, he might well have become one of the world's outstanding theologians and philosophers. Certainly before 1905 he was already one of Europe's most creative leaders in these fields. The broad scope of his outlook and scholarship may be seen in various ways; but behind it was his own special approach to life and knowledge.

In 1900 he accompanied his aunt to the world-famous Passion Play at Oberammergau. To many people, this is a religious highlight that must be seen if only once in a lifetime. To watch the drama unfold and to reflect on the holy moments in the life of the Lord and Saviour of Christendom are experiences of sufficient depth for most people; few examine the drama critically, but rather simply accept it as an affirmation of their faith. Dr. Schweitzer affirmed his faith at Oberammergau also, but he was very upset by aspects of the play. Scenes from the Old Testament which were used to "frame" the Passion events bothered him; he knew well what a distance separated Jesus from the Old Testament world. He was also bothered by what he considered theatricalism, a poor text, and absolutely banal music. One thing touched him: the evident sincerity of the players.[4]

Dr. Schweitzer, even in pursuit of religious affirmation, could never put reason aside nor ignore the fruits of scholarship. He felt always as he had at the time of his Confirmation, that "the fundamental principles of Christianity have to be proved true by reasoning, and by no other method." Accordingly, when he studied the Last Supper of Jesus, and then examined the historical evidence for the life of Jesus, he relied on reason. He had no use for sentimentality, cheap charades, false theatrics or banal music in his quest for religious truth.

Indeed, he was to write later:

How strong would Christian truth now stand in the world of today, if its relation to the truth of history were in every respect what it should be! Instead of allowing this truth its rights, she treated it, whenever it caused her embarrassment, in various ways, conscious or unconscious, but always by either evading, twisting or suppressing. Today, the condition of Christianity is such that hard struggles are now required to make possible that coming to terms with historical truth which has been so often missed in the past.[5]

The need for absolute truth, for historical and verifiable truth, was a necessity of Schweitzer's intellectual outlook. The more he studied, the more he came to realize how often misplaced zeal for the defense of Christianity had often interfered with the truth of history. He saw clearly that much of the trouble Christianity faced in academic and intellectual quarters came because of its failure to grapple realistically with historical tuth. If any one factor marked the course of his studies and writings, it was this love of truth. His approach was objective rather than subjective, but it was the objectivity of one who loved the Christian message rather than one bent on undercutting it. He noted that "hate as well as love can write a life of Jesus, and the greatest of them are written with hate: that of Reimarus, a series of essays known as the Wolfenbüttel fragments, and that of David Friedrich Strauss. It is not so much hate of the person of Jesus as of the supernatural nimbus . . . and their hate sharpened their historical insight."[6]

Dr. Schweitzer, in contrast, wrote from love even though he used the same objective historical standards which challenged Christianity in other hands. Unfortunately, the Church as an institution was ill-prepared to find a friend acting and writing with complete objectivity. In consequence, Dr. Schweitzer almost immediately became suspect in those church quarters which were hostile to academic discipline. He was viewed as an enemy masquerading as a friend. But his was the greater confidence: he believed that truth would support the Church, not undermine it.

As a student Dr. Schweitzer had the advantage of learning from teachers who were great biblical scholars. The most noted was Heinrich Julius Holtzmann under whom he studied the Synoptics—the first three Gospels. Holtzmann has gained renown for his espousal of the theory—now almost universally accepted by scholars—that Mark's Gospel is the oldest.[7] This "Marcan hypothesis" inspired New Testament studies for the theological student. It gave him, for the first time, a key to systematic study of the life and person of Jesus. Using this key, Albert Schweitzer was challenged to probe further into the historical life of Jesus: this was to become the field of his first major scholarly contribution. Schweitzer differed from his teacher and did extensive research to prove that Matthew was the oldest Gospel.[8]

There are four basic problems relating to Jesus that Schweitzer and every other student of theology had to face. First, there was the problem of historicity. Did Jesus really live? If so, were the recorded events actual? If the Wise Men came from the East, with so long and difficult a journey, why did they not spread the word of his birth throughout their realms, and create a world consciousness of the birth of a "Heavenly King?" After the events following the Crucifixion, why did not Pilate and his officers alert and report these great events to Rome, so that all the Empire would be aroused? Why was there such silence about Jesus except among His personal followers? These are questions of history that the scholar must wrest with and answer!

Secondly, there was the question of the miracles. How could they be understood and explained? Did they actually happen? Are there other ways of interpreting the reports? Is it necessary to accept them in order to believe in Jesus?

Third was the question of the world-view of Jesus and of his time. "Whenever we hear the words of Jesus," Schweitzer

➤said, "we tread the ground of a world-view that is not ours."[9]

Schweitzer had pondered the words of Matthew in the Greek testament which he was studying while on maneuvers. In Chapter 10 he read this passage from verses 5 through 13:

These twelve Jesus sent forth, and commanded them, saying, Go not into the way of the Gentiles, and into any city of the Samaritans enter ye not; but go rather to the lost sheep of the house of Israel. And as ye go, preach, saying, The kingdom of heaven is at hand. Heal the sick, cleanse the lepers, raise the dead, cast out devils; freely ye have received, freely give. Provide neither gold, nor silver, nor brass in your purses, nor scrip for your journey, neither two coats, neither shoes, nor yet staves: for the workman is worthy of his meat. And into whatsoever city or town ye shall enter, enquire who in it is worthy; and there abide till ye go thence. And when ye come into an house, salute it. And if the house be worthy, let your peace come upon it: but if it be not worthy, let your peace return to you.

This passage continues through familiar words that we have all heard, but Schweitzer seemed to read them for the first time in the Greek: "Beware of men: for they will deliver you up to the councils, and they will scourge you in their synagogues; And ye shall be brought before governors and kings for my sake, for a testimony against them and the Gentiles."

And after this warning, Jesus continued with his disciples to give them this instruction, or advice:

But when they deliver you up, take no thought how or what ye shall speak: for it shall be given you in that same hour what ye shall speak. For it is not ye that speak, but the Spirit of your Father which speaketh in you. And the brother shall deliver up the brother to death, and the father the child: and the children shall rise up against their parents, and cause them to be put to death. And ye shall be hated of all men for my name's sake: but he that endureth to the end shall be saved. But when they persecute you in this city, flee ye into another: for verily I say unto you, Ye shall not have gone over the cities of Israel, till the Son of Man be come.

This, it suddenly dawned on Schweitzer, was an amazing passage: "till the Son of Man be come." Here is Jesus telling the disciples in his instructions that he sends them forth with nothing, for they will need nothing, but that before they finish going to the cities and towns, the Son of Man shall have come. The messianic kingdom, the messianic reign, the kingdom of God on earth will have been created. How could this be? Obviously this was an expectation that was not fulfilled.

But how could these words be explained away? Schweitzer said, "He tells them also that the appearance of the Son of Man will take place before they have gone through the cities of Israel, which can only mean that the celestial, messianic kingdom will be revealed while they are thus engaged. He has, therefore, no expectation of seeing them return.

How comes it that Jesus leads his disciples to expect events about which the remaining portion of the narrative is silent?

"I was dissatisfied with Holtzmann's explanation that we are dealing not with an historical discourse of Jesus, but with one made up at a later period, after his death, out of various 'Sayings of Jesus.' A later generation would never have gone so far as to put into his mouth words which were belied by the subsequent course of events.

"The bare text compelled me to assume that Jesus really announced persecutions for the disciples and, as a sequel to them, the immediate appearance of the celestial Son of Man, and that his announcement was shown by subsequent events to be wrong. But how came he to entertain such an expectation, and what must his feelings have been when events turned out otherwise than he had assumed they would?"[10]

It is at this point that Schweitzer emphasizes that when we consider the words of Jesus, "we tread the ground of the world-view that is not ours." To Jesus, this concept of eschatology was a real, a genuine belief, an honest expectation of the things that were coming and of the imminent end of the world. Schweitzer at this point finds the answer to questions that Christians for centuries had been confused about. He brings Christian thought back to an understanding of what it was that Jesus was actually saying and Schweitzer makes comprehensible what Jesus and his followers believed and understood.

The following chapter is a sequence to this passage. Here, even before the disciples have gone forth, the disciples of John the Baptist come to Jesus and ask him who he is. The eleventh chapter of Matthew reported it this way:

Now when John had heard in the prison the words of Christ, he sent two of his disciples, and said unto him, Art thou he that should come, or do we look for another? Jesus answered and said unto them, Go and shew John again those things which ye do hear and see: the blind receive their sight, and the lame walk, the lepers are cleansed, and the deaf hear, the dead are raised up, and the poor have the gospel preached to them. And blessed is he, whosoever shall not be offended in me.

Schweitzer gives this explanation: "Matthew 11 records the Baptist's question to Jesus, and the answer which Jesus sent back to him. Here too it seemed to me that Holtzmann and the commentators in general do not sufficiently appreciate the riddles of the text. Whom does the Baptist mean when he asks Jesus whether he is the 'one who is to come?' Is it then quite certain, I asked myself, that by 'the coming one' no one can be meant except the Messiah? According to late-Jewish messianic beliefs the coming of the Messiah is to be preceded by that of his forerunner, Elijah, risen from the dead, and to this previously expected Elijah, Jesus applies the expression of the Coming One, when he tells the disciples (Matt. 11:14) that the Baptist himself is Elijah who is to come. Therefore, so I concluded, the Baptist in his question used the expression with that same meaning. He did not send his disciples to Jesus with the question whether he was the Messiah; he wanted to learn from him, strange as this may seem to us, whether he was the expected forerunner of the Messiah, Elijah.

"But why does Jesus not give him a plain answer to his question? To say that he gave the evasive answer he did give in order to test the Baptist's faith is only an outcome of the embarrassment of commentators, and has opened the way for many bad sermons. It is much simpler to assume that Jesus avoided saying either Yes or No because he was not yet ready to make public whom he believed himself to be. From every point of view the account of the Baptist's question proves that at that time none of those who believed in Jesus held him to be the Messiah. Had he already been accepted in any way as the Messiah, the Baptist would have so framed his question as to imply that fact.

"I was also driven into new paths of interpretation by Jesus saying to the disciples after the departure of the Baptist's messengers, that of all born of women John was the greatest, but that the least in the kingdom of heaven was greater than he (Matt. 11:11).

"The usual explanation, that Jesus expressed in these words a criticism of the Baptist and placed him at a lower level than the believers in his teaching who were assembled round him as adherents of the kingdom of God, seemed to me both unsatisfying and crude, for these believers were also born of women. By giving up this explanation I was driven to the assumption that in contrasting the Baptist with members of the kingdom of God, Jesus was taking into account the difference between the natural world and the supernatural, messianic world. As a man in the condition into which all men enter at birth the Baptist is the greatest of all who have ever lived. But members of the kingdom of heaven are no longer natural men; through the dawn of the messianic kingdom they have experienced a change which has raised them to a supernatural condition akin to that of the angels. Because they are now supernatural beings the least among them is greater than the greatest man who has ever appeared in the natural world of the age which is now passing away. John the Baptist does, indeed, belong to this kingdom, either as a great or a humble member of it. But a unique greatness, surpassing that of all other human beings, is his only in his natural mode of existence."[11]

This world-view of Jesus' time involves eschatology which means "the end of things" and implies the rejection or negation of this world in which we live, and the judgment by which it is found wanting. For the ancient Jew, this meant that the natural world would come to a catastrophic end, and a new messianic world would be established by God, under a Son of David. Jesus spoke to this expectation, which is absent from modern thought. The modern response to this affirmation is of a spiritual world as the kingdom of God or kingdom of heaven.[12] In Jesus' own time it was the kingdom of the Messiah, a sociopolitical kingdom, which was expected. The uniqueness and originality of Jesus lay in offering a third alternative: the ending of the present imperfect world with the establishment of a new ethical world, a world based on love, which would be redeemed by man. Individual men and women could transform and save the natural world through their actions. The answer offered by Jesus was ethics; this is the basis of his humanism.

The fourth concern which faced Dr. Schweitzer was the extent to which Jesus was successful in his quest. The answer, Schweitzer reluctantly gave, was that Jesus was not successful. He was too original, too far ahead of his time, and too optimistic. The world was not automatically coming to an end, and indeed did not end. Ethics had not saved the world, Dr. Schweitzer felt, but remains a splendid vision which a few sensitive persons in each generation have grasped, but which the Christian Church has never succeeded in putting into practice. He wrote:

Jesus does not require of men today that they be able to grasp either in speech or in thought who he is. He did not think it necessary to give those who actually heard his sayings any insight into the secret of his personality, or to disclose to them the fact that he was that descendant of David who was one day to be revealed as the Messiah. The one thing he did require of them was that they should actively and passively prove themselves men who had been compelled by him to rise from being as the world to being other than the world, and thereby partakers of his peace.

Because, while I was investigating and thinking about Jesus, all this became a certainty to me. I let my *Quest of the Historical Jesus* end with the words: "As one unknown and nameless he comes to us, just as on the shore of the lake he approached those men who knew not who he was. His words are the same: 'Follow thou me!' and he puts us to the tasks which he has to carry out in our age. He commands. And to those who obey, be they wise or simple, he will reveal himself through all that they are privileged to experience in his fellowship of peace and activity of struggle and suffering, till they come to know, as an inexpressible secret, who he is. . . ."[13]

Dr. Schweitzer prepared three works as he carried on these studies, which became the basis for his greatest theological work, *The Quest of the Historical Jesus* (1906). They were: *The Problem of the Last Supper, A Study Based on the Scientific Research of the Nineteenth Century and the Historical Accounts* (1901), followed by *The Mysticism of the Kingdom of God, The Secret of Jesus' Messiahship and Passion* (1901), and in manuscript form, *Baptism in the Early Christian Church* (1902).

These studies were all specialized research projects into the questions which as a historian interested him, and led to the development of the work which the world knows as *The Quest for the Historical Jesus*.

While Dr. Schweitzer was pondering these questions and preparing his great study, other duties were to constantly intrude. He was offered the opportunity to teach, and accepted. On March 1, 1902, he began to lecture as a member of the theological faculty at the University of Strasbourg, and on October 1, 1903, he took over permanently the post of principal of the Theological College of St. Thomas.[14] It was a tribute to his scholarship, leadership and ability in human relations that he attained this high position in an important university so soon after graduation.

All the while he continued his organ work, researching the

life of Bach, playing with Widor and the Paris Bach Society during Easter vacation and the school recesses. Meanwhile, also, many other books were forming in his mind: his *Philosophy of Civilization*, intended as a four-volume study, was being outlined.

Schweitzer was suddenly being lionized. His concerts and recitals in the capitals of Europe made him famous everywhere, and people wished to meet him, shake his hand and talk with him. After they saw him play or heard him speak, they noted his disarming modesty, his unconscious mannerisms and perceived the depth from which he spoke and thought. Then they wanted to read his works. Thus, he found a growing audience and became a personality with a message, known, respected and honored all over Europe.

At thirty, Albert Schweitzer was famous. He was a consummate musician, a leading scholar, one of the world's great theologians and philosophers.

Still, he lived, thought, yearned in the present moment. His needs were seeking fulfillment in projects which satisfied him, not others. And this was the cause of continued unrest in him.

6

Second Decisions: Africa and Mission Service

All the outward signs of success and academic achievement could not subdue the inner ache, restlessness and spiritual dissatisfaction that now gnawed at Albert Schweitzer. While his books were being sold and apparently read, he wondered if his ideas were really being understood. And facing him as well were the searching questions that confront every sensitive scholar: Was formal teaching, the daily lectures to enrolled students enough of a challenge? And, could he add to this the normal frustrations and nuisance that belonged to every principal as he sorted out paperwork?

He relished the excitement that was generated by a musical event, the emergence of regional festivals or the publication of new materials. But even these were apparently not adequate or challenging enough in themselves for his ideal of the full life. Whether it be in theological debate or a musical interpretation, he longed for a depth of human experience that included involvement with others. Soon he was to feel almost imprisoned within the walls that proclaimed his academic degrees, awards and achievements. At such moments the memory returned to him of a spring morning in Günsbach, when he was home for a visit from college.

It was Easter vacation, 1896. Schweitzer lay in bed, hardly awake, as the bright rays of the sun slanted into his room. In the silence and loveliness of this early hour he was full of a sense of peace and absolute tranquility. He had often called his college days a time of endowed leisure. The scholar's life was for him not a bind but a blessing. He himself enjoyed school completely, but he frequently considered the state of mind of some of his friends. Many were not happy at all, many more not so financially secure. Their studies were not the pleasant exercise that he savored. Some had failed and dropped out the first term. Others struggled late and long to maintain a passing grade, living on the edge of failure and dismissal. Here he was celebrating the shining springtime while others lived in the dread of dean's reports and probationary threats. It didn't seem just. Should not one have to pay for the good life? Didn't *he* owe something, to someone for all *he* had received?

In this moment of epiphany, Schweitzer decided that he must pay back life for all its goodness. With careful analysis, he decided that he would enjoy this richly endowed life for another decade. Then he would find some field of service and sacrifice where he could repay Creation for all he had received.[1]

Schweitzer had not moved from his bed during this sequence of spiritual reckoning. Outdoors the world was stirring, birds finding their song, the sun climbing into the morning sky. He would look back to this time of decision for years to come: a course was now set. For the next ten years, he would live for science and art. He would capture the musical inspirations that moved him. He would search philosophy. He would write and be published. But all of this would find its final expression in some form of service to humanity. He would pay life back by serving it with heart and hand.[2] At thirty, he would give his life to the world.[3]

Over the years, when Schweitzer thought about this career, he recalled this decision. As he approached his thirtieth birthday, his vow to serve recurred more frequently. He felt he had really committed himself. But at times, he was not quite sure.

Pierre Teilhard de Chardin, like Schweitzer, was struggling for new ways to express the call of service to the world. He was to be an excellent priest and a superior scientist. In his personality, profession, and growth, spirit and matter were to unite. The old dualism, between material and spirit, flesh and soul, would dissolve in a blend of the two. This would one day cause great consternation in his Order, The Society of Jesus, and swift rejection from the Church in Rome. He would experience, as a reward for his unflinching pursuit of truth in science and an unyielding spirit of inquiry in religion, prohibition of all his written works. His scientific discoveries and personal theories of evolution as a part of true faith would bring near banishment and separation from the Catholic Church. He would survive only by the devotion of friends, the philanthropy of private organizations, and the care of fellow churchmen.

Early in his priesthood (1918), in a self-appraisal so like that of young Schweitzer, he charted the course he would follow:

As far as I can, because I am a priest I would henceforth be the first to become aware of what the world loves, pursues, suffers, I would be the first to seek, to sympathise, to toil; the first in self-fulfillment, the first in self-denial. For the sake of the world I would be more widely human in my sympathies and more nobly terrestrial in my ambitions than any of the world's servants.

On the one hand I want to plunge into the midst of created things and mingling with them, seize hold upon and disengage from them all that they contain of life eternal, down to the very last fragment, so that nothing may be lost; and on the other hand I want, by practising the counsels of perfection, to salvage through their self-denials all the heavenly fire imprisoned within the three-fold concupiscence of the flesh, of avarice, of pride: in other words to hallow, through chastity, poverty, and obedience, the power enclosed in love, in gold, in independence.

(*The Hymn of the Universe* 1918)[4]

Schweitzer's first translation of commitment into action was inconclusive. Indeed, this initial attempt at implementing his conviction was disheartening. He had joined the Reverend Augustus Ernst about the year 1903 in a special project of working with paroled prisoners and derelicts. For these forgotten men, the two secured lodging, offered counsel, and provided employment opportunities. They also made cash loans and collected second-hand clothing. Yet this personal effort on the part of these two concerned Christians did not yield much success or attract any spectacular support. The fund-raising aspect of the program was a nightmare to Schweitzer, who detested the begging of funds and the necessary door-to-door solicitations. Not many of their friends, and few within the religious community, were excited over their activity. For one thing, there was no real on-going program of rehabilitation. Also, they lacked a center for their operations and the derelicts were embarrassed by their unavoidable feeling of personal indebtedness. The vagrants were not anxious for work and the prisoners were merely looking for a community center or shelter that would provide the umbrella protection of an impersonal agency or social service. As a result, the ministers' effort sagged and Schweitzer became discouraged about his ability to give to others.

In addition, Schweitzer became bothered by another question: Should he pursue the ministry at all?

As the son of a pastor, he had felt especially close to the call of the ministry. He respected and admired his father's profession. College studies had prepared him for preaching as well as teaching and although his personal theological bent was untraditional, he nevertheless felt constrained to preach and did. But there were doubts.

"All this while," he later said, "I had been studying and thinking about the life of Jesus and the meaning of Jesus. And the more I studied and thought, the more convinced I became that Christian theology had become overly complicated."[5] As has been noted earlier, he sensed that in the early centuries after Christ, the beauty and clarity of his religion incredibly had become excessively complicated.

Schweitzer was certain that the personality and life of Jesus Christ had become grossly obscured by the rash of conflicting theories put forward by those who thought they were clarifying the "life" of the man from Galilee.

Of course, as his published works demonstrate, Schweitzer was not beyond making his own interpretations and comments about the life and meaning of Christ. Even as a child he had not been satisfied with the historic assumptions or dogmatic manuals of faith.

When I was eight, my father, at my own request, gave me a New Testament, which I read eagerly. Among the stories that interested me most was that of the Three Wise Men from the East. What did the parents of Jesus do, I asked myself, with the gold and other valuables which they got from these men? How could they have been poor after that?

And that the Wise Men should never have troubled themselves again about the Child Jesus was to me incomprehensible. The absence, too, of any record of the shepherds of Bethlehem becoming disciples, gave me a severe shock.[6]

These youthful thoughts and critical examinations were to be the basis for an adult struggle of large and significant proportions. They were to mean nothing less than the final break of Albert Schweitzer from conservative, fundamentalist interpretation of Scripture and eventually a lifelong clash with orthodoxy that would resolve itself decades later—in his favor.

The young theologian was asking this sort of question as he looked out upon the clergy in his training:

Is Jesus actually God or the Son of God? If he is God, why did he suffer? If he was the Son of God, why was he made to suffer? What do we mean by the spirit of Jesus? And what about his mother, Mary; what is the real place for her in Christian theology?[7]

Schweitzer believed that the basic questions of Christian theology did not need to be intricate or elaborate. He was almost angry that the Church fathers and scholars were not as explicit in their thoughts as Jesus himself had been. The words of Jesus were powerful in their truth—and simplicity. A learned theologian or an adolescent could study them with excitement and understanding—why should the religious community confound the world when man was simply looking for bread?

Schweitzer believed that Jesus saw his mission as one to

awaken the people to the coming of the kingdom of God. It was not to proclaim himself the Son of God—or God, but to express the power and intensity and imminence of the coming kingdom. Eschatology. But even the use of such technical terms was a source of uneasiness to Schweitzer, as were the questions he raised.

He told Norman Cousins that "in my effort to get away from intricate Christian theology based on later interpretations, I developed some ideas of my own."[8] That was an understatement. For these ideas and insights were to send vibrations throughout the Christian community. They would also later make it necessary for Schweitzer to agree not to preach but only to practice medicine while operating his hospital under the auspices of the conservative Paris Missionary Society.

It was one thing for Schweitzer to pursue his concerns and challenge established doctrine in the quiet of his library and quite something else to do so as the principal of a seminary charged with the teaching and training of young men for the ministry. He faced a great dilemma. He could not deny his own academic integrity by ignoring pressing questions and doubts, yet the school was founded by churches that were solid in traditional theology and desired the promotion of classic, biblical studies. The other members of the faculty did not share his more liberal concepts and were bent on the teaching of fundamentalist faith. Schweitzer thus felt it would be improper for him to campaign for his own beliefs and further the confusion which surely would increase when his students found themselves caught between the old and the new.

Faced with this dilemma, he resolved to leave the seminary. "I decided," he later told Cousins, "that I would make my life my argument. I would advocate the things I believed in terms of the life I lived and what I did."[9]

These then were the circumstances that forced Dr. Schweitzer to arrive at the full and final expression of his life's work: his need to give humanity service; the staleness

and safety of traditional teaching that held for him no ultimate challenge; and the necessity he saw to faithfully pursue
his own intellectual curiosity and retain the academic integrity which would be considered heresy if he stayed where he
was. But Schweitzer still was unsure how to express all this,
how to make dynamic living witness to his inner convictions.

Mere happenstance would fashion the direction of his
life: one evening in the autumn of 1904, he casually glanced
through the magazines that his librarian, Miss Scherdlin, always placed on his desk prior to their circulation in the reading room. In the pile was the familiar green cover of the Paris
Missionary Society monthly. Miss Scherdlin recalled that although Dr. Schweitzer had been critical of the mission
societies, he admitted to a seminar group that the Paris society
was somewhat more liberal than the others. Thus she saw to
it that the publication reached his desk, along with the other
scholarly journals and secular publications.

That evening he picked up the magazine—but only to move
it aside and set to work. Absent-mindedly he opened the
journal, and the title of an article caught his eye: "The Needs
of the Congo Mission." He began to read the vivid account of
the mission work in the Upper Congo described by Alfred
Boegner, President of the Paris Missionary Society. The
writer spoke of the special problems that created so much
suffering and disease in this French sector of Africa—now
Gabon. The Africans were in desperate need of doctors—men
and women who could face the crippling ailments, illnesses
and injury that had plagued so many people. The article was
a powerful emotional appeal, inviting, pleading, shouting for
someone to come forward in service and assistance. Who
should these people be? "Men and women who can reply
simply to the Master's call, 'Lord, I am coming,' those are the
people whom the Church needs," the article said.

Of all the hundreds of young men and women who read
this piece, none could have been more affected than Albert
Schweitzer. When he had finished the article, he put the
magazine aside and quietly began his work. But his search

was over.[10] He saw his time and place; his future, his life, took clear shape.

On January 6, 1905, Schweitzer preached a sermon at St. Nicholai's Church entitled "The Call to Mission" in which he recalled that in the mid-nineties, Professor Lucius, a devoted friend of missions, "was lecturing about the history of missions on a summer afternoon between three and four o'clock. It was very hot, and barely a half dozen students were present. In his words that day I heard, for the first time, the idea of atonement. It was so strange. Dogmatics and New Testament exegesis found it difficult to explain why Jesus died for the sins of the world. Everything we had been told about the crucifixion was cut and dried, lifeless. And we could tell that those who lectured on the subject were not too confident about its meaning themselves. But now, as a call to service in Jesus' name, the significance of missions became alive. The word cried so loudly that we could not escape understanding and grasping it. And from that day on, I understood Christianity better and knew why we must work in the mission field."[11]

Thus Schweitzer had reached the point of view that atonement for the wrongs that the Christian—the white man—had done to underdeveloped peoples—the black man—was in itself a justification for missions.

Schweitzer summarized: "And now, when you speak about missions, let this be your message: We must make atonement for all the terrible crimes we read of in the newspapers. We must make atonement for the still worse ones, which we do not read about in the papers, crimes that are shrouded in the silence of the jungle night. Then you preach Christianity and missionary work at the same time. I implore you to preach it."[12]

Schweitzer had now articulated the position he had reached upon reading in the fall of 1904 about the needs of the Congo mission. By the winter of 1905, he clearly knew his future course. This knowledge was to lead to the action he would shortly take. The dream was to become a reality for as he wrote, "The next several months I acted like a man in a dream."

The next several months he did indeed act like a man in a dream. The emotional aftereffects of the decision to go to Africa upset him constantly . . . was he equal to such a radical reorganization of his life? Not a few complications loomed before him: the cost, the involved planning and training and preparation that was required to truly be of service there. He turned all his energy toward plans for his chosen mission.

The first major moves began on October 13, 1905, when he posted some letters to his parents and certain close friends, informing them that at the beginning of the winter term, he would enroll as a medical student. His destination was to be Africa. His profession would not be music or philosophy or theology but the practice of medicine.[13] In another letter, he resigned as principal of the Theological College at St. Thomas in Strasbourg. The finality of this move was disturbing but Schweitzer felt it to be the only means to put his plan into action.

Shock, puzzlement, and alarm were the responses to these first letters.[14] The faculty of St. Thomas was stunned. The administration officers felt that he had made a serious mistake in his decision and expressed their disapproval. Friends around Europe could not accept it either and wrote him of their immediate, strenuous objections. His parents were, of course, the most personally affected. They had celebrated proudly and joyfully the achievements of young Albert Schweitzer. Barely out of his twenties, he was already recognized as a scholar, musician and philosopher. Now he was ready to cast these attainments aside.

Schweitzer's father could only express disappointment. The family suggested that the whole enterprise was foolish. They could not conceive that he could bury his life and his talent in the jungle while there were others who could easily take the Congo assignment.

Churchmen looked upon Schweitzer with awe and envy. He had mastered the normal demands of theology and then marshaled his intellect and sensitive spirit to carve out new advances with his studies in the life of Jesus and his questions of dogma and tradition. They were amazed that this man was to bury himself in the trackless jungles of Africa when all of the rewards of Western society were his for the taking.

His mentor, Widor, loved him like a son and scolded him like one as well, accusing Schweitzer of behaving like a general who wanted to take up a rifle and go into the front line of combat instead of staying behind at headquarters where he could use his great skills to organize the attack.[15]

A lady friend told him that he could do much more for the Africans by lecturing on the need for medical assistance, thus raising the funds and inspiring the army of young people necessary to really accomplish so vast an undertaking.

What irritated Schweitzer more than anything else was the unexpected shallowness and conservatism of so many Christian friends and acquaintances. These people were active, concerned churchmen. Yet they were aghast that anyone would seriously respond to the words of Jesus Christ. All the days in conference, prayer and study, all the services of baptism, communion and committal, all the sermons and vespers and carols—all added up to a Jesus that for most was forever distant, beautiful and safe. It seemed frankly irrational to find a man in the twentieth century who actually felt constrained to *live* the words and witness of Jesus. For many, Schweitzer was the first to try. Schweitzer was to remember the struggles and the letters of protest and scolding. He wrote:

In the many verbal duels which I had to fight, as a weary opponent, with people who passed for Christians, it moved me strangely to see them so far from perceiving that the effort to serve the love preached by Jesus may sweep a man into a new course of life, although they read in the New Testament that it can do so, and found it there quite in order . . . Several times, indeed, it was my experience that my appeal to the act of obedience, which Jesus' command of love may under special circumstances call for, brought me an accusation of conceit, although I had, in fact, been obliged to do violence to my feelings to employ this argument at all. In general, how much I suffered through so many people assuming a right to tear open all the doors and shutters of my inner self![16]

Only Helene Bresslau understood and supported him.

One thing that should be noted is the fact that Albert Schweitzer had been many things to many people. His particular relationship to others gave them much—his family, his associates, his students, his wide and varied and appreciative musical audience. All found something thrilling, gratifying and inspiring about Schweitzer. Suddenly and radically he was taking himself out of their lives. He had given their lives a perspective, and now he was to vanish from their existence. Many were not thinking of him and his service, but of themselves and their emptiness without his guidance, entertainment, wisdom or care. Greatness, they feared was passing them by and for many, Schweitzer's was the only greatness and goodness they had ever experienced.

In truth, the more they opposed his intentions, the more he sensed that the ethics of Jesus had to become, for him, unlike for them, a way of life. He felt he had to prove *his* faith by living it—the only method that would, in the end, redeem Christianity from its inward, ingrown journey and take it out into the world for the practice of it desired by God.

Dr. Schweitzer once told Norman Cousins that his decision was not the result of having heard the voice of God. Rather it was a completely rational decision, consistent with the patterns and projections of his life.[17] Of course, there were theologians who had told him that they had had a direct word from God, regarding their lives. He never argued. He only remarked that their ears were sharper than his.[18]

When a young man—as Schweitzer did—acknowledges the source of creation and his participation in it, he has surely approached the most deeply spiritual aspect of religion. As Jean Mouroux wrote:

In the religious act, I become aware of my situation with respect to God, I take up an attitude towards him; by making an act of affirmation with my intellect, I adhere to the truth of God and the truth of my being in relation to him. Adoration, humility, and love are necessarily involved in this act in its profoundest depths.[19]

And then, as if Schweitzer were speaking with him, Mouroux concludes:

The experience also includes a voluntary element. It is necessarily an act of freedom—to be more precise, an act of generosity —that founds and posits the relationship . . . I wager my whole destiny and vocation, I abandon myself to God so that I may serve him. For God is love, and the only way I can respond to the gift which he has made me of my being, and of himself through my being, is by the gift of myself in return.[20]

When Schweitzer finally was prepared to go to Africa, he preached a "farewell sermon" to his faithful flock at St. Nicholai's on March 9, 1913, where he summed up his position:

In our age, reason is belittled and slighted—in Catholic and Protestant churches alike. People seem to think such irreverence will make religion easier. In this age I have come before you, daring to speak of religion with joy and reverence. I have tried to use reason to illuminate everything that concerns faith and religion, for I know from personal experience that this is the way my own religion has been kept alive and deepened. The more I understood Jesus, the clearer it became to me and more I was impressed by the way he combined faith and simple common sense. The more I studied the history of Christianity, the more I realized the extent of the errors and disagreements which started because men from the first generation to this day played up faith and piety at the expense of reason, and so put asunder what God had joined together harmoniously.[21]

In his own life, Schweitzer would combine the whole together again—harmoniously.

Breaking from Europe

The function of the poet, wrote Pierre Emannuel, is "to disclose the fatal sickness of his epoch long before it declares itself openly, to unmask beneath unequivocal symptoms, the underlying corruption of energy, and to prevent the latter from flourishing blindly. . . ."

We have reached that point in the life and work of Albert Schweitzer that his friends and interpreters call the "great renunciation." It can be seen as a culmination of ideas Schweitzer expressed in lectures and sermons as well as in conversations he shared with colleagues and family: specifically, his decision to go to Africa represented as much a rejection of European civilization as it did an eagerness to repay the gift of life. And Schweitzer was a man who knew what he was setting aside: personal fulfillment in the arts; academic, scholarly achievements that had brought him world-wide honor; close family ties. In Germany and France, he was an acknowledged and respected young philosopher-theologian. At the time of his decision, he already had begun the serious study of English in order to respond to the invitation of a Cambridge lectureship.

Yet Schweitzer was not happy in Europe; he felt ill at ease and at loose ends. He wrote, "I often had to recognize that the need 'to do something special' was born of a restless spirit. Only a person who feels his preference to be a matter of course, not something out of the ordinary is capable of becoming a spiritual adventurer. There are no heroes of action, only heroes of renunciation and suffering."[1] His family was proud of cousins who had emigrated to America, one of whom, Eugene Debs, had already been elected to political

office and leadership in the railroad workers union. Debs'
early letters, articles, speeches, and later books, revealed the
integrity of a stalwart individualist who was to become a
leading socialist and pacifist. Later when Americans such as
Adlai Stevenson visited Schweitzer, he would tell them, "I
had a cousin who ran for President of the United States."

What many people did not realize is the fact that Schweitzer became deeply concerned with the plight of Western
civilization during the dazzling years of his rise to scholarly
achievement. His education had not been simply an academic exercise for grades, honors and diplomas. He required far more than the satisfaction of succeeding in
doctrinal exams and department orals. He needed to be chal-
lenger as well as interpreter. And when he ranged across the
vast wealth of Western philosophical and theological resources, he was correcting as well as codifying. The easy
explanations, the traditional answers, the orthodox confessions were not acceptable to him unless they became part of
his own experience. He had the courage of his convictions
and came to the conclusion that the intellectual leadership
of Europe was faltering, as he wrote of "the fact that I have
been born into a period of spiritual decadence of mankind."[2]

Later he wrote, "Our institutions are a failure because the
spirit of barbarism is at work in them."[3] As to why he felt
this way, he explained, "Our society has also ceased to allow
to all men, as such, a human value and a human dignity;
many sections of the human race have become merely raw
material and property in human form."[4] Of cities he wrote,
"It is doubtful whether big cities have ever been foci of
civilization"[5] but the spirit of our age says, "There is
nothing, therefore, for us to do but to take the causes of this
(outrage) as quite natural, and to do our best at any rate to
find interesting the unedifying phenomena of its senility,
which testify to the gradual loss of the ethical character of
civilization."[6] "The demoralization of the individual by the

mass is in full swing."[7] These quotations are from the book he said he wished to write when he went to Africa.

Schweitzer sensed the general decay of a society that he saw as willing to gloss over its injustice and discrimination, to condone its glaring inequities and shortcomings. The churches, the universities, the professions, the leadership of business and commerce had finally been content, he felt, to press only so far in their self-criticism of Western civilization. They completed the compromise of their integrity in his view by feeding the rise of nationalism, an attitude that was accepted by every nation in Europe.

Leibnitz triggered the scorn of Schweitzer with his embarrassed observation that the world was indeed not good but at least the best one possible.[8] Schweitzer would however not settle for a morally mediocre world. His sermons preached at Strasbourg revealed his inability to accept the platitudes of the day. Whether his theme was education, immortality, music or funeral practices, the independent critique of society by a man of high standards was always visible. Indeed, his strength and constant popularity as a preacher lay in his ability to fire his audience, to give them a solid spiritual lift so that they could not rest comfortably with the mediocre nor allow society to blow out the fires of free thought in their minds and hearts. For Schweitzer, the Christian faith was a liberation movement and he felt ordained to be its practitioner as well as its preacher.

It should come as no surprise to read later that he claimed never to have been completely happy in his life. "With the spirit of the age I am in complete disagreement," he wrote. "Doubts, therefore, could well arise as to whether thinking would be capable of answering current questions about the world and our relation to it in such a way that would give a meaning and a content to our lives." Viewing such a statement, it is hard to separate Schweitzer from other seers and prophets who have sounded the depths of a given society and found it hollow and empty.

A generation later, a young German pastor, Dietrich

Bonhoeffer, was to sense under Hitler the same sickness, the same imbalance in a culture that found comfort in ignoring the difficult questions and avoiding the real issues that meant life or death for a whole age. Bonhoeffer wrote:

These things come home to one particularly when one realizes the unprecedented state of our public life in Germany. The outlook is really exceptionally grim. There is in fact no one in Germany who can see ahead even a little way. People generally, however, are under the very definite impression that they are standing at a tremendous turning point in world history.[9]

Schweitzer's response to his own criticism of Western civilization was to be a personal statement, a commitment of his life. He was not a social reformer and never sought the role and influence of political leadership. He would seek meaning in his own life, and the society, culture and church that deprived him of this fulfillment was to be renounced and forsaken. European society was the cause of his rebellion, and his commitment in Africa would be the response he could most effectively make.

Schweitzer had explored the cultures of the ancient and Middle Eastern worlds as a student. His writings on Jesus, Paul and the kingdom of God reveal his concern for as well as his mastery of these subjects. In the end he was to discover that the modern world must yield its own answer to these frequently debated biblical subjects for itself. His last manuscripts, published as *The Kingdom of God and Primitive Christianity* returned to this debate of biblical authority that he started in his youth with the appearance of *The Quest of the Historical Jesus*.

Schweitzer believed that, viewing the Bible accurately, the seeds of ethical awareness that were sowed in the prophets appear in the teachings of Jesus. The Sermon on the Mount he saw as the fulfillment of the ethical imperative to love.

When he reached the concluding section of *The Kingdom of God and Primitive Christianity*, Schweitzer saw St. Paul as the resolution of certain primary questions.

Paul, the thinker, recognized as the essence the Kingdom of

God, which was coming into existence, that it consists in the rule of the Spirit. We learn from this knowledge which comes to us through him that the way in which the coming of the Kingdom will be brought about is by the coming of Jesus Christ to rule in our hearts and through us in the whole world. In the thought of Paul, the supernatural Kingdom is beginning to become the ethical and, with this, the change from the Kingdom to be expected into something which has to be realized. It is for us to take the road which this prospect opens up.[10]

Albert Schweitzer took that road and sought the answers which civilization had never found, yet which still lay before it. They preoccupied his mind, his action, his driving energy for a lifetime.

Although separated from Schweitzer and often also working alone, others too were involved with the ultimate questions in philosophy and religion. Such a contemporary who shared priorities with Schweitzer was Martin Buber.

Throughout his life, Buber's primary concern was the advance of Zionism. In Berlin in 1900–1 and in Vienna in 1902 Buber actively pressed his platform for a Zionism founded on the ideas of inner renewal and spiritual growth rather than on a Jewish nationalism which was being advanced by "political Zionist" leaders such as Herzl. The development of a Jewish state was the avowed intention of Herzl and his followers. They considered Buber too idealistic, too romantic, too much the mystic to organize and extend the kind of Zionism that was to capture the imagination of Jewish people around the world. Yet Buber persisted. He envisioned a Zionism that went far beyond being Jewish, nothing less than a global spiritual renewal that welcomed Christians as well as Jews. Buber's concept of freedom within community constantly raised tensions between political and "cultural" Zionism.

During World War I, Buber felt constrained to isolate the issues again and make clear where he stood. The similarity of his view to Schweitzer's is evident:

I would simply say this: that the idea of a Jewish State, with flag and cannon and so forth, I will have nothing to do with—not

even in my dreams. How things turn out will depend on what
people make of them; therefore those who are concerned about
the person and about humanity must give themselves to the task
—here, now that once again it lies with men to build a community, a fellowship.[11]

And Buber again, like Schweitzer, fought for an openness,
a dialogue with a religious community that encompassed the
world. He would not let his particular religious tradition or
loyalties encroach on the opportunities that God sets before
every generation for growth and renewal. So he could also
say:

An Israel aspiring to renewal of her faith and a Christendom
striving for the renewal of hers should have much to say to each
other which has not so far been said, and they could offer to help
each other in a fashion which at present we are scarcely able to
conceive.[12]

When confronted with American life, Schweitzer felt it to
be only a pale reflection of its European source. Emerson,
Thoreau, Parker—great spokesmen of an earlier generation had
called on the American experiment to strike out in new directions. But it seemed to Schweitzer to be merely a dupli-
cate, a later model of the European failure. Philosophers
such as Thoreau found an audience in America yet received
little more for their ideas beyond polite applause. Thus,
when Schweitzer speaks of the European failure, he includes
the collapse of American civilization as well. Only once did
he visit the United States, in 1949, but he found no superior
answer in the American brand of Western culture. Individuals and groups were friendly, but America seemed to him
exactly like Europe except that it had four-lane highways and
high-rise buildings.

Schweitzer read extensively in Oriental culture and philosophy. Indian thought helped him in his personal development and in his rejection of Europe. But its passivity and
alienation from the world were not to add to the enlarged
freedom he sought. In addition, a systematic study of Chi-

nese thought became a lifelong endeavor for him. At his death, several unpublished manuscripts on Chinese philosophy were still in the study-library. Yet China, like India, offered no final solution for Schweitzer. And Africa, he found to be an oral and activist society, without a notable written tradition or heritage.

Well after the announcement of his decision to go to Africa as a doctor, there continued the verbal duels with his friends who still could not accept this drastic change in his professional career. "It was no use allowing them to have a glimpse of the thoughts which had given birth to my resolution."[13] Schweitzer was a man of independent thought, and he was to remain this way for ninety years.

In 1906, the year of his momentous decision to go to Africa, another significant event occurred in the birth of Jean-Paul Sartre, his second cousin. The infant (grandson of his father's brother Charles) was to grow up during the period of Schweitzer's medical studies in Strasbourg and Paris, and Schweitzer saw him frequently as a child. As a young man, after World War I, Sartre became close to his cousin whom he always called Uncle Albert. Later, Jean-Paul Sartre was of course to emerge as the chief exponent of the school of French existentialism that flourished in the postwar years of World War II.

In 1905, Schweitzer had begun his first reading in the works of Søren Kierkegaard, the Danish theologian and first existentialist. His works had just been translated into German and while his religious piety never influenced Schweitzer, his critique of Christianity and culture helped Schweitzer in bringing his own philosophical position into focus.

Schweitzer now was questioning the whole theological framework of Christian thought as well as rejecting its concept of a purposeful universe. He felt compelled to develop a new world-view, which as he noted, lay in part in a return to the world-view of the Stoics. They believed that purpose lies in mankind, not in the world itself.

It is not known to what extent he discussed these ideas

with Sartre. In recent years, Robert Mindel of the Collège de France in Paris, and Dr. John Everett, President of the New School of Social Research in New York, have pointed out the existential nature of Schweitzer's position. This position is the reason, Dr. Everett insists, that Schweitzer is not dealt with as a philosopher in the formal schools of philosophy, which, rigidly adhering to the approach of linguistic analysis, have tried to avoid existentialism.

The long-time associate of Dr. Schweitzer who shared his last decade at Lambaréné, Dr. Richard Friedmann, a philosopher, physician and psychiatrist, claims that most of Sartre's teachings came from his older cousin—though he feels they lacked Schweitzer's added insight. The depth and meaning of his quest carried Schweitzer far beyond the position taken by most modern existentialists. For he could never settle for the notion that existence was basically purposeless. The universe might be purposeless, Schweitzer felt, but man could create purpose and meaning in life. This was to be the great imperative of his own life: man could supply compassion amidst raw, brutal nature; man could be a moral person in an immoral universe. Upon these principles, Schweitzer was to restructure and reshape his life.

During his time of conflict, questioning and search, Schweitzer was to meet the one person who would fully understand him and his philosophy: Helene Bresslau. Her father was the distinguished Professor of History at the University of Strasbourg. His home became for Schweitzer one of the primary settings for his intellectual encounters as Schweitzer shared his concerns and ideas with this brilliant scholar of Jewish background, and atheist conviction. Dr. Bresslau had rejected the Hebrew tradition and indeed all forms of religious institutionalism entirely.

As Schweitzer continued his frequent visits to Dr. Bresslau's study, he came to appreciate and enjoy the companionship of the professor's quiet, studious daughter. And her militance. For Helene, like Albert, had chosen a difficult and unusual course upon graduation from the College of Teachers at Strasbourg. She had studied social work and then had entered this field, one which was not yet welcoming women into its professional ranks. More specifically, Helene had become vitally involved with helping unwed mothers who were at that time most often regarded as "fallen women." Her classmates and friends had offered nothing but criticism of her involvement in such a project. This pioneering, dark-haired, often unsmiling young woman was to become the friend and confidante of Albert Schweitzer during the most turbulent period of his life. At first a quiet observer of discussions between her father and Schweitzer, she gradually became a participant in and partner to the emotionally charged decisions that were to be made by Schweitzer. And gradually she fell in love with this young man that she most admired.

Schweitzer had never really been involved with a girl in his student years. His social life had been limited by his larger interests in the world of ideas and great music, and the challenges of higher goals and career aspirations. It was thus with bewilderment and exasperation, that Schweitzer received the word of some, critical of his African dream, who hinted that he was leaving Europe because of an unhappy love affair. They might as well have cited a total lack of love affairs, for Schweitzer had been thoroughly immersed in academic and musical commitments.

He was, however, experiencing a courtship of sorts with Helene Bresslau. They shared ideas, hopes and dreams of Africa, and they were inspired by the courage and determination that each saw in the other. To talk seriously of philosophy, religion, psychology and culture brought deep personal satisfaction to them both. Their relationship would not be based on the giving and sharing of their physical bodies so much as the long years of mutual understanding and support given often in loneliness by each between the continents of Europe and Africa.

Schweitzer could offer nothing that would appeal to a young woman who had built her life on the expectations of

living in her home town, surrounded by family and familiar
sights. His would not be the steady hours and the predictable
income. Nor could he offer stability of residence, of even the
absence of danger and disease for the future. He always had
the aspect of one who was estranged, often thinking thoughts
that had a taint of heresy, sedition or arrogance. When one
goes against society, culture and the Church, one is essentially
inviting the world to combat. Helene Bresslau understood
these storms of conscience. She had felt throughout her life
the insecurities of being a Jewish girl in a dominant Christian
culture, always admiring a father who had the power to reject
both Judaism and Christianity.

When Albert Schweitzer came into her home and her
father's life, he also brought to her a sense of joy and excitement that she had never known. He was not only one of her
father's most distinguished students but one of the most
famous scholars in Strasbourg. In the university he was a topic
of discussion, whether one argued religion or commented on
his last recital. His books were well known within the circle
of her friends and his preaching was far and away the most
challenging that many had heard in local pulpits. Yet Helene
was so quiet, reserved and unsure of herself socially that it
was years before she and Schweitzer were seen publicly. He
had at that point visited her home for almost a decade and
she had followed with fascination and excitement his un-
folding plans for work in Africa.

As these plans became more specific, she realized that Albert had become an essential part of her life. Although people
spoke openly of their friendship—and they had thought of
it as only a companionship—they felt it would be terminated
with Schweitzer's departure for Africa. But Helene now
found so much of her attitude toward life and its meaning
expressed in the person of Albert Schweitzer. She was not
alone in this. His parents had gone through despair to think
of parting with their son. Friends, colleagues, musicians, students—all felt emptiness when they recognized the firmness
of his resolve to leave Europe and literally and physically

renounce its way of life. But for Helene Bresslau, parting from Albert would mean the virtual loss of her life and values.

What she was to do would not be easy or very coy. Some would call her scheming, for she would ask Albert Schweitzer to marry her. If she did not, she felt they would never be husband and wife, and she would never see him again. If there had been a tragedy in either life it might have been this lack of romantic or emotional involvement with one another, but as good companions neither ever complained. It was during the hectic days of decision for Schweitzer that Helene made known her intentions—but not fully. Now that he was about to enter medical school, she told him she was prepared to study nursing. He would need competent assistance in Africa if his hospital and clinic were to succeed. There would be no likelihood of any skilled personnel being present in equatorial Africa. Aside from a few merchants and river traders, no one would even be educated, and medical skills and training would have to be supplied from Europe. Schweitzer knew these facts—thus, when Helene offered to change her own career, he saw it primarily as a means to further a common cause.

During the years of their joint studies, Helene and Albert were in constant touch. And the closer they came to an actual departure date, the more logical it seemed that they should marry. Their values and sense of service were identical. Their appraisal of Western culture meshed in their mutual feelings of estrangement and rejection. Helene had never felt her destiny to be wrapped up in Germany or the rest of Europe. The excitement and reverie of involvement in the struggles of Albert Schweitzer had brought a dimension to her life that nothing could dampen. He was thoroughly immersed in Africa, in the specialty of tropical medicines, in the fundamentalist politics of mission society intrigue. Helene was throughout his preparation both listener and supporter. But she wanted, finally to become his wife, and she began to ask him how he felt about their going to Africa as Doctor and Nurse. Would this jeopardize his standing with the sponsoring Society? What would his friends think about their being together in Africa if they were unmarried? Had he ever thought about a lifelong commitment that was more than professional or ethical?

Of course, their most intimate thoughts and conversations on these matters were never recorded. But we do know that in the final months of preparation, Albert Schweitzer said to Helene, "We must go to Africa as husband and wife. It is not proper or good thinking to arrange it any other way. We will be married." And they were, as she had planned and hoped.

Little did she realize how many years they would be separated, continents apart. For although Helene had devoted every ounce of her energy, determination, and will power in her desire to be part of the doctor's life, her own physique would rebel. She was never able to maintain the grueling, exhausting pace of the determined man who had married a Jewish girl to accompany him on a Christian mission in pagan Africa. But what she would have, even in her declining years and confining months of old age, was the abiding joy of having married Albert Schweitzer and having been part of one of the great dreams of the century. The two would become one in their toil and their triumph. They were married on June 18, 1912. This is also supposedly the date of the first time that Albert ever kissed her.

As a medical student, Schweitzer plunged into his new studies with a total dedication. Nothing less would have been adequate. He had to acquire a basic knowledge of the physical and biological sciences. This meant learning physics, chemistry and biology as the necessary requirements for medical school acceptance. Here was a man with two earned degrees, now beginning again. And the scientific subjects did not come easily to one who had specialized in theology and philosophy. Long, late hours of study were his path to medical school.

Helpfully, the theological faculty voted to retain him as a full professor while relieving him of the administrative duties of principal. It was still necessary for him to lecture, grade papers and hold student conferences. Also, Schweitzer's dean's quarters had to be vacated but again the faculty showed its understanding by arranging for a rent-free apartment for him on the top floor. The student body showed their affection and interest in his project by providing the manpower in carrying his books and furnishings to the new fourth-floor apartment.

Although his administrative load had been reduced, Schweitzer still could not cut down on his other activities. For one thing, the income from concerts and recitals was required so that he could build reserve funds for his trip. Yet his minimal teaching assignment meant a smaller salary, barely enough to cover living expenses. It was here that the medical faculty helped by waiving the normal tuition and laboratory fees for his studies in their school. When Schweitzer later took up the specialty of tropical medicine in other schools, he found it necessary to increase his schedule of recitals to pay the unexpected costs. All of these activities—the research and writing projects, the medical studies, the recitals, made for a grueling schedule.

And Schweitzer no longer was a young, adolescent student with time and energy for everything. Now a man in his thirties, he found his long night hours of study terribly exhausting. In order to keep himself from dozing at his desk, he asked the housekeeper to leave a basin of cold water in his room. She thought that he applied this to his forehead when he became drowsy. It was only months later that she learned that he plunged his feet into the water and soaked them there when he felt sleepy. This not only kept him awake but gives us an example of his typical perseverance in completing work that simply had to be done.

When Schweitzer arrived at the medical school administrative office, he created a sensation. He recalled the occasion with these words, "When I went to Professor Fehling, at that time dean of the medical faculty, to give my name as a student, he would have liked best to hand me over to his colleague in the psychiatric department."[14] As stated, the university council waived the student fees since he was a fellow faculty member, and various other normal student restrictions were also set aside, but there were legal difficulties connected with Schweitzer's enrollment to be resolved, due to the bureaucratic nature of German-run universities. In time, the faculty found a way to settle all such problems. Consequently, in the final week of October 1905, Schweitzer attended his first lecture, in anatomy.

German medical training required five terms each of lectures in the fields of anatomy, physiology, chemistry, physics, zoology and botany. Following this study, Schweitzer would take the natural-sciences examination, called the *Physikum*. He plunged into his courses with teachers who came to mean much to him later as he practiced in the equatorial jungle. Stern disciplinarians, they required careful study and accurate information.

On May 13, 1908, he took his *Physikum;* it was a rainy day, but in spite of this and other factors, it proved to be a memorable occasion. He found that the memory of a man over thirty is not that of a student of twenty. In addition, old scholar that he was, he almost hurt his performance by ignoring the urging and invitation of the other younger students to join them in their cramming sessions, the *"Paukverband."* They assured him that he could not pass without the review and memorization of recent examinations for each course, together with the answers expected by the professors. It seemed too juvenile at first to Schweitzer to enlist in such activity, but then he remembered the virtue of humility. Perhaps his professional status was getting in his way. He remembered that he was not now a professor, but a student. He was confronting a strange new discipline and it was imperative that he succeed as a student; consequently he attended the cramming sessions, and was grateful he did. As a result, the examination went better for him than he expected, although he was going through the worst crisis of fatigue he had ever experienced, perhaps even worse than that which would follow the First World War.[15]

Yet he had found his subjects to be invigorating and challenging. To him, "study of the natural sciences brought me
even more than the increase of knowledge I had longed for.
It was to me a spiritual experience."[16] The rigorous challenge
to prove all facts, and to take nothing for granted was enervat-
ing, but mentally invigorating as well. The search for truth
in the humanities, in the fields of history, philosophy and
religion, he wrote "is carried on in constantly repeated endless duels between the sense of reality of the one and the
inventive imaginative power of the other. The argument from
facts is never able to obtain a definite victory over the skill-
fully produced opinion." Rather, he thought progress in
such fields was often merely the result of skillful argu-
mentation. "Now I was in another country. I was concerned
with truths which embodied realities, and found myself
among men who took it as a matter of course that they had
to justify with facts every statement they made. It was an
experience which I felt to be needed for my own intellectual
development."[17]

Philosopher that he was, one danger was that he would
pursue the natural sciences for their own ends, for he wrote,
"I had stupidly got into my head the idea of studying pure
science only right to the end, instead of preparing for the
examinations."[18] This would have brought his downfall had
it not been for the cramming sessions with his fellow
students.

After the *Physikum*, Schweitzer had to undertake the clin-
ical program of his medical education. This proved to be far
less of a strain for him than the academic work. His principal
studies included medicine, gynecology, bacteriology, pathological anatomy and pharmacology.

One of his professors, Schmiedeberg, was a kind, gentle
man. Years later Schweitzer saw him on a railroad platform
with a group of Germans being evacuated from Alsace following the Armistice, clutching one clumsily wrapped bundle. Schweitzer knew the Germans were being sent hastily
across the border without having the opportunity to properly

pack or salvage their household goods and furniture, so he went up to his old teacher and asked if he could be of any service to him. Instead of asking for help with his furniture, he handed Schweitzer the package he was carrying. He said it was his lifework on digitalis, and that he was worried it would be confiscated by the French soldiers. Would Schweitzer keep it for him? He did and later mailed it to the doctor in Baden-Baden, who lived just long enough to see it published.[19]

As always, Schweitzer continued to find memorable relationships through his student activities. He lived for a time as a medical student in the residence of Professor Frederick Curtius, the Lutheran superintendent and son of the well-known Greek classicist who had formerly taught in Berlin. Professor Curtius had married Countess Louisa of Erlach—by birth Countess de May—was now old, nearly blind and infirm, but a great lover of music. Schweitzer would spend an hour many evenings playing the piano for her, while she talked of the grand days of her life in Berlin. From her, he reported that he learned much and his courtly nature and manner that charmed so many in later years undoubtedly was part of her legacy to him. He wrote, "This distinguished noblewoman gradually acquired a great influence over me, and I owe it to her that I have rounded off many a hard angle of my personality."[20]

When one is as busy as Schweitzer was, the years move rapidly, and the time came for his final semester in Medical School. He chose as his thesis topic, *The Psychiatric Study of Jesus*.[21] In reaction to some papers and books that had already been published on the subject, Schweitzer wanted to respond to claims that Jesus was an unbalanced, neurotic personality. Not a few people were taking this position that had been encouraged by scholars in the fields of psychiatry and psychology. They, of course, had not been trained in the field of biblical scholarship, and Schweitzer had a natural combination of varying disciplines to sort out the issues.

He felt that these critics failed in their understanding of

the uneven material found in the four Gospels. He did not claim that these first four books of the New Testament formed a logical unity. The impossibility of discovering a balanced personality of Jesus was due to the fact that the Gospels did not offer a systematic or chronological biography of Him. Each Gospel was of course a separate document, written at a different period of time after the crucifixion of Jesus, and not necessarily using the same source materials.

As a result, one simply cannot create a blend or find a unified, rational life of Jesus by using all of the material. When one attempts this, he finds the simple country leader presented in Mark almost in conflict with the Greek Logos presented in John, the royalty-conscious upper-class leader portrayed in Matthew (whose appeal is constantly to the status-conscious Hebrew) to be at odds with the peasant teacher from the provinces reported by Luke. But if one takes each Gospel story separately, from strictly the vantage point of its author, one finds a rational personality in *each* of the four Gospels. Dr. Schweitzer's thesis was that Jesus was a sane man, well balanced and able to give direction and guidance to us if we can understand and accept the differences in viewpoint between his culture and ours. The world is indebted to Schweitzer for his scholarship concerning Jesus—but it also was the basis for conflict with Christians who wanted to retain the view of the life and witness of Jesus in conceptions of the Middle Ages.

In October 1911, Schweitzer took the state medical examination, paying for it with the fee he earned playing the organ at the French Music Festival in Munich—establishing a pattern he was to follow later: earning necessary medical and hospital expenses by lecture or concert fees. Schweitzer had completed the Medical College examinations the previous December 17, and was relieved to know that he had met the demanding requirement of qualifying as a medical doctor. He reported, "Again and again I had to assure myself that I was really awake and not dreaming. Madelung's voice seemed to come from some distant sphere when he said more than once, as we walked along together, 'It is only because you have such excellent health that you have got through a job like that.' "[22] Now he had to spend a year as an intern, followed by residency. In the spring of 1912 he went to Paris to specialize in tropical medicine, and began purchasing supplies for his expected African mission.[23] Feeling the need for still more training, he arranged, with the hospitals, for extra time to go to Berlin for additional study of tropical disease. Finally in the year 1913, at age thirty-eight, he would emerge a fully qualified doctor, a specialist in tropical medicine.

On June 18, 1912, now a medical doctor as well as a doctor of theology, philosophy and music, Albert Schweitzer and Helene Bresslau were married. He wrote she "had already before our marriage been a valuable collaborator in the completion of manuscripts and correction of proofs, was a great help again with all the literary work which had to be got through before we started for Africa."[24] Hardly the usual description a man would write of his wife, but it was in character for Schweitzer and the woman he had chosen as his helpmate and life's companion. Following the marriage they moved out of the bachelor's quarters on the St. Thomas Embankment "in order that with my wife . . . I might spend the last months, so far as I was not obliged to be traveling, in my father's parsonage in Günsbach."[25]

Helene was now a graduate nurse, and he a medical doctor: the preparations for Africa were now complete—except for sponsorship.

8

The Renegade Missionary

After the appeal of the president of the Paris Missionary Society for volunteer doctors to go to the Congo, one would think that he would have been extremely pleased to learn that Albert Schweitzer had become a physician, and was prepared to enter the Society's service. This was not to be the case. Earlier Schweitzer had met Monsieur Boegner, the director of the Society. Now he wrote to him, telling of his decision to work for the Congo mission. Boegner was quite moved and pleased to learn that his article had inspired Schweitzer to such a course of action. But Boegner was also a skilled and sensitive administrator and saw immediately that Schweitzer's request would meet difficulty.[1] Boegner thought of his board and its donors and supporters. His mind reviewed the board's membership, especially those who made up the personnel committee voting on all applicants for overseas appointment. They were firm in their religious orthodoxy and in requiring it of new members.

Only recently they had rejected a young scholar who had, they said, "Christian love but not correct Christian belief."[2] Boegner had strenuously disagreed with the chairman on this decision, pointing out that missions were badly in need of manpower and that they had turned down a well-qualified young pastor. But the chairman was adamant. No one would represent the Society if they could not affirm, without reservation or qualification that every word of the Scriptures was divinely inspired.

Boegner knew Schweitzer's writings and theological position. He would never be able to answer dogmatic questions affirmatively. Moreover, Schweitzer's own book was considered

one of the likely reasons for the earlier candidate's reservations and the board would hit on this immediately in review-
ing his application.

Schweitzer had shown clearly that the Fourth Gospel was
written a century after the birth of Christ. It could not have
been the work of John, the beloved disciple, the long-
standing acceptance of this traditional view to the contrary.
Biblical studies were moving to a new frontier and Schweitzer
had been in the front rank of this advance. This alone would
disqualify him with conservative mission societies.

He was not unaware of these conflicts or difficult ob-
stacles.[3] Yet Schweitzer would not retreat from the primary
considerations of his own decision: to do something practical
and concrete, to be a doctor rather than a preaching missionary; to heal the sick, alleviate suffering, and aid those struggling with malaria, sleeping sickness, leprosy and other
dreaded tropical diseases. These very goals had been the main
point of the article written by Monsieur Boegner.

And Schweitzer had another reason for being a doctor. He
had written that when mission societies were first established,
their principal support had come from the orthodox branch
of the Christian Church. The liberal camp had not been
represented in these efforts, and thus a fundamentalist flavor
had dominated the organizations. Schweitzer wrote, "The
faith that was in the fetters of dogmatism was first in the
field."[4]

Although the societies found support for missions in
liberal circles, these societies had protected themselves
against liberal concepts. Schweitzer was to remember that
these "societies accepted, indeed, all the material help offered them by Liberal Protestantism—how hard my father and
his liberal colleagues in Alsace worked for mission societies
which had quite a different doctrinal outlook!—but they sent
out no missionaries who would not accept their own doctrinal requirements." He added, "It was always interesting to
me to find the missionaries themselves usually thought more
liberally than the officials of the societies."[5] His father had

discerned a slightly more liberal cast to the reports of the Paris Missionary Society than to those of others, and so he worked on its behalf. "But that the question of orthodoxy played the same role in the committee of the Paris Society, I at once learned, and very explicitly, when I offered my services," Schweitzer himself recalled.[6]

Boegner tried to persuade Dr. Schweitzer to change his field of interest, but Schweitzer cut him short, explaining that his mind was made up. He had already prepared by becoming a doctor, specializing in tropical medicine, and now was ready to depart. Dr. Schweitzer explained he wanted to go "merely as a doctor," part of his decision expressing the desire "to work with my hands." He said, "I wanted to be a doctor that I might work without having to talk. For years I have been giving myself out in words, and it was with joy that I had followed the calling of a theological teacher and preacher." But, "this new form of activity" would not be merely talking about "the religion of love, but actually putting it into practice."[7]

Boegner promised to talk with the officials who would make the decision.[8] After all, there was no physician for the mission within a thousand square miles, and mission reports continued to stress the pressing need for doctors. Schweitzer was making a highly valuable and practical proposal in offering his services to the Society and for so distinguished a person to thus present himself "for approval" touched and humbled Monsieur Boegner. He promised to do everything possible to advance his candidacy.

When he met again with Dr. Schweitzer, he had the sad task of telling him that the committee members had rejected his candidacy. Not only were they alarmed by his ideas, but as they saw it an even greater threat was posed by the fact that Schweitzer was such a renowned critic of orthodoxy and traditional concepts; his acceptance might taint the Society. Thus, Schweitzer's fame had damaged his standing with the committee instead of helping it, contrary to Monsieur Boegner's expectation. The director had hoped that the committee members would not dare to reject such an eminent leader as Schweitzer. Boegner had stressed his academic achievements and world recognition: if such a famous man gave up all to go to the Society's African mission, his commitment might well attract others.[9]

A committee member refused to consider that argument, and retorted that it would only intensify their problem by encouraging intellectuals and freethinkers who could only disrupt the mission enterprise and confuse the natives with their theological improvisations. Others agreed. They were not about to sponsor Schweitzer and open the floodgates to other liberals and radicals. Schweitzer had lost, but other plans were already running through his mind. More engagements would follow.

He could ask for support from the more liberal General Union of Evangelical Missions in Switzerland. But he would not retreat before the formalism and dogmatism of the Paris Society.[10] He had worked long and hard to prepare, and, in addition, his father had labored a lifetime for this group, raising money and believing in its enterprise overseas. Schweitzer refused to believe the Society would take a liberal's money but reject a liberal's offer of service. Neither would he bow to its bureaucracy nor admit that this tiny group could blacklist anyone whose ideas threatened their own. A major principle was involved and he could not in self-respect submit to this treatment or conclusion.

For the time being he had to withdraw his application. The more he analyzed the situation, the more he realized the Society's strength of position. He had gone to them, hat in hand, requesting to be sent to Africa at their expense.[11] But what if he offered to give his services, at no cost to them? Would they still reject his skills as a doctor because they could not abide his theology or advanced ideas? He began to make plans for raising his own funds.

All of his life it had cost him something to stand up for what he believed, to face vital issues. He had always paid the price of going forward when others turned back. From that day on the hillside in Alsace when he roused his conscience to warn the birds of danger, his beliefs had demanded the integrity of action. The confrontation with his pastor at confirmation class when he refused to submit his intelligence to the all-purpose dogma, *take on faith*. So many of his experiences had involved ethical encounters—classroom debates in which he stood alone, written articles that challenged old positions and proposed new ones, examination by the Ordination Council, even appeals to building committees to restore old organs instead of buying factory-made replacements—constantly he had faced adversity and created controversy.

And he was learning that controversy could not destroy him. Delay him, yes, but not defeat him. He was battle-hardened. He could not be placed in the ranks of vacillating young pastors who were uncertain of their actions and unsure of their beliefs. He knew himself well and was confirmed in his theological beliefs. He would return to the Paris Missionary Society not as a beggar soliciting support but as a self-sufficient doctor offering his professional services. They, not he, as he saw it, would have a chance to redeem themselves; there would be another confrontation with the Society.[12]

Helene was stunned to learn that he had been rejected. It was inconceivable to her that any Christian body would turn down the volunteered services of Albert Schweitzer. Her anger matched her bewilderment. Here was a man so widely known and respected in the religious community. He was corresponding with some of the greatest scholars in the Christian Church. Only recently the theological faculty of Cambridge University had reissued their invitation, urging him again to come to England for lectures and teaching. Helene was puzzled—and furious.

How could a mission board of a church society deny such a man as lacking "correct Christian belief?" Her Jewish, non-sectarian background perhaps made it difficult for her to grasp the intransigence of Christian doctrine. But she did understand Albert Schweitzer, and his rejection aroused her to aid him in finding another means to overseas service.

She eagerly joined her husband in a program of fund-raising to supply a hospital and underwrite the expenses for its first two years. They compiled lists of friends who might help. They could give them a start that could be supplemented when they returned from Africa by a concert or lecture tour in Europe. And if they could successfully raise the money, then Albert could tell the Society[13] that it would cost them nothing. He would merely be asking permission to go only as a worker, a doctor among the Africans who came to the mission, not as a preacher. Their list of names expanded. There were members of St. Nicholai, his church in Strasbourg, and others in that city who had supported his work in the Theological College of St. Thomas. These people knew him well, had believed in his leadership and supported his programs by generous grants for scholarships, teachers, lectures and church activities. He could count on them. To his delight, the professors at the medical school instituted a public fund for his venture.[14]

Then there was his family throughout the entire province. His father, his uncles and other members of the liberal school of Alsatian (Zwinglian) ministers would surely contribute. There would be other donors: those who had sponsored his concerts, his patrons and benefactors excited by his musical accomplishments.[15] He remembered that Charles Widor had already suggested that the Paris Bach Society give some benefit concerts for his work. Schweitzer was also prepared to play himself at any concert that his friends could arrange.[16]

But as he started the personal calls he remembered how unhappy he had been in the earlier project of begging funds for prisoners.[17] Now he was asking aid not for others, but for himself and his own project, a far more imposing task he felt. He recalled that frequently when he rang a bell and was met at the door, his hostess or host would at first be pleased to think that he was saying a personal good-by before sailing for Africa.

The tone of my reception became markedly different when it came out that I was there, not as a visitor, but as a beggar. Still,

the kindness which I experienced on some of these rounds out-
weighed a hundredfold the humiliations which I had to put up
with . . .[18]

The major objection of potential contributors seemed to
be that he was asking for support of a plan that had not yet
been proved feasible. As yet, no authorization had come from
the mission board. He was not even certain where he would be
stationed in Africa. In addition, he had no record at all in
medical practice. He was offering only his good intentions.
Fortunately, many of his close friends came through with contributions because they believed in Albert Schweitzer and
wanted his program to succeed.

But not everyone was as emotionally involved and this
created problems. They wanted to see a balance sheet. What
would the expenses be to operate such a plant?[19] How much
money would be required for the initial two years? These
queries made it necessary for Schweitzer to start planning the
inventories of supplies that he would take with him. Poring
over drug and surgical house catalogues and price lists, he
learned that to ensure receipt of goods he had to place his
orders at least six months in advance. This situation really
necessitated an act of faith on his part, because he had to
start immediately making out his requests.

As contributions came in, they were immediately transferred into payments for orders placed. Now he was a man
working alone; no church or society had offered him assistance. For eight years he had studied and prepared for his
journey. He had resigned from his academic posts, canceled
long-term concert and lecture contracts and was totally dependent on a small band of friends for help. Only their love,
support and encouragement made it possible for him to go
forward and continue his long-term planning.

Placing orders for medical equipment and supplies provided
Schweitzer with his first real taste of administrative work as
a doctor. Until now, medicine had been intellectual work,
"but now I had to make out from catalogues lists of things to

be ordered, go shopping for days on end, stand about in the shops and seek out what I wanted, check accounts and delivery notes, fill packing cases, prepare accurate lists for the custom-house examinations, and occupy myself with other similar jobs. What an amount of time and trouble it cost me to get together the instruments, the drugs, the bandages and all the other articles needed for the equipment of a hospital, to say nothing at all of the work we did together in preparation for housekeeping in the primeval forest. At first I felt occupation with such things to be something of a burden. Gradually, however, I came to the conclusion that even the practical struggle with material affairs is worthy of being carried on in a spirit of self-devotion. Today I have advanced so far that the neat setting out of a list of things to be ordered gives me artistic satisfaction. The annoyance, which I do feel again and again, is only at the fact that so many catalogues, including those of chemists, are arranged as unclearly and unpractically as if the firm in question had entrusted the compilation to its porter's wife."[20]

Finally, the time came for Helene and Albert to go over their accounting books. Schweitzer decided that "The financial difficulty was for the present surmounted. I had money enough for all purchases necessary for the voyage, and for the running of the hospital for about a year. Moreover, well-to-do friends allowed me to anticipate that they would help me again, when I had exhausted my present resources."

He then made a definite offer to the Paris Missionary Society stating "he would come at his own expense to serve its mission field on the Ogowe River from the centrally situated station in Lambaréné."

His friend, the kindly Monsieur Alfred Boegner, was no longer the director of the Paris Missionary Society. Old age and health problems had forced his retirement, so Dr. Schweitzer did not have the satisfaction of reopening the application procedure with him. Boegner had certainly never appeared to Schweitzer as an adversary, but rather as a helpful intermediary with the Society's board. He always indeed con-

sidered him an ally, although Schweitzer recognized that
Boegner could not greatly influence the board. The new director, Monsieur Jean Bianquis, however, turned out to be
just the person that Dr. Schweitzer needed. He had infused
the Society with new concepts, and is now remembered for
his efforts to win a broader following for the Society.[21]

He not only reported Schweitzer's new application (with
his offer to go to Africa at his own expense) but "maintained
with all the weight of his authority that they must not lose
the opportunity of obtaining, free of cost, the mission doctor
whom they had been so ardently hoping for."[22] Nevertheless,
the most orthodox members of the board still objected.

Dr. Schweitzer recalled: "It was resolved to invite me before the Committee and hold an examination into my beliefs.
I could not agree to this, and based my refusal on the fact
that Jesus, when He called His disciples, required from them
nothing beyond the will to follow Him. I also sent a message
to the Committee that, if we are to follow the saying of Jesus:
'He that is not for us is against us,' a missionary society would
be in the wrong if it rejected even a Mohammedan who offered his services for the treatment of their suffering natives.
Not long before this the Mission had refused a minister who
wanted to go out and work for it, because his scientific conviction did not allow him to answer with an unqualified 'Yes'
the question whether he regarded the Fourth Gospel as the
work of the Apostle John.

"To avoid a similar fate, I declined to appear before the
assembled Committee and let them put theological questions
to me. On the other hand, I offered to make a personal visit
to each member of it, so that conversation with me might
enable them to judge clearly whether my acceptance really
meant such terrible danger to the souls of the negroes and to
the Society's reputation. My proposal was accepted and cost
me several afternoons. A few of the members gave me a chilly
reception. The majority assured me that my theological standpoint made them hesitate for two chief reasons: I might be
tempted to confuse the missionaries out there with my learn-

ing, and I might wish to be active again as a preacher. By my assurance that I only wanted to be a doctor, and that as to everything else I would be *muet comme une carpe* (mute as a fish), their fears were dispelled, and these visits actually brought me into quite cordial relations with a number of the Committee members.

"Thus on the understanding that I would avoid everything that could cause offense to the missionaries and their converts in their belief, my offer was accepted, with the result that one member of the Committee sent his resignation."[23]

In February 1913, the Schweitzers shipped seventy packing cases of medical equipment and supplies to Bordeaux from Paris. They returned to Günsbach to say their farewells. As they packed, Helene objected to Albert's converting all of their money into gold coins. But Dr. Schweitzer insisted, "we must reckon on the very serious possibility of war before we return." As events were to prove, his assessment of world events was correct.[24]

On the afternoon of Good Friday, 1913, Helene and Albert, carrying their luggage, walked with his father and mother to the depot in Günsbach. Neighbors came out and followed, and by the time he arrived on the station platform, Schweitzer, with tears in his eyes, realized that virtually the whole town was there to see them off. After embracing his parents, Albert and Helene stepped aboard the train. He turned to wave a handkerchief to the throng, taking a last long look before swinging through the narrow door leading into the fourth-class section.[25]

Arrival in Africa

Easter weekend of 1913 was exciting for the Schweitzers. Following their departure from Günsbach, with its emotional farewell by the townspeople, they stopped in Paris for the holiday. There they visited Charles Widor who had organized a farewell concert given by the Paris Bach Society; then they entrained on Easter Sunday for Bordeaux. Here the shipping crates containing their precious medical supplies had arrived and were being stored. Their ship was anchored at Pauillac, which was an hour and a half by train nearer the mouth of the Gironde River.[1]

When they arrived at the steamship offices at Bordeaux, a great problem suddenly arose; the warehouses were closed for the Easter Monday holiday.* The supply cases could not be moved. Dr. Schweitzer pleaded with one person after another to try to do something until finally an official, seeing Schweitzer's distress and cognizant of the fact that a doctor embarking on a long voyage to open a new hospital had to bring along his own medical supplies, took matters into his own hands. He waived aside all regulations and with keys in hand escorted Dr. Schweitzer to the warehouse. Men were found to load the huge crates onto the train as the passengers for the Congo voyage climbed aboard. There was a sudden flurry of activity as a guard blew his whistle; French soldiers on their way to African assignments pushed forward to take their seats. Dr. Schweitzer, meanwhile, carefully directed the gentle handling of every crate, checking off each against the bills of lading. Finally, the last huge box slid through the doors of the freight car, and Schweitzer breathed

* A legal holiday in France.

a sigh of relief as the baggagemen closed, locked and sealed the doors. Then, he rushed forward to join Helene and they hastily boarded the train that would take them to the waiting ship at Pauillac.[2]

As the train chugged along, the Schweitzers looked in excitement at the countryside. This was a part of France that they had never before visited, one with rolling hills, quaint peasant homes and yellow fields of spring flowers in bloom. Soon, they were at the quay where they stepped from the train amid the bustle and confusion of emigration, customs, military and baggagemen. All served one purpose: to get cargo and passengers quickly aboard the small steamer, *Europe*, anchored ten feet away, before the tide ebbed. Dr. Schweitzer wrote, "Then came a time of crushing, shouting, signalling to porters; we pushed and are pushed till, over the narrow gangway, we get on board, and, on giving our names, learn the number of our cabin which is to be our home for three weeks."[3] Helene and Albert were pleased with their cabin, which was roomy, and well forward, away from the engine's noise and vibration. They barely had time to refresh themselves before the luncheon bell sounded. On they went to the dining salon to find their table and meet their fellow passengers.

The Schweitzers were assigned to a table with several officers, the ship's doctor, an army doctor, and two wives of army officers who were on their way to rejoin their husbands stationed in Africa. The Schweitzers were the only inexperienced travelers in the group; all the others had lived in Africa before and were quite familiar with it.[4] Accordingly, as novices on their maiden voyage, they found themselves the object of regular counsel, advice and solicitude from the more experienced. Listening to their tales and knowledge about not only where each was going, but where each had been, Schweitzer thought of his mother's chicken yard. He could not help but recall how the new hens walked among the others shyly and humbly for the first few days until they found their places in the pecking order. He good-naturedly likened himself to one of those shy hens, not quite sure of his place yet among the professional travelers.[5] But one thing he noticed almost immediately: a feeling of determination, direction, and energy among these experienced travelers.[6] Over the years, he was to observe the vitality of such people who seem at home anywhere in the world. Moving out into the world himself, he, too, acquired this vitality and became as well less of a European and more of a world citizen.

Most of the passengers seemed to take it for granted that this would not be an easy voyage. Schweitzer wondered if all trips to Africa were rough, or if they sensed something in the wind as the ship put out to sea. At any event, he did not have long to wait and see; the second day at sea a severe storm hit and the ship pitched and tossed from port to starboard and back.[7] The ship had been built low since it not only had to cross the ocean, but had to sail up the shallow Congo River as far as Matadi as well. Hence, it was built to draw less water than the usual ocean liner, and was more at the mercy of the storm.[8]

That night Schweitzer rapidly acquired some sea-travel experience. He had neglected to make fast with rope his steamer trunks and other baggage. In the night they began to crash against the cabin walls and roll back and forth across the floor. It seemed dangerous to the Schweitzers to get out of bed. All night they listened to the banging and crashing. Schweitzer later recalled that as he lay in bed, he had counted the seconds between smackings against the walls. As the night wore on, they became aware that not only in their cabin, but in others too, a similar crashing was echoing throughout the ship. Other passengers, even the more seasoned, had apparently not made their trunks fast enough to withstand the strain of the lurching and rolling at sea. The next morning the steward showed Schweitzer the seaman's way of lashing down his trunks and luggage.[9]

Three full days the storm raged, and the ship tossed. Finally, as it neared the island of Teneriffe, the storm abated. Here the ship stopped to refuel, and take on additional cargo, potatoes, vegetables and bananas. Pleasant seas ushered them as they sailed south of Teneriffe.

Dr. Schweitzer was enjoying himself and learning from his talks with African natives on deck. Among other things, they urged him to wear a sun helmet from now on, as the sun could be deceiving in the tropical climate. An older African warned him that there was danger from sunstroke (whether or not the sky was overcast) especially at sunrise and sunset. He must never become careless and leave his head uncovered. They also showed him the different fruits and vegetables brought aboard at Teneriffe, and explained how the Africans prepared them. Finding him intensely interested in every detail they had mentioned, they showed him their personal equipment of native gadgets, charms and amulets. These had been used by Africans from time immemorial in their struggle for survival against the jungle and its threats.[10]

Dr. Schweitzer was eternally grateful to the Africans for befriending him on this voyage. They were his teachers of things unknown and unobserved by the more sophisticated passengers who never had time or inclination to talk with the natives.[11]

But Dr. Schweitzer also learned quite a lot from the white passengers. A French Army lieutenant who had served many tours in West Africa in locations on the Senegal and the Niger and at Madagascar was now on his way to the Middle Congo, just south of Gabon. He had a personal theory, which he expounded to Dr. Schweitzer, on the effect of Mohammedanism on the African. He believed the African who was not "infested" with Mohammedanism to be a good servant, soldier and guide. However, the Moslem convert was a totally different person in his opinion. "You can build him railways, dig him canals, spend thousands of pounds on the land he is to irrigate, but it all makes absolutely no impression on him; he is absolutely and on principle opposed to everything European,"[12] the lieutenant said. This unsuitability of the Moslem for European civilization, Dr. Schweitzer was to later observe and note himself. The old antipathy between the

Christian and the Moslem was appearing south of the Sahara, as Islamic teachers and preachers from Morocco and Libya came to Africa to spread the message of Islam. Actually, he was to learn as he became more of a student of African culture that the Moslems had been south of the Sahara for hundreds of years, long before the Portuguese explorer, Vasco da Gama, introduced the first European Christian missionaries to Africa.

The lieutenant went on, "But let a marabout—a traveling preacher of Islam—come into a village on his ambling horse, with his yellow cloak over his shoulders, then things begin to wake up! Everybody crowds around him, and brings his savings in order to buy with hard cash charms against sickness, wounds and snakebites, against bad spirits and bad neighbors.[13] Dr. Schweitzer was in due course to learn the need to deal with three principal religious groups of Africans: Christian, Moslem and native. He had fully expected to find the first and third groups, but had not been prepared for the large numbers of Moslems who were formidable rivals with Christianity for converting the African dissatisfied with the animism of tribal religion.

Schweitzer became acquainted with a military doctor aboard who had already served twelve years in equatorial Africa, and was now on his way to Grand Bassam where he was to direct the Bacteriological Institute. Together, they worked out a schedule for a two-hour daily seminar during which they discussed tropical medicine.[14] Schweitzer found he had many questions he wanted to ask, and wanted very much to draw on the vast experience of the doctor. After years in Africa, the military physician had definite ideas of what doctors serving in Africa should know and how they should act in specific situations. But the two men had entirely different convictions as to the curing of the Africans, derived from their different personal motivations.

The military doctor felt that it was imperative that the army and company physicians devote as much time as possible to treatment and curing of the diseases ravaging the

African, because only if they were wiped out among the natives could the whites be protected from them.[15] Only by
completely controlling sleeping sickness among the blacks, for
example, could the Europeans be safe from this dreadful
scourge, the doctor stated. Dr. Schweitzer had come to Africa
with far different motivation and purpose. He knew he would
be the first man in the entire area principally serving the African, and he was dedicated entirely to the cure of the African
population as an end in itself. His reason for doing so was
not merely to make life easier for the Europeans by controlling
diseases which also crippled them. He was to be the African's
doctor. He found time from the first for white people who also
needed his ministrations whether in the missions, the lumber
camps, the military camps or on the river boats. Nonetheless,
he remained primarily a doctor to the people of Africa and
only incidentally a doctor to the Europeans. Schweitzer felt
the European was indebted to the African and had not repaid
his debt. His motivation then in coming to work among the
natives was to administer to *their* suffering.

The ship's second stop was Dakar, where Dr. and Mrs.
Schweitzer set foot on the African shore for the first time.[16]
Africa. Here in this ancient world, which appeared to have
stood still since time began, man still lived as a child of nature.
And the natural was overpowering. The great harbor, above
which stood Dakar, then the capital city of Senegal and Gam-
bia, illustrated this sense of vastness, as did the wide ap-
proaches of the great sandy shores, and the density of the
vegetation—trees, underbrush and flowers. Here was an ancient
port village with unchanging ways, hardly touched by the
effects of the white colony which made Dakar a capital. The
town lies on a steep slope, and as Dr. and Mrs. Schweitzer
walked up its badly kept streets, he realized that the African
way of life was altered only at the moment of its contact with
the European, and then instantly reverted to its seemingly unchanging patterns. When Africans were working or otherwise
involved with the white man, it might appear that they were
becoming a part of his culture, but once the work was done,

the black returned to his native quarters; and there all was just as though he never had left them. The doctor wondered at that time if Africa would always be this way. Imperceptibly, changes were taking place, and he was to be one of the first to recognize this. The African revolution of the 1960s was not to be such a surprise to him as it was to most, and accordingly his view and appraisal of it differed from those who were to lack his many years of observing Africa.

Dakar is remembered by Dr. Schweitzer for two reasons: it was there for the first time that he set foot on African soil; secondly, it was there for the first time that he was shocked by the cruelty of the natives to their animals. The city's very steep hills were negotiated by donkeys under the heavy whip of unsympathetic black drivers. Dr. Schweitzer was appalled at the way they forced these beasts to carry their heavy supplies up the slopes, frequently hitched to an awkward two-wheel cart, also overloaded. On one of these steep inclines, he came upon such a cart in which sat two Africans beating and shouting at their struggling donkey. Dr. Schweitzer could not bear the situation. He spoke sharply in French to the Africans, ordering them to dismount, had one help in pushing the cart and had the other lead the animal by the bridle up the hill. Though surprised at this European's strange interference, the Africans were too stunned to do anything but obey. With mutterings and harsh looks they did as they were told, and with Dr. Schweitzer's help, they successfully reached the hilltop. When the Schweitzers rejoined the rest of the ship's party, a lieutenant advised, "If you cannot endure to see animals ill-treated, don't come to Africa. You will see plenty of that kind of horror here."[17]

As the ship made its way southward, the passengers watched the shoreline with its lush foliage, massive trees and dense undergrowth. The voyage down the African coast thus served to give Dr. Schweitzer a wonderful view of Africa. They passed the Pepper Coast, the Ivory Coast, the Gold Coast and on to the Slave Coast—areas today called Sierra Leone,

Guinea, Ghana, Nigeria, Cameroon and now Gabon—as they sailed into the Gulf of Guinea.

Early on Sunday morning, April 13, 1913, the ship arrived at Libreville, capital city of Gabon, the land that Dr. Schweitzer for most of his life was to call home. The Schweitzers were surprised and delighted to be welcomed there by a Mr. Ford, the American missionary, who came aboard with a welcoming gift of flowers and fruit from the mission garden.[18] Eagerly, the Schweitzers accepted his invitation to visit his mission at Baraka, situated on a hill a short distance outside of the city. They arrived there just as the doors of the chapel opened at the close of Sunday morning services. Mr. Ford graciously introduced the newly arrived doctor to some of the black congregation as they came out. He found a dozen friendly hands eagerly extended to him. Now, at last, to be inside a mission in Gabon, seemed to him the end of a long period of preparation, and the beginning of a new life. But this was only a temporary stop. There was still a long journey upriver ahead before he finally would arrive at his own mission in Lambaréné. On Monday the Schweitzers were back on board ship as it weighed anchor for the voyage from Libreville to Port Gentil, situated at the mouth of the Ogowe River. The following day they were on that river, the one which was to become their life line, and like all African inhabitants, they would begin to learn that strange mystique by which one becomes deeply involved with the role and importance of "our" river.

Fear of high taxes that might be charged by the custom officers at Port Gentil had Dr. Schweitzer worried. During the latter part of the voyage, the passengers had spoken of the high taxes collected by colonial administrators for everything brought into Africa. "It will be 10 per cent of everything you bring," they would say. One old African told him they charged as much for old or used materials and possessions as they did for new ones. Dr. Schweitzer, with great concern, considered the value of his packing cases of medical supplies as well as of their personal property. As it turned out, the customs officials were really quite understanding and not nearly so officious as he had been told. They also did not charge excessively as he had been led to expect.[19]

The Schweitzers slept overnight on the ship and transferred to a river boat in the morning.[20] This boat, the *Alembe*, would carry them up the Ogowe River while the *Europe* went on to the Congo River. The *Alembe* was an even narrower and shallower boat than the *Europe* with two huge paddle wheels at its stern. There was no room on board for the packing cases and it was arranged that they would follow two weeks later on the ship's next trip. All personal luggage was taken aboard, the Schweitzers embarked, and the ship's crew waited for the rising tide to carry the shallow boat over the sandbars. Some of the passengers, misjudging the rise of the tide, had lingered too long ashore, and the boat had to leave without them. Later, the tardy passengers arrived by motorboat and climbed aboard for the journey upstream.[21]

Now Dr. Schweitzer would see the virgin forests and great jungles he had dreamed about. Here was the primordial Africa which has withstood the centuries. They were south of the equator; from now on the equatorial heat was to become part of their life. The Ogowe River valley runs inland in a slightly northerly direction, so that by the time they reached Lambaréné, they would once again be close to the equator which they had crossed four days earlier. Dr. and Mrs. Schweitzer watched the changing scenery with anticipation, noting many details of this new homeland they were entering. The antediluvian aspect of the scenery—tangled and thick underbrush, tall trees and grasses, and the spongy shoreline—all suggested a density of nature and a primeval element which surpassed their expectation.[22]

Dr. Schweitzer described this first day's voyage up the Ogowe:

"It is impossible to say where the river ends and the land begins, for a mighty network of roots, clothed with bright-flowering creepers projects right into the water. Clumps of palms and palm trees, ordinary trees spreading out widely

with green boughs and huge leaves, single trees of the pine
family shooting up to a towering height in between them,
wide fields of papyrus clumps as tall as a man, with fan-like
leaves, and within all this luxuriant greenery, the rotting stems
of dead giants shooting up to heaven . . . In every gap in the
forest, a water mirror meets the eye: at every bend in the river,
a new tributary shows itself. A heron flies heavily up and then
settles on a dead tree trunk; white birds and blue birds skim
over the water, and high in the air, a pair of ospreys circle.
Then—yes, there can be no mistake about it!—from the
branch of a palm, there hang and swing—two monkey tails!
Now the owners of the tails are visible. We are really in
Africa."[23]

After a long stretch of travel, the boat would put into
shore at a small native village. Stacked up waiting for it were
several hundred logs for the boiler fire. This fuel was stored
on deck by the villagers, under the direction of an elder of the
town. The transaction would hardly begin before the captain
was accusing the suppliers of not having enough logs ready.
After a sharp and insulting exchange, the African would humbly excuse himself with weak gestures and bows before the
cutting demands of the river captain. It was then agreed that
the villagers would not be paid in cash for this insufficient
load, only in alcoholic spirits.

The Africans believed, according to Schweitzer's fellow
travelers, that the white men got a better buy on liquor than
they could and that they would benefit accordingly—by taking
the alcohol instead of cash. This was untrue and Schweitzer
watched the transaction critically. Others told him that the
whiskey payments had demoralized the blacks along the
Ogowe, causing them to become shiftless and lazy. Later on
in the trip, deserted villages were pointed out to Schweitzer
as an example of the havoc created by the alcohol currency.

"When I came here fifteen years ago," said one trader pointing to the abandoned huts in a clearing, "these places were
all flourishing villages."

"And why are they so no longer?" I asked.

He shrugged his shoulders and said in a low voice, "L'al-
cool. . . ."[24]

An old refrain ran through Schweitzer's mind: the white
man's inequitable treatment of the black. Whites must begin
their reparations he felt, and he expected to do his share.

Later the next day the slopes of Lambaréné came into view.
As the steamer sounded its siren, Schweitzer neared the end
of his journey. Only time would tell if he would be successful
and equal to the tasks that lay before him.

10

The First Mission Hospital

In April 1913, the ship landed at Lambaréné amidst the confusion of an excited populace which showed up at the sound of its siren, many to claim baggage or cargo. The island of Lambaréné had many stores and apparently most of them were expecting shipments. The presence of the many merchants intensified the confusion and racket.[1]

There was no one to meet the Schweitzers so they stood aside to watch the frenzied activity on the dock. Then, above the commotion, Schweitzer caught sight of a long narrow canoe, rowed by singing boys. It headed straight for the ship. A white man in the boat's stern was almost thrown off balance as the canoe swished to a sudden stop.

He shouted to Schweitzer who returned his greeting. This was a Mr. Christol, a teacher in the lower grades of the Lambaréné mission school. His class had just won a race with the young men from the upper class in their sprint to the docks of Lambaréné. The prize for the winner was to be the privilege of rowing the Schweitzers back to the mission. The youngsters swarmed around the visitors from Europe who shared their excitement and would, of course, rather soon share their life. The Schweitzers stared at their canoes, hollowed out of tree trunks, and wondered how safe and comfortable this last hour of traveling would be.[2]

Cautiously, they took their places in the hollow trunk, sitting on the canoe's bottom, with only a flimsy backrest for support. Schweitzer insisted that his wife sit in front of him . . . behind the forward rowers, so that he could look out for her safety. The boys stood up and rowed with long thin paddles, which added to the Schweitzers' uneasiness. Gradually,

1. The town of Günsbach, Alsace, home of Albert Schweitzer's family, as seen from one of his favorite sitting places. The spires of his father's church dominate the skyline.

2. The lovely Schweitzer family home in Günsbach. It was built in 1926.

3. Pastor Louis Schweitzer, Albert Schweitzer's father in a photograph taken about the year 1915. He was among the most respected liberal Protestant ministers of his day.

4. Albert Schweitzer's mother, a handsome and hardy woman. She died in 1918 in a tragic accident.

5. Schweitzer, age five. He had just begun to attend school at Günsbach.

6. The legendary black African statue by Bartholdi at Colmar. It was
Schweitzer's strong and sustained emotional reaction to this statue as a
boy and young man that helped motivate him in making the commitment of his life to Africa.

7. Schweitzer at eighteen, an undergraduate at the University of Strasbourg.

8. The young pastor of St. Nicholai's church in Strasbourg.

9. Albert and Helene Bresslau Schweitzer, planning for the journey to Africa. He had completed his study of medicine, and they married in June 1912.

10. Lambaréné, 1913—
Schweitzer had arrived
in the spring and had
built his first hospital.

11. Native African living quarters at the first Schweitzer hospital in Lambaréné, Gabon. Food was supplied, but the Africans preferred to prepare it themselves.

12. Schweitzer in 1923, back home in Günsbach with his daughter, Rhena. He had survived the hardships of internment as a prisoner of war during World War I.

they became more at ease and began to enjoy the ride. Later, they were to find it a relaxing experience traveling up or down the Ogowe this way. At first, the yellow water of the river seemed perilously close to them, but later it seemed most natural and convenient to travel in this fashion. The boys sang as they paddled, and would call back and forth every now and then to the older crew with Mr. Ellenberger, the group which had lost the race.

Christol and Ellenberger were teachers, not ministers, and therefore, not strictly missionaries as such. It was heartening to Dr. Schweitzer, after his many struggles with the mission society in Paris, to find so pleasant a welcome and so friendly an atmosphere, to have this wonderful first impression even before seeing the mission itself.

Soon they turned from the main stream of the Ogowe to one of its branches, and one of the front rowers turned and quickly pointed out to the Schweitzers some white structures on the slope of the hill toward which they were heading. Dr. Schweitzer looked ahead eagerly, surmising that this was the mission. The setting sun was flooding the hill with light and the gleaming whitewashed buildings glowed and sparkled. This first impact, spirited young boys, a happy instructor, and now this sunwashed hill, filled Schweitzer with joy as he realized that this was to be the place of his service and of the new life he had planned at such great cost.

At Andende, a welcoming party of Africans and Europeans greeted him, with friendly hands extended to assist the Schweitzers ashore and up the bank. Mrs. Christol was there, Miss Humbert, the schoolmistress, Mr. Kast, the "industrial missionary," and others. It was an exciting occasion. Hardly were they on shore, when the bell rang for evening chapel which was held in a room where the sacred music was accompanied by chirping crickets. Schweitzer sat on a packing box outside, deeply moved, holding Helene's hand. After supper, the children gave a musical program in honor of the doctor's arrival, singing original verses composed by Mr. Ellenberger.[3]

The Protestant Mission of the Paris Missionary Society was actually at Andende, nearly two miles upstream from Lambaréné. Lambaréné is a large island, nearly two miles long, which, viewed from the shore, looks like a great green egg half exposed above the waters of the vast Ogowe River. The river is at least a mile wide on each long side of the oval island. The Ogowe is one of the immense river systems in equatorial Africa, a great flowing body of water, with many arms, inlets, islands and peninsulas, appearing at times to be almost a system of connected lakes along the shorelines. It flows in a clearly defined stream only in the wide channel in the middle. For many years, explorers had thought the Ogowe was a northern branch of the Congo River, and Trader Horn, Du Chillu, and Count de Brazza had all explored it with expectations of finding connections with the Congo proper. There was also a widespread theory that they could follow its upper reaches and find Victoria Falls, as a part of a vast inland water system supposedly even linked with the Upper Nile on the opposite side of the continent. All such theories were to prove invalid. The Ogowe is a large but self-contained river, draining several thousand square miles of this portion of Africa.[4]

In it swim crocodiles and hippopotami, and along its banks are numerous other large creatures of the tropics. The equator is only forty miles north of Lambaréné. Huge snakes swim in its waters or dangle from trees along its shores. One learns quickly never to paddle dugout canoes under trees or he finds an unwelcome guest dropping into the boat. This was and is the land of the leopard, gorilla and elephant.[5]

The Protestant Mission of Andende was situated on some hills that sloped gradually to the river, offering a commanding view in all directions.[6] In three directions, one looked out over the lush, extravagant terrain and foliage of the branch rivers with their lakelike recesses, islands and oxbows, and the flowing central river. Up and down it traveled the boats of the river trade, of the lumber and logging industries. One could see the ancient Lambaréné Ford, where for centuries the Africans had crossed the Ogowe. The pathway on both sides of it was worn smooth by many feet, and it was legend that the trail crossing here went south to Capetown or north to Algiers.[7]

There was sufficient activity along the river that enterprising natives found it good business to remain at the ford with pirogues to transport travelers across. Sitting in a pirogue—dugout logs, twenty to forty feet long—the waiting oarsman would hold onto an overhanging branch with one hand and leisurely talk with the other boatmen who, in orderly fashion, queued up to wait their turn to transport passengers. Sometimes they would beach the pirogues and stretch their legs, passing their time in games or gossip with local villagers. When a potential passenger showed up, the boatman whose turn it was would make his offer, "A boat to the other shore? The river is dangerous, but I will cross you safely." Then would begin the bargaining palaver to establish the price. Back and forth traveler and boatman would argue and, if it appeared that the traveler would not meet what were considered fair terms, the other boatmen would crowd around and support the demands for a fair payment. Eventually, the argument would be settled and off would go the boatman with his passenger and cargo, skimming over the water, a gay expression of triumph shining in his face because he had earned a fare.

The great rivers were the roadways of Africa, running from the interior to the coast. One must follow a river's course to enter or leave the country. The vast African jungles with their tangled underbrush, gnarled roots and marshy, spongy soil cannot be permanently or deeply penetrated, except along a river or one of its tributaries. With the exception of taking the one ancient route that crosses the Ogowe at the Lambaréné Ford, traversing the jungle is looked upon as impossible in equatorial Africa. A river, therefore, is always a focal point for the tribes, industry, missionaries, government officials, the military and the populace.

The Ogowe was the great father river of the tribes and

people with whom Dr. Schweitzer was to live, off and on, for over a half century.

The morning after their arrival, the Schweitzers explored the mission grounds. Standing on the hill in front of Dr. Schweitzer's house or on its spacious veranda, one can look directly out over the junction of the branch and the main stream of the Ogowe. Above and behind the house are the homes of the missionaries, dormitories which look like barrack buildings, schoolrooms, gardens, cleared fields, and high trees with thick brush below forming a barrier at the edge of the clearing. All around the houses are coffee bushes, and cocoa, orange, lemon, mango, palm oil, pawpaw and mandarin trees. These were planted by the first missionaries at Lambaréné, Americans from New Jersey who had established the mission in 1874. The middle of the three hills on which the mission stands is still known as "American Hill." Here was the doctor's house and the river was its, and the whole mission's, only avenue, highway or street.[8]

Schweitzer was anxious to get to work but was immediately frustrated by the lack of an interpreter which had been promised. A native teacher at the mission school at Samkita had volunteered to act in this capacity. His name was N'Zeng and he was also to act as an orderly, but he was not to be found.[9]

The pressure of the delay began to mount as the doctor discovered that the location of the hospital had yet to be decided. Building materials were not on hand. He felt behind already and thus was hardly prepared for the young student who ran up to him with the news that patients were gathering in front of his house.

Schweitzer was angry. He was not ready to see patients and his orders to the mission had been that a three-week period of organization would precede any medical duties. Helene walked along with him to the house and suggested that they at least see the patients. The two walked with the young man who brought the word that the people had gathered. He seemed bright and interested. Schweitzer hoped that perhaps he could be of further help to him.[10]

The doctor was not even moderately prepared to see the patients. His medicines and equipment were in packing cases at Port Gentil. He did not speak any of the native dialects and was entirely dependent on French, and that for communication only with those who had attended mission schools. There was no interpreter or orderly present. Most of all, there was no hospital facility of any kind. It looked as if it would be a grim, fruitless beginning. Yet Schweitzer knew how important this first meeting would be to the people. In other days as organist, lecturer and preacher he had learned one lesson well: at the very start of an undertaking, one must command respect and confidence. If this happened, these attitudes would then carry over to other times.

Dr. Schweitzer came around the corner of the building with Helene and the youngster. He instructed the boy to tell those who spoke French to gather at one end of the porch. To the French-speaking group Schweitzer explained that he would be happy to consult with them and to treat them as required as soon as his medicines arrived. He explained that that would not be until the next river boat arrived from Port Gentil, and reminded them that a doctor without his medicine was like a fetishman without his charms.

This made sense to the group of natives and they replied that they would wait to hear the ship's siren. Schweitzer spoke again to the group, this time telling them of his need for men to work with him in preparation of the hospital. Shelter for the sick was essential. Also, someone present was needed to go to Samkita to spread the word about the delay in the doctor's beginning his work. The sick and the injured there and in the other villages must be told not to come to Lambaréné until the shelter was constructed and the medicines and equipment had arrived.

The next three weeks would be needed for these preparations and only those who were able to work should come to the hospital, Dr. Schweitzer told the group. He was adamant about this. All who came must be willing and able to work and those who stayed must bring their own food or they would starve. He impressed upon his listeners the urgency of his requests and then dispersed the crowd. Shortly afterward he noticed the pirogues on the river departing with those who had come.

Schweitzer then asked his young friend if he felt that there were any natives who did not speak French who had still been able to understand what he said. The boy said that he thought that everyone, French-speaking or not, had roughly gotten the message. Even the drums, he felt, were telling distant villages about the new doctor and his plans. Indeed, as they talked, Schweitzer could hear the rhythmic throbbing of the drums, echoing over the water, off the hills, and seemingly being caught up again in relays.

The drums, he learned later, called him Oganga, the fetish-man. The drum telegraph system had said simply that the fetishman was powerless until the next boat arrived with his charms. Whether it was via French, native dialect or drums, the message announcing his arrival was being spread much faster than Schweitzer had dreamed possible.

Ellenberger and Christol, the two teachers at the mission complimented Schweitzer on his handling of what was a most delicate situation. Schweitzer asked them about his interpreter and orderly, N'Zeng. They replied that the pirogues returning by way of Samkita would pass the message at once—and that he would arrive shortly. Ellenberger went on to say that there was something Schweitzer would have to learn about N'Zeng and the blacks—they would let him down every time.

Schweitzer quickly and angrily responded by asking about the whites—where was the hospital, the materials for construction, and the laborers that had been promised? The two teachers backed away from any responsibility for these matters and said he would have to ask the missionary administrators about them when they had their next meeting.[11]

Schweitzer could see that without corrugated metal and

lumber no hospital could be constructed that would be ready in time to handle the first group of patients. He inquired about some of the buildings in the mission; perhaps there were some unused rooms that could house a temporary clinic. Nothing was available. The teachers' classrooms were overcrowded, and they were waiting for requests to be filled. Christol then mentioned, jokingly, that an old fowl house was vacant. Schweitzer laughed with him but did not rule this out as a possibility. He simply had to have some temporary quarters.

When he had finished his exploration of the mission building and grounds he came to the deserted, run-down, filthy chicken coop. He walked around the shelter and then went inside. The basic structure was sound if unkept. He arranged to have the coop's sides enclosed. With brush and shovel the Schweitzers cleaned out its interior. The roof was checked during a rainstorm and repairs made where needed. Then came the job of whitewashing the inside walls. The work went on. Before long, the three weeks had passed and on the evening of April 26, the Schweitzers heard the siren of the packet ship returning from Port Gentil. The precious supplies had arrived. Hastily, arrangements were made to send boys with the larger pirogues to fetch them.[12]

The steamer captain had thoughtfully unloaded the cases at the riverbank by the Catholic mission since he dared not enter the branch river. The mission store had a huge pirogue, able to carry up to three tons weight. This was borrowed to transport Dr. Schweitzer's seventy packing cases, and it then made a return trip for the zinc-lined piano sent by the Paris Bach Society. Messrs. Champel and Pelot, two more industrial missionaries from the station at N'Gomo, had come, and they supervised the transportation of the cases and piano. The children joined in helping move the cases up the hill to Schweitzer's residence; there the doctor and his wife began the involved task of unpacking and checking the condition of the medical and surgical provisions.

The next morning when Schweitzer emerged from his house, he was greeted with the questioning, saddened eyes of the sick and injured Africans who had mysteriously arrived during the night to await their turn for medical aid. These pathetic, ill people with their distressed faces touched his heart. He could no longer delay; now he must begin medical practice. Almost every day since he had given his ultimatum, he had cared for a few patients. Now, there were dozens, enough to fill a hospital.

Thus, outside the doctor's house, the hospital came into existence that morning. Initially, supplies were moved out onto the veranda. Then, taking a position on the steps, with Helene standing just inside the screen door to pass him materials and instruments he called for, Dr. Schweitzer began medical treatment. It continued all morning until nearly lunchtime, when the skies suddenly opened and a torrential downpour began. During the rainy seasons, storms began suddenly and just as suddenly ended. But they came with no warning. Fortunately, Schweitzer's supplies were under cover or they would have been ruined. This experience made clear to him the need to open a temporary hospital in the enclosed, sheltered chicken coop.[13]

There were many diseases and illnesses peculiar to the tropics that needed treatment and much surgery to be performed. Dr. Schweitzer could see ahead of him a full, busy medical practice. Malaria and sleeping sickness were two of the worst ailments he had to treat. Others were dysentery, ulcers, mental illness, pneumonia, leprosy, framboesia and other types of skin diseases. Many patients had severe injuries caused by snakebites, animal attacks and accidents which had occurred in the whites' lumber camps where the natives worked.[14] Abdominal tumors among the women, and strangulated hernias among the men were also prevalent. The doctor would have an incredible variety of medical problems to solve.

On August 15, 1913, while Schweitzer was still using the makeshift operating room, a patient with a very severe and painful strangulated hernia was brought in. It needed immediate attention. He had not yet done any major surgery in the fowl house, but Mr. Christol offered his students' room and it was hurriedly cleaned with antiseptics. Mrs. Schweitzer prepared the anesthesia while the doctor gathered together the necessary instruments and drugs. The operation was a success, the first major surgery Dr. Schweitzer performed in the jungle. He had hoped to delay surgery until the new hospital was built. Now, he knew he must press for its hasty construction.[15]

Doctor in the Jungle

Before the hospital building was ready, Dr. Schweitzer's work nevertheless went on. For the first time he dealt with lepers, whose large lesions, open sores, tough hidelike crusts and dismembered hands, arms and feet showed the ravages of this dread scourge. If the disease had advanced far enough in a patient, his fingers, toes or a hand or foot would be missing with only a stump remaining. Many damaged feet were bandaged in large quilted bags so that the pain could be eased by padded protection of the afflicted.[1]

All matters requiring medical attention were not so gruesome, however. The birth of babies was a delight to Schweitzer. One of the first and most amazing discoveries he made in his practice was that parents and family immediately painted a new baby white, and sometimes the mother as well. "Is it because they wish they were white?" the doctor asked incredulously the first time he saw a whitewashed infant. The natives howled with laughter. "No, it is to frighten off the evil spirits who, if they see the white color, will be afraid and not harm the baby or the mother!" That white should be a dreaded color amused Schweitzer. Eventually, as he delivered a wriggling infant, held it by its feet, slapped its buttocks, he would say as a standard reminder to the parents, "Don't forget to paint it white."[2]

But there were far more of the unpleasant cases for the doctor to deal with than there were pleasant ones: these patients were members of what Schweitzer called "the fellowship of those who bear the mark of pain." Thinking of one man suffering with a strangulated hernia, he wrote:

"How can I describe my feelings when a poor fellow is

brought to me in this condition? I am the only person within hundreds of miles who can help him. Because I am here and am supplied by my friends with the necessary means, he can be saved, like those who came before him in the same condition and those who will come after him, while otherwise he would have fallen a victim to the torture. This does not mean merely that I can save his life. We must all die. But that I can save him from days of torture, that is what I feel as my great and ever new privilege. Pain is a more terrible lord of mankind than even death itself."[3]

The doctor's first assistant in his practice was a willing worker named Joseph, discovered among his first patients, an intelligent, bright young man who had previously served as a cook to Europeans in Africa and through this work had learned French.[4] In May, Dr. Schweitzer asked him to be his orderly until N'Zeng arrived. Joseph eagerly consented. His knowledge of anatomy, or rather his French-language descriptions of the parts of the body, came from the kitchen and butcher shop. Thus he would amuse Dr. Schweitzer by saying, "This man's mutton hurts," or "She suffers with pain in her left loin."

Joseph became the doctor's chief psychologist, in a sense, for he understood his fellow Africans, knew how they thought, what they feared and what expectations they had. He could understand their emotional and intellectual limitations and appreciate their sincerity. He also knew when to be suspicious of them. Consequently, he would advise Dr. Schweitzer to be considerate, gentle, stern or strict with the various patients as each individual situation required. He warned Dr. Schweitzer of those who would take advantage of him, if they could, and of those who would be loyal and faithful—as patients or as workers.[5]

The uniform distrust of Africans that had been expressed by the missionaries was counteracted, therefore, by Joseph. Dr. Schweitzer realized quickly that the general European suspicion of Africans was based on the tendency to generalize, to lump all people into one category. But he was enough of a teacher to understand why, if unfairly, the Europeans felt this way: he knew that all people including Africans did not perform intelligently when they did not comprehend fully.

Joseph became a kind of an admissions counselor for Schweitzer as well as a first-class aide. Sometimes he would overreach his authority, advising the doctor not to see a particular patient. In one such instance he argued against treatment because he knew that the ailing person had been refused help by the fetishmen and witch doctors of the local tribes. The man was going to die. The neighborhood medical consensus was that nothing could save him, and Joseph did not want the large and powerful clan to bring reprisals on Schweitzer if his treatment did not prove successful. Treatment would carry with it a high risk, but the doctor could not back away from what he saw as his duty. He admitted to Joseph that this man and others would die. The practice of medicine was not perfect and yet much could be accomplished by easing suffering and reducing pain. This was to be part of his work for terminal cases. On the other hand, he told Joseph, a white doctor did have means of curing unknown to the fetishmen. Thus Schweitzer refused his native aide's advice and gave his attentions to the suffering patient.

This exchange with Joseph revealed to Schweitzer a very crucial point early in his medical career. He discovered that he had to be firm with his friends and associates who tried to turn away fatal native medical cases for political reasons. To them the matter was simple: Schweitzer should avoid the patients that the witch doctors had given up on. They felt that he needed to build his reputation in this early period and this to them meant that he could have no medical failures or defeats on his record. Schweitzer could not accept this counsel. Fortunately, all of his early operations were successful. His competence matched his compassion.[6]

Nothing amazed the African more than to hear how the white doctor would "kill" a person, cut him open, take something out, sew him up and then bring him back to life—a life with no further pain. This to them was truly marvelous. Even the best of the fetishmen could not match such a feat.[7]

"So, when the poor moaning creature comes, I lay my hand on his forehead and say to him: 'Don't be afraid! In an hour's time you shall be put to sleep, and when you wake you won't feel any more pain.' Very soon he is given an injection of omnipon; the doctor's wife is called to the hospital, and with Joseph's help, makes everything ready for the operation. When that is to begin, she administers the anesthetic, and Joseph, in a long pair of rubber gloves, acts as assistant.

"The operation is finished, and in the hardly lighted dormitory, I watch for the sick man's awakening. Scarcely has he recovered consciousness, when he stares about him and ejaculates again and again: 'I've no more pain! I've no more pain!' His hand feels for mine and will not let it go."[8]

Dr. Schweitzer often told his native staff how he had been moved to follow the example of Jesus, to come to the Ogowe to help cure the sick.

"The African sun shining through the coffee bushes into the dark shed, we, black and white, sit side by side and feel that we know by experience the meaning of the words: 'And all ye are brethren' (Matt. 23:8). Would that my generous friends in Europe could come out here and live through such an hour!"[9]

Operations took place in the tiny room of the chicken coop. The patient's family and other patients sat in silence on the ground outside while the doctor operated, assisted by his nurse and Joseph who plunged the operating instruments into a boiling kettle before handing them through the door to the doctor. This drama appeared as magic to the natives. The African's understanding of sickness and disease was simple. He had one explanation. Pain was caused by a worm.[10] If pain was in the chest, there was a worm in the chest, writhing under the skin. If pain was in the leg or arm, the worm was in that area, etc. What the fetishman did was to use some method to entice the worm out of the body and give the patient a charm to keep it out, once removed. Accordingly,

Dr. Schweitzer was used to the Africans saying, "There is a worm here," as they pointed to the area of their discomfort.

Medical records of the patients presented a problem. Most Africans did not know when they were born or how to spell or write their names. As early as May of 1913, Dr. Schweitzer devised a system of numbers for the patients from the two different tribes he cared for as well as for the villages they came from. He would keep each patient's records in a huge daily ledger opposite his designated number.* The number was put on a cardboard tag, attached to a string and hung around the patient's neck. He was told, when discharged, to keep the tag and if he ever returned to the hospital, to bring back the tag. To the African, these simple tags became fetishes to ward off the evil spirits tamed by this doctor, and they placed a very high premium on the tags; none were ever lost. They were visible evidence of the protection given them by the white "Oganga" as Dr. Schweitzer was known to the Africans throughout the jungle. Thus, Dr. Schweitzer, unwittingly, came to qualify by native standards as a fetish-man.[11]

One unexpected problem developed when Schweitzer noticed that the sick people in his care would not eat any of the food prepared by his wife. He asked Joseph about this one day and learned that food was a special concern of the African people. The second most common source of sickness for them was caused by food poisoning and they believed that this was usually brought about by an enemy. Schweitzer protested that he hardly fit into that category, but Joseph said that his people were terribly suspicious. One could never be sure who had come near the food while it was being prepared—even touching the ladle or walking past the kitchen could induce poisoning in the view of the natives.

To solve this dietary dilemma Joseph suggested that the families of the patients cook their food. They would be on guard to see that no strange hand touched the ladle or ap-

* See appendix for these records.

proached the cooking area.[12] Schweitzer agreed to this and
announced that a member of every patient's family would be
in charge of the cooking as well as the securing of the food.
All he would do would be to issue the provisions in the morning in a line outside of the storehouse. This was characteristic
of the imagination and adaptation of which Schweitzer was
capable, and in winning the respect and confidence of the
natives, these qualities were of inestimable value in assisting
the growth of his hospital. To this day one can see the small
cooking fireplaces where many families prepare and serve their
own food.

After this move, Dr. Schweitzer took other steps to develop
an African hospital, not a European hospital, not a city
hospital, not a regulation hospital, but a workable jungle
hospital. The tag system, the family-feeding program and,
later, other necessary procedures were added. Schweitzer did
move cautiously, observing, and developing his own philosophy of the relationship between black and white; African and
missionary; preindustrial and "civilized." He saw in Lambaréné the encounter of cultures and hoped, in his person and his
service, to bridge gaps between them.

Most whites, including those at the mission, felt that there
were peculiarities difficult to deal with in the African outlook
and way of life: the natives' carefree abandon, their living
primarily in and for the moment, their trustfulness that everything in life would work out well, their belief in spirits, charms
and magic. They did not see these patterns of behavior as
parts of a genuine and significant culture deserving of respect.
Rather, they thought simply that the white man had "culture"
and the African did not. To Albert Schweitzer, however, it
was already clear that the African very definitely had a culture
that was vital and deserving of full respect. Unlike the missionaries, colonial administrators or industrial developers,
Schweitzer did not believe it was the white man's duty to
superimpose an alien culture on the African, in the name of
"civilization."[13] This attitude was to make Dr. Schweitzer
a minority of one—a white person standing apart from almost

all other whites in Africa, often misunderstood by other white men, and as well by Africans who had come to expect uniform reaction from all white persons.

The disappointment Dr. Schweitzer felt on arrival that the hospital had not been built turned out in the end to be good fortune. Those first weeks working out of the chicken coop had taught him that a hospital building could not be conventional if it were designed to serve the particularities of his medical practice and above all the great number of Africans coming to him. He would have to design his own hospital. He began to sketch out his ideas and keep check lists of his projected needs. As a result, from the very first, the mission hospital was different from any other hospital.

The council headquarters plan called for a hospital to be built on the top of a hill, but Schweitzer realized the folly of this idea. His patients came by boat and many could not walk; the carrying of patients up the hill in the glare of the sun would be difficult and impractical. Often a canoe put in to shore and simply deposited the sick person on the bank. When that happened, the total responsibility for transportation and admission to the hospital became the doctor's. In addition, his supplies, which came every two weeks now by steamer in large bulky wooden cases would be difficult to haul up a hill. Furthermore, he discovered that the top of the hill proposed as the hospital site did not have any more breeze than the bottom. The hot sultry air of this equatorial climate was simply like an oven, at either spot. But the sun beating on the roofs of buildings in the open would make them feel all the hotter, and there would be no protection from it, no shading trees, on top of the hill. Finally, if the hospital were on the hill, he and Helene would have the long climb in the sun each morning and afternoon.[14]

Thus Schweitzer reached the decision to have the new hospital built at the foot of the hill in the grove near the landing. Here, there would be only a short distance to carry litters, and a coolness from the water and the shade of the trees. Dr. Schweitzer mentioned these factors in his decision to Mr. Christol and Mr. Ellenberger. They understood his points instantly. However, they told him that many details of the plan had already been worked out and voted on by the missionary council or synod, and there had already been exhaustive discussion over the location of the hospital. Schweitzer asked when the council met again. He was pleased to learn it would be held in early July—just a few days away.

Mr. Ellenberger invited him to join them. "You are welcome to attend with us and present your proposal." It was agreed. Schweitzer would go to the conference to be held at Samkita. He recalled this first trip up the river on that July day in 1913. "We started one misty morning two hours before daybreak, the two missionaries and myself sitting one behind the other in long folding chairs in the bow. The middle of the canoe was filled with our tin boxes, our folded camp-bedsteads, the mattresses, and with the bananas which formed the rations of the natives. Behind these things were the twelve rowers in six pairs one behind the other; these sang about the destination to which we were bound and about who was on board, weaving in plaintive remarks about having to begin work so early and the hard day's work they had in front of them! Ten to twelve hours was the time usually allowed for the thirty to thirty-five miles upstream to Samkita, but our boat was so heavily laden, that it was necessary to allow somewhat longer.

"As we swung out from the side channel into the river, day broke and enabled us to see along the huge sandbank, some 350 yards ahead, some dark lines moving about in the water. The rowers' song stopped instantly, as if at a word of command. The dark lines were the backs of hippopotami, which were enjoying their morning bath after their regular grazing time on land. The natives are much afraid of them and always give them a wide berth, for their temper is very uncertain and they have destroyed many a canoe.

"There was once a missionary stationed in Lambaréné who used to make merry over the timidity of his rowers and challenge them to go nearer to the great animals. One day, just as he was on the point of bursting into laughter, the canoe was suddenly shot up into the air by a hippopotamus which rose from its dive immediately beneath it, and he and the crew only saved themselves with difficulty. All his baggage was lost. He afterwards had a square patch, with the hole that the creature had made, sawn out of the bottom of the canoe, that he might keep it as a souvenir. This happened some years ago, but the story is told to any white man who asks his crew to row nearer to a hippopotamus.

"In the main stream the natives always keep close to the bank where the current is not so strong: there are even stretches of river where one finds a countercurrent flowing upstream. And so we creep along, as far as possible in the shade of the overhanging trees. This canoe has no rudder, but the rower nearest the stern guides it in obedience to signals from the one in front, who keeps a sharp lookout for shallows, rocks and floating or submerged tree trunks. The most unpleasant thing on these trips is the way in which the light and heat are reflected from the water. One feels as if from the shimmering mirror one were being pierced with arrows of fire. To quench our thirst, we had some magnificent pineapples, three for each of us."[15]

They stopped for lunch at midday in a native village, where Dr. Schweitzer was graciously greeted by some of his former patients. The rowers cooked their bananas over an open fire while the three Europeans ate a more hearty meal. Dr. Schweitzer wondered why after such hard work the rowers did not have some more substantial food.

That night, they arrived in Samkita and the next morning Dr. Schweitzer met with the missionaries. There were clergymen, teachers and industrial advisers all helping the natives develop various skills. A number of African missionaries who had been ordained joined in the discussions. The meetings lasted for a full week and Dr. Schweitzer was impressed with the quality and dedication of these men and women. "I felt it inspiring to be working with men who for years had practiced such renunciation in order to devote themselves to the service of the natives, and I enjoyed thoroughly the refreshing atmosphere of love and good will."[16]

The missionaries were interested in personal reports of the initial work at the hospital and many of them would take Dr. Schweitzer aside to ask his opinion about their personal health. He was always glad to listen to their symptoms and, in several cases, examined the men and prescribed on the spot. He also assured them all that they and their families could call on him at any time.

The mission council voted to allow Dr. Schweitzer to change the site of the proposed hospital and voted him the sum of eighty pounds (4000 francs).[17] He would receive this immediately and he could use it as he saw fit. This decision freed them of an administrative burden and gave him some freedom in negotiating with natives and labor crews as well as in ordering supplies. Dr. Schweitzer had rapidly developed into a good, frugal buyer who enjoyed bartering and the palaver, and was able to hold his own and get concessions from those he bargained with. He felt confident that he could get the most for the money allotted him and would be able to stretch it as far as possible.

Shortly after returning to the mission, he learned that Mr. Rapp, a lumberman who had visited his hospital earlier, was stopping at the Catholic mission and had a labor crew with him. Mr. Rapp made eight members of his crew available to Dr. Schweitzer and, upon their arrival at Lambaréné, the building of the mission hospital began in earnest, with the collecting of lumber, clearing of the site, setting of foundation posts, and the plain hard labor of building. Dr. Schweitzer also found other workers to help so that by the time the Rapp crew moved on, a strong beginning had been made, and work was continuing.

Unfortunately, the doctor found that the only way to get the job done was to work along with the laborers. The moment he left the site, they sat down. But the work went steadily on.

In a few months, the new hospital was in full operation.

The structure had two main rooms, each thirteen feet square; the outer serving as consulting room, the inner as operating theater. There were two small side rooms under the roof projections; one was the dispensary, the other the sterilization unit. The hospital's walls were of corrugated iron. The roof was of raffia leaves. After the hospital was built, the waiting room, a shed for patients, and a hut for Joseph were built of roughhewn logs and raffia. The patients' dormitory was forty-two feet long and nearly twenty feet wide. There were sixteen units for the patients, each with a bed and a passage. There was no separation of the sexes: a procedure the Africans considered unnecessary. The attendants were sent out with axes to cut wood for the bedsteads, and the hospital was furnished.[18]

Dr. Schweitzer was pleased with the facilities, but not for long. By January 1914, he realized he must build a new addition to the hospital. There was no place for the infectious cases. New accommodations for them would have to be built. There was also no room for the attendants. Each bed was raised twenty inches above the ground; the attendants were allowed to sleep under the beds or next to them. But when making his night rounds, Dr. Schweitzer sometimes found the attendants had placed the sick persons on the ground and had gotten into the beds themselves. He had allowed space for sixteen patients, but now could see that he needed forty beds. Thus, from the first, he found that nothing would ever be complete or perfect and that he would always be building, replacing, remodeling and planning. This was to be a major occupation for Schweitzer in Lambaréné, a time-consuming job added to his exhausting medical practice. But now, in spite of all its shortcomings, he did have a hospital —the mission hospital—designed and built with his own hands, aided of course by Joseph and many others. This was his beginning in Africa.

Life went on busily at the hospital. Patients continued to come in great numbers and the doctor was kept busy with them, as well as with the needed construction. He had de-

vised a set of rules which he required the orderlies to read
to the patients every morning:

THE DOCTOR'S STANDING ORDERS:

1. Spitting near the hospital is strictly forbidden.

2. Those who are waiting must not talk to each other
loudly.

3. Patients and their friends must bring with them food
enough for one day, as they cannot all be treated early in one
day.

4. Anyone who spends the night on the station without
the doctor's permission, will be sent away without any medicine. (It happened not infrequently that patients from a
distance crowded into the schoolboys' dormitory, turned
them out, and took their places.)

5. All bottles and tin boxes in which medicines are given
must be returned.

6. In the middle of the month, when the steamer has gone
up the river, none but urgent cases can be seen till the
steamer has gone down again, as the doctor is then writing
to Europe to get more of his valuable medicines. (The
steamer brings the mail from Europe about the middle of
the month, and on its return, takes our letters down to the
coast.) [19]

One noon at mealtime, after visiting the hospital, Mr.
Christol asked the missionaries and their families if they
knew the difference between the mission and the hospital.
After various unsuccessful guesses, he told them with a laugh,
"The mission has Ten Commandments but the hospital has
only six."

These commandments were observed; the work of the hospital went forward. As Dr. Schweitzer had surmised, the missionaries in the field were not nearly as concerned with
doctrinal matters as was the mission board at home. He
wrote:

"As I had expected, the questions of dogma on which the
Missionary Society's committee in Paris had laid so much
weight played practically no part in the sermons of the mis-

sionaries. If they wanted to be understood by their hearers, they could do nothing beyond preaching the simple Gospel of becoming freed from the world by the spirit of Jesus, the Gospel which comes to us in the Sermon on the Mount and the finest sayings of St. Paul. Necessity compelled them to put forward Christianity as before all else an ethical religion. When they met each other at the mission conferences held twice a year now at this station, now at that, their discussions bore on the problems of how to secure practical Christianity in their district, not on doctrinal ones. That in matters of belief some of them thought more strictly than others, played no part in the missionary work which they carried on in common. As I did not make the smallest attempt to foist any theological views on them, they soon laid aside all mistrust of me and rejoiced, as did I also on my side, that we were united in the piety of obedience to Jesus, and in the will to simple Christian activity. Not many months after my arrival, I was invited to take part in the preaching and thus was released from the promise I had given in Paris: '*d'être muet comme une carpe.*' "[20]

The two main tribes served by the hospital were the Galoas and the Pahouins. The Galoas were the oldest, longest established tribe of the area, a people whose geographical location and way of life had changed little since prehistory. They were a more docile people than other tribes, which was almost their undoing. When the French arrived in 1843, the Galoas had the area near Lambaréné to themselves, but an unexplainable migration of the Pahouins, or Fangs, from the interior began to take place. Fighting their way into the region, the Fangs, a cannibalistic people, prepared for warfare with the Galoas. These cannibals were intelligent, quite advanced in the skills of war and quick at adaptations to living conditions required for survival. Their greater skills, as well as their belligerence, began gradually to lead to the extermination of the Galoas when the French took matters into their own hands and stopped the warfare and invasion, decreeing that both tribes should share the land. An uneasy peace developed after 1880. The members of the two tribes would work together, but never fully accepted each other.[21]

Once, in 1914, Dr. Schweitzer asked some attendants to carry a litter. Looking down on the patient, they replied, "He is not of our tribe," and refused to give assistance. A very real sense of brotherhood was felt for those of their own, and they would obediently assist a fellow tribesman whether they knew him or not personally. But brotherhood did not extend across tribal lines. A Fang, for example, would not give blood for a Galoa.[22]

Joseph was a Galoa. N'Zeng, who finally arrived, was a Pahouin. Dr. Schweitzer found it very helpful to have an interpreter for each tongue or tribe; among other reasons, they could exercise tribal authority over their members, making personal relations and the work of the hospital go more smoothly.[23]

The doctor continued to participate in the missionary conferences. Once he attended a meeting where a missionary was lecturing to a group of converted Christians. The missionary was emphasizing the need of Christians to give up some aspects of tribal behavior which, for one thing, included having more than one wife. He was belaboring the point of "sacrificing the joys of polygamy." After he first had several times referred to the understandable joys of polygamy, Dr. Schweitzer gently tapped him on the shoulder and with a chuckle whispered, "My brother, what makes you so sure that to have more than one wife would be a joy?"[24]

At Home in Africa

Schweitzer began to feel at home. Africa was the main object of his concern, and the center of his work; now, in addition, he was learning to love the life of the people.

One day he was sitting in the bow of a long pirogue, gliding through the yellowish Ogowe waters, facing the African rowers like a teacher with his class. One of them asked him about the differences between Africa and Europe. Schweitzer was amused by the question. He thought for a moment of the two continents in broad terms, and said that he thought there were three differences.

First he noted that in Europe there were great forest fires, often ignited by a single spark which would quickly burn down a huge woods. This amazed his crew. It was inconceivable to them that a fire could burn on its own, out of control, in a forest. In tropical Africa, even in the dry season, the forests dripped with moisture. Their region was so damp and surrounded by so much damp foliage that large areas were untouched by the sun's rays—a forest fire was an impossibility. Even of dry timber, only small limbs and middle-sized branches could be burned; attempting to burn tree trunks only made them char.

Following the discussion of forest fires, Schweitzer mentioned another difference between continents that brought a chorus of laughter and comment: in Europe people rowed for pleasure. His young crew at first thought that people must row in Europe under orders or at least for gifts. They were startled to learn, as the doctor went on, that exhausting contests were held and that the participants rowed without pay. In Africa, a canoeist might race against someone for a short distance, in the spirit of friendly rivalry. But such races for fun were brief and infrequent. In this tropical continent with its river and lake highways, rowing was the chief means of transportation. One virtually could not travel unless he went by water. Rowing meant survival and it would be senseless to waste any time or effort in useless activity like boating tournaments or contests of endurance and speed. The native African had a grueling life. He needed his strength in the survival struggle—there was no inclination to turn daily labor into sport.

The most startling and amazing difference between continents to the Africans was to come. Schweitzer told his company that in Europe a man married without paying for his wife. This shocked the crew, since in Africa one paid handsomely for a wife. Schweitzer also told them that it was considered good luck to have a son and European families rejoiced, not mourned, at the birth of a baby boy.[1]

These statements were in complete contrast to the taboos of most tribes. In most tribes it was understood that when a young man married, his family had to pay the bride's family whatever price the families' palaver set. Consequently, because of borderline subsistence in most families, the birth of a boy carried with it a hardship. On the other hand, there was rejoicing when a girl was born, for her family of course knew that at some future time they would receive a handsome dowry from some boy's family. No family dared to violate the taboo of paying for a wife. The bride's family decided the price which her future family must meet. Usually, the whole amount could not be paid at once; thus there was a sort of credit arrangement. The young people were married (sometimes at twelve or fourteen years of age) and the first installment was paid. Then at intervals, the girl's family would come around for additional payments. If payment was not made on demand, the wife was taken back and returned only when her family was satisfied with the financial arrangement.[2]

The first time a situation of this kind happened at the hospital, Dr. Schweitzer thought the girl involved had been kidnaped and voiced alarm. None of the Africans got excited. "It is the way. It is proper," they told him and refused to follow or reclaim the girl.[3]

These practices surrounding birth and marriage are similar to other customs. They lie far back in the thought patterns of the African native and are regulated by taboo. They exercise a strong influence over the people of Africa through psychological controls that the white person living there should appreciate but rarely does. The origin of taboos lies deep in the collective experience and unconscious of a given tribe, rests seemingly in the supernatural realm and allows for no change in behavior. To violate one, however, creates for the native a traumatic experience terrifying in its consequences. Schweitzer saw taboos as understandable cultural adaptations to the natural world.

Among the Pahouins, for instance, it is taboo for a man whose wife is expecting a child to eat meat which has begun to spoil; normally they will eat meat that most whites would regard as putrid. It is also taboo for him to touch a chameleon; to fill a hole with earth; to drive nails; to be present at the death of a man or beast; to step over a procession of driver ants, among other things. If he violates such taboos, he believes dreadful things are bound to happen to his child.[4]

It is considered by some tribes a taboo to have the firstborn child be a boy. Tradition says that it will result either in the death of the boy or his mother. The origin of this, Dr. Schweitzer suggested, may lie in the economic hardship expected for the family.

Dr. Schweitzer recalled that during his first stay in Lambaréné, a boy at the Samkita mission station observed a taboo which forbade him to eat plantains or other food taken from a pot that had the residue of plantains previously cooked in it. One day at mealtime, his schoolmates, speaking in jest, told him that he had just eaten fish cooked in a pot having a piece of plantain in it. The boy was immediately seized with cramps and died before the doctor could arrive.[5]

A curse spoken by one person against another is accepted as a taboo. On one occasion, a girl refused to obey the command of her father to give up the man of her choice and marry a man selected by her family, who had already made the payment they had requested. Instead, she ran away with the man she loved. The father, who needed the price of the dowry, uttered a curse upon her, vowing that if she married her lover, either she or a child of that marriage would die. She later gave birth to a healthy baby, and then resolved to die that the child might live. She ate nothing and seemed to wither away, dying an apparently mysterious death from "feebleness," which in the doctor's judgment, although he was not consulted, probably was the result of malnutrition.[6]

One of the missionaries, who had formerly served at Lambaréné, felt himself the terrible strain of a spoken curse. In his class there was one youngster who tended to be of a disagreeable disposition. One day, in exasperation, the missionary told him unthinkingly that he would always have a bad character.

Some years later, the boy, now a young man, came to see the missionary and accused him of making him a most unhappy man because of the curse under which he lived. The missionary, amazed, had forgotten his utterance. The young man repeated what the teacher had said to him, indicating that he completely lacked the energy or will to overcome his bad character, knowing that it had been willed on him by the missionary's curse.

The missionary explained that what he had said was not meant as a curse and that, to the contrary, he had always hoped and prayed that the boy would be happy. Upon hearing this, the young man was visibly relieved. Before leaving the mission that day, it was noticed by many that the boy had suddenly become carefree and buoyant, as though a great weight had been lifted from his conscience.[7]

Spoken blessings are also thoroughly accepted by Africans of many tribes. One can secure the blessing of others by the process of taking on aspects of their "nommo," that is, of their psychic and moral attributes. Dr. Schweitzer was interested by the number of boys born at the hospital who were named "Dr. Albert," and of girls called after his first two nurses, "Mademoiselle Matildi" and "Mademoiselle Emma."[8] They were not called simply Albert, Matildi or Emma, but by the title also. In this way, there could be no mistaking the fact that they had appropriated the blessing of these three particular people who had certain desirable qualities of strength, knowledge and power.

Often, a family observing a taboo against the birth of a girl will give it a boy's name, or vice versa, to help make sure evil spirits are confused.[9] This type of masquerading is a ruse to insure blessings needed to attain a happy life. Nothing is more desired by many Africans than the knowledge that they have the good wishes and blessings of those people they admire and regard as superior—the chiefs, fetishmen, medicine men, witch doctors, and even white people —who exercise various degrees of authority over their lives and have knowledge that is power. Dr. Schweitzer felt that most Europeans were too impatient and thoughtless to take time to express good wishes to the African, when a few kind words would have made a great deal of difference. Recognition of the African alone would go a long way toward proving the "nommo" many Africans desire so much.

One reason that Dr. Schweitzer's hospital has become so well known and probably the greatest value of his hospital through the years to the natives has been that there Africans have been respected and dealt with thoughtfully as individuals. Africans, Europeans and Americans, alike, in trying to isolate the single factor that makes the hospital unique, usually end up simply by saying, "Here one is treated with love," "Greater than all the medication is the love Dr. Schweitzer shares with the Africans," etc. Such tributes were heard by George Marshall from many Africans. The doctor offered his blessings in only one way, through his medical work at the hospital.

Schweitzer felt sadly that most Africans, including those who were pagans, were more full of love and good will than white Christians. They seemed to share a strong sense of well-wishing and concern for one another. Too often, the doctor noted, many Christian white men, including some of the missionaries and teachers, were too preoccupied with specific tasks of their professional service to take the time to express simple human interest in the African or his personal problems.[10]

Many of the Africans Schweitzer met who were supposedly Christians maintained simultaneously a strong belief in taboos and other aspects of tribal religion. Schweitzer was tempted one day to question his orderly and assistant, Joseph, about this double standard.

Joseph had been telling the doctor about the big fishing expedition in which his village participated during the annual dry season. The entire village would leave on a two-week fishing festival in a huge fleet of canoes to encamp on a large sandbank exposed by the receding waterline caused by the drought. Old and young alike would live together in booths, celebrating and singing for two weeks. At every meal they would cook and eat fish in all forms: baked, broiled, boiled, fried, and stewed. Fish not consumed was dried and smoked. When the festival was over, if all went well, the tribe would take home as many as ten thousand dried and smoked fish, according to Joseph.

Schweitzer suggested that Joseph go on the excursion that year and take along a small tub to bring back a few fish for him. Joseph instantly declined and became suddenly very solemn. Schweitzer questioned him, anxious to know why he had no desire to join the festival. Joseph explained that on the first day of the trip there was no fishing but a great deal of preparation of the waters—the elders of the village would pour rum and throw tobacco on the waters to bring good humor to the evil spirits that controlled the fish, allowing the catch to be made. Joseph recalled that several years earlier these rites had been omitted and the fishing was poor. The following year an old woman allowed herself to be wrapped up in a fish net and drowned—a means used to restore good fortune to the tribe. By this gift of human life the evil spirits were supposedly placated.

Schweitzer's amazement at this procedure is seen in his later account:

"But why? Most of you are Christians!" I exclaimed. "You don't believe these things!" "Certainly not," he replied, "but anyone who spoke against them or even allowed himself to smile while the rum and tobacco were being offered, would assuredly be poisoned sooner or later. The medicine men never forgive, and they live among us without anyone knowing who they are."[11]

Thus Joseph revealed the double standard of religious belief held by many Africans.

In 1913, the division between the older Africans who believed in magic and fetishes, and the younger generation, which did not, caused a severe cleavage in communal life. The children attending mission schools and who later became Christians could never be initiated into the lore of their fathers. Some suffered in their villages as a result. In the end, they were the ones who left home to follow the foresters, miners and industrialists, or went to the large cities, having been severed from their tribal associations.

During Schweitzer's first years in the Ogowe River valley, the elders and medicine men dealt with insubordination in a hideous way. A secret organization, called the "Leopard Men," was formed and controlled by them. Its purpose was to put a stop to the breakdown in tribal loyalties. Before the young men of the community could be influenced by the missionaries, they were secretly initiated into this order which demanded blind and absolute allegiance to the fetishmen and the elders. Given a secret initiation at night, dressed in the skin of a leopard, with steel claws that cut flesh like a leopard, they were then sent out to attack the non-believing, rebellious Africans, those losing their allegiance to the old ways or African Christians who had renounced tribal-folk mores. A fearsome reign of terror set in. Schweitzer was called upon frequently to give emergency treatment to patients who had been brutally injured, mangled by the steel claws. Like the animal, Leopard Men tried to sever the carotid artery, and when successful, death was immediate and, of course, Schweitzer could not help.

The irony was that the young men inducted had no choice; they did not volunteer. At a tribal gathering, they were unsuspectingly given a potion to drink mixed in a human skull and afterward were told that it was the leopard potion and that they were now members of the Leopard Band. They feared the Leopard Men and dared not refuse membership. They had an even greater fear of the magic potion against which they believed none could successfully resist. They felt they had to submit to the Band. Their loyalty was first tested by an order to bring a sister or a brother to a grove as a sacrifice. The next time they were tested, they had to perform an actual killing.[12]

After the Armistice in 1918, Schweitzer recalled, the government decided to stamp out the Leopard Band and arrested ninety men on suspicion. They administered poison to one another and all died in prison rather than divulge information about the organization.[13]

In complete contrast to the Leopard Band seeking to retain tribal ways were the blacks who became missionaries and Christian clergymen. These converts renounced the tribal ancestral culture and as a result became "rootless" on their own continent in taking on the white man's beliefs and behavior patterns.[14]

Thus Schweitzer was becoming conscious of a transition taking place in African culture. He saw the efforts to withstand the deterioration of tribal habits of living, to maintain "the old ways," and he saw how Western civilization and missionary efforts were hastening their breakdown. It was perhaps because he saw this process, that Schweitzer, while maintaining close personal ties with the missionaries, never became a zealous participant in efforts at attempting Christian conversion of the Africans. He ran his hospital as though it were a non-sectarian enterprise and joined only as a friend in the missionary councils. The restriction against Schweitzer's speaking, the instruction to be "as mute as a fish," imposed by the Paris Society had been lifted by the missionary synod. At one synod session, after his opinion on a theological matter had been asked by one of the missionaries, he was rebuked by an African convert who said that the conference members should not take the doctor's opinion into account "since he is not a theologian, as we are."[15]

Foremost, however, in Dr. Schweitzer's mind was his continuing commitment as a physician. It was in his practice that he most closely related to the Africans. And they responded to him. They were, for example, overwhelmingly pleased and astonished that he could diagnose heart disease, a very frequent ailment in Africa. Once, in 1913, an old woman arrived at the hospital. Stethoscope in hand, the doctor listened to her heartbeat, examined her chest and back, asked her only a few questions and then prescribed digitalis. When Schweitzer left the room, she looked up at Joseph and said, "Now I know we have a real doctor. He knows that often I can hardly breathe at night, and that I often have swollen feet, yet I had never told him a word about it, and he had not looked at my feet."[16]

Schweitzer was fast becoming an institution in Lambaréné, to be loved and respected by African and European alike.

13

Prisoner of War

For the Schweitzers, World War I began on August 5, 1914.
On that day, word reached Lambaréné that Germany and
France were at war.[1] These were the two countries which
had claimed Schweitzer's native province of Alsace, and both
had contributed to his cultural orientation. He was in
Africa, far from his homeland, yet still a part of it, in a sense,
for he was now a resident of the northernmost of the French
Equatorial African colonies—Gabon—which was bordered
on the north by the German Cameroons. Hence, he found
himself thousands of miles from home on another German-
French border. For Albert Schweitzer, Africa, his new home,
provided no asylum from war. It was also to be fought there.
Now it was just beginning.[2]

The Schweitzers had planned to return to Europe after
one or two years in Africa for a brief rest. They were now well
along into their second year. The exact time of their departure would depend on how well their funds held out, as well
as on Helene's and his ability to endure the African climate.
He had not, however, intended to go home under the conditions that developed.

On the morning of August 5, the Schweitzers learned that
the conflict had started. By evening, they were prisoners of
war. They were informed that they might remain in their
house for the time being, but must refrain from all contact
with both white people or Africans. Native soldiers were assigned to them, and they were told that they must obey un-
conditionally all orders of their guards.[3]

Probably the most unpopular people in Africa were the
guards assigned to hold Dr. Schweitzer as a prisoner. Africans

from the various tribes and villages in the jungle would come
to the hospital with their sick and injured only to be told
they could not see the doctor. The hospital lay idle nearby.
Schweitzer was a prisoner in his own house. Armed guards
took turns watching it, some standing in front of the house,
others on the porch, and no one was allowed to enter. On
the hillside in front of the house sat groups of puzzled natives. Their doctor, a white, was being held prisoner by
black African soldiers assigned by other whites. The situation
angered them. Every now and then a family would appear,
bringing a prospective patient slowly up the hill, only to learn
that the doctor was a prisoner and unable to help. For many
of them, the war was a mystery. What had clear impact, however, was the loss of the care and services of one who had
become vitally important to the lives of thousands. At first,
the war involved the natives little beyond such changed conditions as the closing down of the massive lumber industry
and the stoppage of overseas trade. Later on, however, their
men were to be engaged in helping French troops fighting
on the front in the Cameroons.[4]

But already, packet ships no longer were traveling the
Ogowe. Supplies were cut off. Lumber could not be shipped.
The economy languished. The native laborers brought into
the logging camps from the interior were discharged. These
released laborers, imported from other tribes, were now without homes, and they began wandering throughout the Fang
and Galoa villages and lands creating a whole new set of
problems.[5]

The Bendjabis were the most numerous among this group.
These fierce tribesmen from the interior had been lured to
the logging camps with the promise that they would be returned to their villages when their work was completed.
Now, however, transportation was out of the question and
the lumber companies were unable to send them back. Many
of the primitive Bendjabis appeared to have a complete lack
of discipline and regard for property. They became wanderers
on the ancestral, proprietary lands of the settled tribes and

were becoming unassimilated migrants and vagrants in the otherwise ordered structure of the African village society near Lambaréné. Most of them spoke dialects not understood by the Galoa and Pahouin, so that community problems were complicated by the consequent lack of communication.[6] The breakdown of historic African living patterns was accelerated by their presence. With many of the Europeans going home and the marshaling of others into the local militia, the colonial administrators had to turn all their attention to the war. Local political supervision broke down.

Most of the missionaries and teachers were also being ordered home. One of the Paris Society members, an Alsatian like the Schweitzers, was also under house arrest.[7] American, French and Swedish missionaries were recalled. Communications, transfer of their funds and shipping of their essential supplies were no longer possible. Isolation was returning to Africa. Not only were the missionaries and teachers departing, but nothing was left to fill the vacuum created by the withdrawal of those responsible for supervising and maintaining law and order.[8] The economic and cultural development generated by the century-long interchange between nationals and Europeans was being halted. And the African simply could not revert suddenly to preindustrial ways as though the influence of European civilization had never been on his continent.[9]

The formerly imperceptible changes of the previous century were now apparent. The African's tribal authority had been modified. His economic means of living, his mode of hunting and gathering food, his tribal patterns of migration and territorial development, had all been altered. No missions, teachers or administrators functioned and labor bosses were not hiring in the villages. Their absence left havoc where there had been a promising and creative society bridging two cultures. The war in modern Europe was taking its toll in Africa.

It was only a matter of time until armed conflict itself

came to the African continent with marching armies and killing between white men. European officers began to seek black recruits for training and eventual combat with the whites. This was the "progress" of the war in Africa. First, black soldiers were sent to imprison the white doctor, and now they were being equipped to shoot and kill whites.[10] After a century of virtually total domination by whites who offered natives little opportunity for equality, or free exchange of communication, they suddenly had a strange opportunity for a kind of liberation. War would give the blacks an equality to bear arms and to join the hostilities. In the next war, a new generation was to see the fulfillment of that equality.

Most of the white men in Africa thus returned home and only those involved as administrators of a colonial war (with a few white soldiers and officers) remained to observe the slow but relentless deterioration of African life and culture. Schweitzer, who was interned until September 1917—a period of three years—also was to see the impact of the sudden alterations in African life caused by the irresponsible withdrawal of the European.

As a result, he became convinced that African and Western civilization had become so inextricably tied that sudden, almost total withdrawal of the Europeans posed an untenable situation. A more orderly transition was needed. He was also already of the opinion that the thorough Westernization or Europeanization (and Americanization) of Africa would not work. A new interlocking, intermixed and interacting civilization must be developed, keeping the best of the African culture with its ideals of community stability and personal worth, and blending with it those aspects of Western civilization that would make possible a more abundant economic and sophisticated cultural life. Neither the European colonizer then nor the African liberation patriot later would understand his reasoning.[11]

To the European (and American), Dr. Schweitzer often seemed to be criticizing the colonial, capitalistic and missionary enterprises in Africa; to the African independence advocate, he always appeared to be favoring a subtle continuation of colonial authority. His perspective, a view of compromise, was a stance of cautious support for self-determination and independence developed through three long, hard years of war in Africa. He anticipated the difficulties now being encountered in Africa, and this again shows his wisdom and insight into a continent that he saw as unable to thrive under either political extreme.

Schweitzer was kept under house arrest only a relatively short time because of the protests of the tribal chieftains and the overall popular demand for his badly needed services. Also, there was a growing awareness on the part of the military that Dr. Schweitzer was not emotionally involved with the Germans, but was a humanitarian whose only concerns in the war were with the human suffering it caused, the gaps in understanding and communication it created between civilized men, and the havoc and destruction it brought to African culture.

As an intellectual, the military officers really did not trust him. As a doctor, they could at least appreciate him. In fact, the commandant found it increasingly necessary to grant permission for patients to be allowed to see the doctor.

Consequently, within three months, in November 1914, Dr. Schweitzer was allowed to resume his normal activities at the hospital, to visit the island of Lambaréné and the Catholic mission, and to travel up and down the Ogowe. Therefore, for the remaining period of his African confinement he was relatively free, as long as he restricted himself to contact with and medical service for African people,[12] government officials and the maintenance personnel at the mission stations. But even in this period of relative restriction he developed insight into the condition of African civilization in the light of the withdrawal of European influence.

The Catholic natives of the Ogowe were not very interested in the war when news of it first came because of their emotional involvement in the recent election of a new Pope. But most Ogowe natives, regardless of faith, were soon engaged to serve as carriers for the Gabonese French Army units sent north to fight the Germans in the Cameroons. When word filtered back that ten of the white soldiers from Lambaréné were killed early in the conflict, an old native man remarked, "What, so many men killed in this war? Why don't their tribes meet to talk out the palaver? How can they ever pay for all these dead men?" (In native warfare those who die must be paid for by the opposite side.)[13] This African and many others were simply confused by the war. Later, Dr. Schweitzer listened with sadness for the white man's culture, his own, as this same African expressed the view that Europeans kill merely out of cruelty. "Why, Doctor," another native asked, "do the white men who brought us the Gospel of Love not practice it among themselves?" Gradually, the doctor came to realize that the African was thoroughly disoriented by his expectations of the white man's standards, theology and ethics and the contrast presented by his actual living of them.

Dr. Schweitzer had converted all his funds into gold coin before coming to Africa in the expectation that war might occur. With the high prices the war brought, he found his supply running low. In addition, he was cut off from the source of his funds in Strasbourg. Eventually, he had to tell Joseph that to economize he would have to cut his wages. Joseph reluctantly told the doctor that dignity would not allow him to serve for the small sum proposed and so the doctor lost the services of his invaluable orderly and translator. Joseph was able to find employment with a French officer in his former occupation as a cook.[14]

With the unrelenting continuation of war, Dr. Schweitzer's mind returned to a concern about Western civilization as a whole that had not occupied him for many years.[15] As a student of philosophy and theology, he had heard and studied the thought of Oswald Spengler, a professor at the neighboring University of Munich. Spengler's ideas were an intellectual fad in student circles and his ideas were discussed with enthusiasm wherever young people gathered. Upon reading his works, however, Schweitzer felt Spengler's pessimistic ideas were "without substance," and decided to someday write a book of his own on the processes of decay and disintegration taking place in society. But his studies introduced him to other writings, and his plans to refute the ideas of Spengler were continually postponed. Now that war had come to Europe, and the decline of civilization was not only noticeable but accelerated, he felt he could put off writing the book no longer. Accordingly, during his four months of house arrest, he spent most of his time preparing the first volume of the *Philosophy of Civilization.*

He recalled at the time that during the summer of 1899, while he was spending an evening with some friends at the home of the widow of Professor Ernst Curtius in Berlin, the discussion touched on Spengler's philosophy. Someone had made the remark that "We are all just nothing but *'Epigoni!'*" This thought remained in his mind.[16] *Epigoni* is a Latin word then in vogue in philosophy to refer to the inheritors of a great culture, or more specifically, to the generation which follows a great, creative one, and that merely lives on the accomplishments of the past. He had thought to call his book *Wir Epigonen* (*We Inheritors of the Past*), but now in 1914, as he wrote the book, he realized that the fundamental subject to be discussed was the philosophy of where civilization was going, not merely the heritage of its past.

Dr. Schweitzer for many years had realized that his generation's optimism which stressed "perpetual progress," was a limited world-view that could not be sustained. Some hard-headed examination of this naïve optimism was needed. Its greatest weakness was its failure to allow for the essential drive necessary for society to creatively and constructively meet its problems.

In the early summer of 1915, he suddenly realized that he was becoming too despondent about the future by dealing mainly with criticisms of society. Why not think of Western civilization's positive features and enlarge the hopeful themes of philosophy for the future? It was not enough to point out what was wrong; one must provide constructive alternatives. In searching for the answer to the pessimism one experienced in surveying the crisis of civilization, he concluded "that the catastrophe of civilization started from the catastrophe of a world-view."[17] He felt that the idealistic world-view, the "progress" ethic on which Western civilization rested was no longer sustaining it. Only a few men, such as Søren Kierkegaard, a nineteenth-century Danish theologian, recognized that this Western world-view and life affirmation were at variance, and could not be united. Kierkegaard had in his search turned from a commitment to the external world to a personal pietism which was unacceptable to Dr. Schweitzer. He felt there had to be a more meaningful response to the questions on the meaning of life now posed by the existentialists. He found greater hope for this in the Eastern philosophies.

While Schweitzer had been a student at the Sorbonne, Friedrich Wilhelm Nietzsche had died, and Schweitzer was selected by the philosophical faculty to give the commemorative address at a convocation honoring Nietzsche.[18] He read all Nietzsche's published works in preparation for his address, and was strongly repelled by the philosophical conclusions this brilliant thinker had reached. Schweitzer appreciated his rejection of theological and philosophical pretensions, but considered Nietzsche's conclusions too shallow. On the subject of religion, Schweitzer felt that Nietzsche's denunciation of classical Christianity had elements of brilliant insight. But his rejection of the virtues of piety, love and compassion and substitution for them of nationalism, competitiveness and materialistic science as ideals left Schweitzer cold. In the end, he rebelled against Nietzsche, but he still felt the necessity of offering some definite critique of Western civilization. To him, Nietzsche had voiced valid premises but had emerged with invalid conclusions. This feeling led Schweitzer to address himself to the dilemma of how a critical mind could build a hope for escape from cultural morass without losing itself in pessimism. This became an all-consuming challenge to Schweitzer as a student. Now, with war ravaging Europe, the intensity of his concern about this dilemma returned.[19]

He found that the world-view of the West had been completely severed from any ethical dimension, so that true affirmation of *all* life was lost. All these thoughts were developed fully in Dr. Schweitzer's books which resulted from this period of serious thought and writing. Two volumes were written while he was a prisoner of war in Lambaréné: *The Decay and Restoration of Civilization* and *Civilization and Ethics.* The same philosophical concerns motivated his preparation of a third volume, *Indian Thought and Its Development,* although it was not written until after the end of the war. These three books, together with his autobiographical writings and essays on Goethe, comprise the thorough critique of civilization that is an enduring landmark in Dr. Schweitzer's thought.[20]

Dr. Schweitzer had completed the first volume of his *Philosophy of Civilization,* when he came to the striking realization that man's ethics as he and others had previously thought about them were incomplete; they pertained to man only. *Man had failed to identify with life itself,* and remained egocentric. From this position, there evolved Dr. Schweitzer's contention that true ethics must involve all of life, all the living.

It was while pondering this, in a world torn by war (as he was paddled down the Ogowe, the crew carefully picking their way through a herd of hippopotami), that the dictum "Reverence for Life" first occurred to him. Reverence for Life became the basis of the ethical imperative that Dr. Schweitzer was to offer to the world. The ethic had been the basis of his boyhood prayer, "protect everything that breathes." Now from this concept came the second volume of his trilogy, *Civilization and Ethics.*[21]

He had barely completed the material, when word came

that he and Mrs. Schweitzer were to be interned in Europe. Schweitzer feared that his manuscripts would be confiscated by the French so his wife suggested that he wrap the material in newspapers and give it to a missionary for safekeeping. Since America was not yet at war, Schweitzer decided to entrust his new work to his Presbyterian missionary friend from the United States, Mr. Ford. He had stayed on after the Americans had turned the missionary station over to the French, although he could not continue to teach because of his inability to speak French. The missionary, known for his deep evangelical faith, wondered aloud about taking a manuscript on philosophy. He thought it surely must contain challenges for himself and other people who held his belief. Yet he admired Schweitzer and agreed to take charge of the writings, "although he admitted to me, he would have liked best to throw the heavy packet into the river, because he considered philosophy to be unnecessary and harmful."[22]

During the period immediately preceding his deportation, Schweitzer was visiting the Catholic mission upriver. Orders arrived for his internment and transfer to Europe. He and Mrs. Schweitzer were taken aboard the river steamer for the trip. Later he wrote:

"Just as we had been taken on board the river steamer and the natives were shouting to us an affectionate farewell from the land, the Father Superior of the Catholic mission came on board, waved aside with an authoritative gesture the native soldiers who tried to prevent his approach, and shook hands with us: 'You shall not leave the country,' he said, 'without my thanking you both for all the good you have done it.' We were never to see each other again. Shortly after the war he lost his life aboard the *Afrique,* the ship which took us to Europe, when she was wrecked in the Bay of Biscay."[23]

They were transferred to Port Gentil where they were interned with other prisoners on their way to the concentration camp at Garaison in the Pyrenees. Here and at Saint-Rémy-de-Provence, Dr. and Mrs. Schweitzer were to spend the last year of the war. It was at Garaison that he practiced playing the organ by using his fingers on the dining-room table, keeping his hands agile and his mind active.[24]

The doctor wrote about one of the most interesting events that occurrred at Garaison: "Not long after our arrival, some newcomers arrived from another camp which had been broken up. They at once began to grumble at the bad way in which the food was prepared and to reproach their fellow prisoners who occupied the much-envied posts in the kitchen with not being fit for their job. Great indignation arose thereat among these, who were cooks by profession and had found their way to Garaison from the kitchens of the first-class hotels and restaurants of Paris! The matter came before the Governor, and when he asked the rebels which of them were cooks, it turned out that there was not a single cook among them! Their leader was a shoemaker, and the others had such trades as tailoring, hat-making, basket-weaving or brush-making. In their previous camp, however, they had applied themselves to doing the cooking and declared that they had mastered the art of preparing food in large quantities. With Solomon-like wisdom, the Governor decided that they should take over the kitchen for a fortnight as an experiment. If they did better than the others, they should keep their posts. Otherwise, they would be put under lock and key as disturbers of the peace. On the very first day, they proved with potatoes and cabbage that they had not claimed too much, and every succeeding day was a new triumph. So the non-cooks were created 'cooks' and the professional cooks were turned out of the kitchen! When I asked the shoemaker the secret of their success, he replied: 'One must know all sorts of things, but the most important is to do the cooking with love and care.' So now, if I learn that once more someone has been appointed Minister of some department about which he knows nothing, I do not get excited over it as I used to, but screw myself up to the hope that he will prove just as fit for his job as the Garaison shoemaker proved to be for his."[25]

When he was admitted at the Garaison Prisoner of War Camp, the non-commissioned officer who inspected his bag-

gage picked up a copy of Aristotle's *Politics*, which Schweitzer had brought along with the hope of using it in the further
studies he planned in preparation for the continuation of his
Philosophy of Civilization. " 'Why, it is incredible!' he
stormed. 'They're actually bringing political books into a
prisoner of war camp!' I shyly remarked to him that the book
was written long before the birth of Christ. 'Is that true, you
scholar there?' he asked of a soldier who was standing near.
The latter collaborated my statement. 'What, people talked
politics as long ago as that, did they?' he questioned back.
On our answering in the affirmative, he gave his decision:
'Anyhow, we talk them differently today than they did then,
and so far as I'm concerned you can keep your book.' "²⁶
Schweitzer may well have felt relieved, recalling his decision
not to bring his own manuscript on *The Philosophy of Civilization* with him because "it would be just my luck to be under
the control of the dumbest sergeant in the French Army."²⁷
In March 1918, the Schweitzers were among a group of prisoners transferred to the prisoner of war camp at Saint-Rémy-de-
Provence, an ancient monastery with a walled-in garden. Its
windows that fitted so loosely that its inhabitants were at the
mercies of the winds that blew constantly through the cracks,
keeping the stone walls and slate floor damp and chilly.
Helene caught a chill and fever. Overall living conditions
were not good, but the Schweitzers carried on as best they
could.

From his first entrance into the monastery commons, a
large reception room on the ground floor, now used as the
dayroom for the prisoners, Schweitzer felt he knew the room
from some past experience. He could not lay his finger upon
his strange sense of acquaintance and intimacy with the room,
and began to wonder if he was losing his mind as well as his
health. He did know for certain that he had never been in this
part of France before. Then, he awoke one night, the mystery
solved: a Van Gogh picture glowed in his mind's eye. There
was "all the unadorned and bare ugliness . . . the iron stove,
with the flue pipe crossing the room from end to end," the

great dark cracks in the walls, and he remembered the Van Gogh drawing of which he had vaguely been thinking and recalled that the tortured artist had once been confined for a mental breakdown in the south of France. Upon inquiry in the morning, he learned that the monastery indeed, when it had been serving as a mental institution, was the very building where he had spent four miserable, hopeless months before his suicide.[28]

In Saint-Rémy the slow, dismal months of internment dragged on. Then, just before the war ended, both the Schweitzers were adjudged non-political and included in an exchange of prisoners, so that for the last two months of fighting they returned to Alsace, physically, mentally and spiritually exhausted. The long period of inactivity and the gloom of the world in chaos, both conditions so trying to one whose character demanded moral commitment and work for a world at peace, combined to take its toll on the fatigued mind, body and spirit of Schweitzer. When the prisoner exchange took place and the Schweitzers were released at Saint-Rémy, they walked through the gate carrying the heavy valise that contained all their worldly goods. Outside the monastery, they found themselves in an alien world, ravaged by war, still bearing the scars of destruction and havoc. Arriving at the railroad station in Tarascon, a distant platform was pointed out to them as the place to wait for their train. Weak and sick, his wife exhausted, Schweitzer was so burdened by the weight of the heavy luggage, he could hardly manage to keep walking along the tracks to the designated waiting spot. A poor cripple whom Dr. Schweitzer had once treated at Saint-Rémy came forward and took the suitcase without a word and walked along beside him. Dr. Schweitzer wrote, "While we walked along side by side in the scorching sun, I vowed to myself that in memory of him, I would in future always keep a lookout at stations for heavily laden people, and help them."[29] He did this and on one occasion was even suspected of having thievish intentions.

In 1949, for example, while in America, Schweitzer was

being interviewed by a group of reporters in a Chicago rail-road station, when he suddenly excused himself, broke through the press ranks, moved quickly up to a woman, tipped his hat and asked if he could carry her bags. He took both of her heavy suitcases, and walked along beside her, she apparently unaware that one of the world's most famous men was carrying her bags. The reporters followed behind him, and one asked, "Why did you do that? Is this part of your philosophy of Reverence for Life?" The doctor simply replied that it was a little joke he had with himself.

Now, however, in 1918, the war and his internment had robbed him of most of his sense of humor. Upon returning to Günsbach, his joy at being home turned to grief. His aged mother, walking along the road outside of Günsbach, had been crushed to death by a troop of German cavalry. The speeding horsemen had rounded a curve at breakneck speed and tramped her before she could evade them. She had been a sweet, gentle and intelligent woman of iron-willed deter-mination. While it was an accident, her violent and needless death seemed unpardonable to Schweitzer; it somehow showed a disregard of the goodness and worth she had per-sonified. Schweitzer's father, an eloquent, wise spokesman for the ethical and rational in society, was overwhelmed by this heartless blow. Louis Schweitzer never bothered there-after to even take shelter from the bombs falling about him after the death of his beloved wife. His family and friends felt he had lost the will to live.[30]

Günsbach was the closest unevacuated town to the trenches on the Western Front and horrible reminders of the war were seen everywhere. The sound of the great guns boom-ing over the Vosges could be heard. One could not walk with-out seeing machine-gun installations. Main roads were rimmed with barbed wire. Albert and Helene Schweitzer found they were living in still a third phase of the war.

The vicarage of Schweitzer's father was commandeered as a barracks for German officers, and Louis Schweitzer was re-duced to serving almost as a houseboy at the parsonage in which he had previously lived as a proud pastor. To see this destruction of values and the general condition of his father brought further anguish to the son.[31] His buoyant hopes, his dreams for Africa, his pursuit of music, his shaping of philosophy of civilization—all seemed destroyed by the mauling armies and the tragedy of war that had fallen upon Europe and the Schweitzer family. Schweitzer had lost his mother in a savage, senseless act. He had seen his father become a subdued neutral in his own home. He and Helene had survived the indignities and uncertainties of internment. The cost of all this was more than he was emotionally able to bear.

The waste of life, the killing of thousands of young men and women, the shattering of a continent—all of this grief drove Schweitzer into a deep depression. As one of the most sensitive and compassionate of men, his suffering, personally, became unbearable. He was to sink lower and lower into the depths of fatigue, physical weakness and spiritual ennui.

For Helene, as well, life came to a standstill. A constant fever had left her terribly underweight and without strength. She went through a daily cycle of apprehension, alarm, hypertension, and then hours of perspiring and anxiety. Schweitzer did not need to be a physician to see that he himself was in a serious depression and that his wife, without the normal support of which he was capable, was made all the more unstable and fearful. She would never fully recover from this period, and her partnership in marriage would be restricted in every way.

Schweitzer himself battled an alternating high fever that had first attacked him at the camp at Saint-Rémy. His return to Günsbach had not helped. He wrote:

"I kept hoping in vain that among my native hills I should get rid of my langour—but I got worse and worse," till at the end of August, the high fever and torturing pains, led him to conclude that he needed an operation for an infection that resulted from the dysentery he had developed while in prison camp. He continued, "I dragged myself six kilometers in the direction of Colmar before we could find a vehicle of any sort." There he gained transportation to Strasbourg. His operation was successful but did not help in reducing his chronic depression.[32]

Schweitzer's thoughts returned to Lambaréné, where his life had been so full. There he had found the joys of serving the poor with his own hands. He had grappled with pain and sorrow and seen it yield to both the surgeon's hands and the compassion of those who believed the ethics of Jesus. His dream had become reality in Lambaréné, it had shown itself to be the answer to so many bewildering questions he had raised about his life and now he seemingly had to yield all in the wake of a destructive war. And the war had damaged not only the beginnings of his work in Africa but his family in Europe. He felt alone. He had prepared in the past to do everything and now was able to do nothing.

When the mayor of Strasbourg visited him to offer an appointment to the municipal hospital, Albert accepted with hesitation—"I did not really know how I was going to live. In learned circles, I could have believed myself entirely forgotten but for the affection and kindness shown me by the faculties of Zürich and Berne."[33]

But he was to be released from this agony of 1919 by an invitation to lecture at the University of Uppsala in the spring of 1920. Out of Sweden came the invitation from Archbishop Nathan Söderblom and it was to return to Schweitzer the gift of life; it marked the turning point in his ailing, depressing days. And he knew it, later confessing that Söderblom's kindness was his salvation. In Sweden, Schweitzer gained more than a recovery in health—he recovered his vision and purpose of life so that he could return to his life commitments with new energy and inspiration.[34]

The Swedish experience was also, in a broader sense, a watershed point for Christianity in the twentieth century. Sweden was a country that had responded to the leadership of Bishop Söderblom—an intellectual giant not unlike the younger Schweitzer with an array of interests that included not only theology and philosophy, but art, literature, music and international relations as well.

Söderblom was the son of a Lutheran minister. Like Albert, he had known the special problems and joys of being raised in the home of a minister. His academic pursuits closely paralleled Schweitzer's. Following his ordination, he had studied at the University of Uppsala for advanced degrees. He served as pastor of the Paris Swedish church in 1894. Several years later, in 1901, he received his doctorate in theology at the Sorbonne, sharing some of the same courses and professors that later stimulated Schweitzer. And like his Alsatian counterpart, Söderblom had an abiding concern for the Church and for a free expression of the Christian faith which meant the embrace of new developments in the fields of biblical study and theology.

Söderblom was a charismatic leader. His sermons and addresses struck a powerful note among the young people of Sweden which led to a great resurgence of their interest in the Church. But his faith was not a pious orthodoxy or a reworked fundamentalism. Rather it was creative and innovative and resulted in the first strong steps into the ecumenical age. Indeed, Söderblom became the father of the ecumenical movement with his hosting of the Stockholm Conference in 1925.

Nathan Söderblom had followed the career of Albert Schweitzer. His writings had been studied in Sweden. His African mission may have been frowned upon by the Paris Missionary Society, but it was highly regarded in the Swedish Church. Söderblom had helped to keep the Church together during the calamity of World War I. Now as Archbishop of Uppsala, he was not only at the center of ecclesiastic progressivism, but was also very much in harmony with the increased expectations and expression of them by university youth of Stockholm and the rest of Europe as well.

Christians have traditionally looked to the Holy Land for their historic inspirations concerning the Faith. Yet Sweden would qualify as one of the launching places for great effort by the Christian Church on behalf of humanity.

It was here that Albert Schweitzer was to find life and to claim it joyfully. Sweden was a society, especially in the university city of Uppsala, of youth eager and open for a challenging, liberal philosophy of life. And it was here Albert Schweitzer fully expounded his theme of Reverence for Life.[35]

As this open society was willing and happy to receive his message, so was he needful of all the love and life the students could pour into his beaten soul. Schweitzer's stay in Sweden was a total experience of renewal and refreshment. Spring comes with a rush in Sweden and the countryside ignites with laughter and celebration. The long winter yields to a sun-filled sky. The days become longer and longer and the exuberance of living touches all people everywhere. These tonics of nature, of scholarly eagerness and acceptance, in this nation untouched by the tragedy of war, and in this Church uncoerced by literalism and fundamentalism, were to provide the inspiration for Schweitzer's return to Africa.

His health improved almost immediately. His battered ego found students vying with professors for his counsel. In a country where elderly people are alert and athletic, Schweitzer began to think that forty-five was rather young. He began to speak of returning to Africa for the first time. Such comments brought instant encouragement from Bishop Söderblom. New friends became lifelong supporters of his mission as individuals like Baroness Greta Lagerfelt and her husband extended generous aid. Later the baroness was to invite the doctor and his wife to her home. She also offered to translate his works into Swedish as well as to recruit friends and further funds for the hospital. Her enthusiasm was matched only by her aid, which was substantial and became another factor in the recuperation and recovery of health for Schweitzer. He wrote later: "I came to Sweden a tired, depressed, and still ailing man . . . I recovered my health and once more found enjoyment in my work."[36]

In reporting this, the idea remained that his extended depression had been the result of an infection and the surgery that followed. In later years, he admitted to something more: he had had a nervous breakdown.

There were thousands of shell-shocked victims of the war and one of them, just as broken and shocked, was Albert Schweitzer. He was shocked by the inhumanity of man to his fellow and the pessimism grown out of the decay of society that caused it to decline and go to war.

We should note that so many people look upon Dr. Schweitzer as an emotional titan totally lacking despair or apprehension. They see his work and labors in a difficult setting, surrounded by opposition both in Africa and in Europe, and think that his triumphs came without personal cost. They find it hard to believe that he, like they, had tasted disappointment and defeat. The fact is that he almost succumbed to the shock of war and the dissolution of his dreams. Death haunted him. The atmosphere of Sweden provided a catalyst for Schweitzer's recovery, but it was only one step in the process.

One reason that Schweitzer took up the physical activity of rebuilding old organs was for its therapeutic value. He found it easier, for several years, to apply himself to a project such as this requiring manual labor, rather than undertake work involving ideas, words, or music. Many found it incomprehensible that Schweitzer chose to do the actual physical work of rebuilding and restoring organs. But he simply could not settle down with ideas. His nervous tension required physical release of a kind that was also creative and expressive of his inner feelings. Thus he combined the effort of hand and mind to an activity that had worth and excitement. Gradually, he was able to return to thorough normal and purposeful living.

But "gradually" here meant years not months. One of the people that helped in his recovery was a Swiss psychoanalyst, Dr. Oscar Pfister of Zürich, who persuaded Schweitzer to undergo therapy.[37] He felt that by probing his memory, he could release the hidden sources of his malaise. Schweitzer agreed to this for "research purposes only," unwilling to admit that he needed psychiatric help. When Schweitzer later reported on his sessions, he wrote:

"He relieved my thirst and gave me an opportunity to stretch out and rest my weary body, but at the same time made me narrate to him, just as they came into my mind, some incidents of my childhood, that he might make use of them . . . Soon afterward he sent me a copy of what he had taken down in shorthand during those hours. I asked him not to publish it, but to leave it to me to complete. Then, shortly before my departure for Africa, one Sunday afternoon when it was pelting rain and snow alternately, I wrote down, as an epilogue to what I narrated, thoughts that used to stir me when I looked back."[38] These were later edited and published as *Memoirs of Childhood and Youth*. This volume has never been recognized for what at least in part it is: a psychiatric study of Albert Schweitzer.

Those who view the albums of photographs of Schweitzer taken during the period of his therapy will appreciate what a marked change came over this handsome, self-assured, virile, robust young man, who had been reduced to a doubting, fearful and introverted person.[39]

A less robust and less stable person would never have made the great recovery he did. Yet even with his great inner strengths, the recovery took a full five years. In 1949 when Dr. A. A. Roback, the Harvard University psychologist, asked Dr. Schweitzer if his illness had been psychological, he replied, "Who can say? Who can say? I was tired and sick."

One of the English interpreters of Schweitzer, George Seaver, wrote:[40] "Pfister has since confessed the inability of psychoanalysis to explain the personality of Schweitzer:

In spite of all we know of Schweitzer's inner life and development, the actual problem of his personality as a whole remains unsolved. Even if we were to possess far more material for analysis than that with which Schweitzer actually provides us, even if such analysis could be undertaken in ideal circumstances, and even if it were to penetrate to the depths of the unconscious and furnish us with the key to many important data, it would nevertheless remain patchwork. In the last instance it is bound to stop short somewhere in deference to those creative powers which spring from the realm of the eternal Logos, from Eternal Freedom.[41]

The Return to Lambaréné

Finally, Schweitzer recovered sufficiently to enter more and more again into intellectual activity. His emotional despondency and depression started to recede. His mental exhaustion as well began to become a thing of the past—part of the horror of the war. He lectured in Sweden at Uppsala, and in England at Oxford, Cambridge and Birmingham universities. He was honored at Prague and visited Copenhagen. He was also invited to give organ concerts throughout England, Sweden, Denmark and Switzerland. With the funds he thus obtained, he was able to pay the debts of the Paris Missionary Society incurred by him for his hospital during the war, and to put aside enough to support his wife and himself.[1]

His books of lectures: the two volumes of *The Philosophy of Civilization, Christianity and the Religions of the World,* and his account of his first period in Lambaréné, *On the Edge of the Primeval Forest,* had been published. The latter was a compilation of his notes, letters and recollections. He also promised that upon returning to Africa he would write regular circular letters about his activities and the hospital which subsequently were published as a companion volume, *More From the Primeval Forest.* The American edition which includes both works,[2] *Memoirs of Childhood and Youth* was sent to the publisher on the eve of his return to Africa.[3]

Both he and Helene slowly began to feel that they were emotionally and financially prepared for activities in the postwar world. During their European period of renewed activity, Dr. Schweitzer continued to assist churches, cities and architects in rebuilding and restoring organs damaged by the war. He gave concerts to raise additional funds for this purpose and lectured wherever necessary to encourage these restorations.

Helene at this time found a new purpose also. On January 14, 1919 she gave birth to a daughter, Rhena, a birthday present for her husband. Helene was still weak, and the birth was difficult, but her wonderful spirit and sense of humor carried her through. Schweitzer was delighted with the new addition to the family. Among other things, he thought the child might overcome the separation developing between Helene and himself.[4]

The Schweitzers were now settled in Strasbourg, where the doctor was preaching at his old church of St. Nicholai, as well as serving on the hospital staff as a surgeon, an appointment that pleased him very much.

Not long after this appointment Helene asked her husband about his thoughts concerning Africa; he had not for a long time mentioned the hospital nor talked about possible future plans. Schweitzer admitted to her that his concern for her health and the birth of Rhena had brought an indefinite postponement to any thoughts he had about a return to work at Lambaréné.[5]

But Helene reminded him of the work yet to be done there and of the new sources of income that were now available to them for support of that work from friends and donors. She expressed particular concern for the countless African patients who needed his medical ministry and guiding hand in the affairs of the hospital. Helene was prepared to urge her husband's return to Lambaréné—but without her. It was no longer possible for her to be in the tropics during the rainy season. She would remain in Europe with Rhena but felt he must return to the primary area of his life's work in Africa. What Schweitzer was unable, indeed at the time perhaps unwilling to request, his wife was free to give—the opportunity, almost the command to resume the work in Africa for both of them. He wrote: "Unceasingly I thank her in my heart that she rose to the sacrifice of acquiescence in my return under these circumstances to Lambaréné."[6]

Those who travel and serve at great distances from home must suffer the separations from their loved ones. Pierre Teilhard de Chardin in his travels went through some of this same kind of suffering that Schweitzer was now to face. Although De Chardin was not married and did not carry the special burden of guilt that belongs to married partners during long years of separation, he was close to a happy, eminent family. One by one they were laid to rest while he was away. He would receive word by letter or telegraph. His sister Françoise preceded him to China where she was to serve as Superior of the Convent of the Little Sisters of the Poor in Shanghai. In 1911 she died during a smallpox epidemic.

In 1936 De Chardin had returned to Peking, China, as international tensions were increasing. Upon arrival, he learned of his mother's death. He could not then return to France, nor could he when word came, that same year, of his sister Marguerite's death, following years of illness. These separations and sorrows were borne, as with Schweitzer, by a man who found virtually his sole consolation in a powerful faith in the ultimate goodness and greatness of God.

As word spread that Schweitzer was to return to Lambaréné, his friends exhibited a variety of reactions. Some told him that at forty-seven he was too old to continue such a venture. Others offered assistance as he entered a new round of preparations. Unlike the first excursion, he now had a successful record on which to build and tangible results to show for purposes of fund-raising. When he said farewell to Helene and Rhena, his companion for the trip was a chemistry student from Oxford University, Noel Gillespie, who planned to spend some months with him. He proved to be an invaluable assistant.

The journey back up the Ogowe in April 1924 was marked by spontaneous greetings and expressions of joy from those who remembered his former period of service and were happy to see him returning in good health. The satisfaction of Dr. Schweitzer's return to Lambaréné was marred, however, by the condition of the hospital. It was a shambles, reclaimed for the most part by the jungle. Only two buildings had remained standing. The doctor's cottage, like the rest, was in a dilapidated condition due mostly to the damage to the roof. It almost appeared as though he would have to begin again to construct the hospital. Schweitzer wrote: "We get on shore about midday, and while Noel superintends the unloading, I walk up to the hospital like one in a dream. It might be the Sleeping Beauty's place of concealment! Grass and brushwood are growing where once stood the wards which I constructed with so much trouble. Above what is still standing are stretched the boughs of big trees which I remember as little saplings. There are still standing the buildings of corrugated iron in which we had our operating room, consulting room, and dispensary, and another in which we housed some of the patients. These two are still in fairly good condition, though their roofs of palm leaves are hopelessly damaged.

"The path from the hospital up to the doctor's little house on the hill is so overgrown with grass that I can scarcely follow its winding."[7]

The mission was still staffed by the same Swiss missionaries and schoolteachers, Messrs. Herrmann and Pelot, and Mme. Herrmann and Mlle. Arnoux who had been there when Dr. Schweitzer had left for Europe during the war. M. Herrmann reported that they had maintained the roofs until about a year before Schweitzer's return when a shortage of men for the making of the roof tiles occurred. Now the hospital looked as if it had been utterly abandoned.

The roof tiles are made by the natives by stitching raffia leaves over bamboo, a process that requires careful and prolonged work. These are then overlaid. There had been two international exhibitions of African woods since the war and the timber merchants were having a difficult time filling orders. Every able-bodied man who could swing an ax or knew how to float log rafts down the river to the ocean could expect and demand high wages. But as a result, African huts suffered from neglect. The only tiles not used by private business were those supplied to the government as a compulsory service.

Schweitzer took one look at the hospital and concluded to Noel that leaf tiles had to be found at any price. The roofs simply had to be repaired. Though it was Easter eve, the two men climbed into a long canoe and started for a village about an hour and a half away where the doctor was well known. After much handshaking and exchange of compliments and greetings, the doctor went from hut to hut, looking in and talking with each family. Finally, behind one cabin he found a pile of twenty stitched leaf tiles. When the people discovered he was interested in getting them, they told him of more, and soon he had assembled a stack of sixty-four.

In order to obtain them, a long palaver with the elders of the village was required. Flattery of the natives was one tool the doctor had to use. He had brought along some small presents for this purpose, and began to display them, making his bids. But the elders were firm bargainers too. Moreover, they could not agree with each other on price, much less *le Docteur*. Finally, Schweitzer resorted to threats. Unless he received the tiles, he said, he could not open the hospital. When he did, he added, only those people from the villages that had helped him would be treated. If he left empty-handed, no one from their village need come to the hospital. But the elders couldn't believe this threat. They howled with laughter. Some play-acted or mimicked sick people being refused treatment by a stern doctor. They assured him they knew he would never refuse treatment to anyone.

The matter was finally settled as a tropical storm hit. Hastily, the villagers loaded the leaf tiles in the canoes, and urged Schweitzer to return again, leaving Noel and him in the downpour as they scurried for shelter. Thus Noel had his first experience at a palaver, a way of life for most Africans, a business procedure at which they are very adept.[8]

On Easter Monday, the first patients were standing outside Dr. Schweitzer's door as he emerged for breakfast. He could see that there would be no time to make repairs before seeing patients regularly. He was depressed as he noted the sick and feeble condition of these people. There were, on this morning alone, cases of sleeping sickness, leprosy, ulcers, framboesia, infections covering the entire bodies of children, and injuries caused by encounters with wild animals. Calling Noel, he went to work as soon as he had eaten a hasty breakfast.[9]

Dr. Schweitzer sat up most of the first night of his renewed practice administering injections of caffeine, ether and camphor to a man suffering from an advanced heart condition. A small native girl, apparently unable to sleep, who had come with one of the families, had wandered past the workroom door, and in the dim light saw the doctor injecting a needle into the patient. Sitting back in the darkness she watched this procedure continue throughout the night. In the early hours of the morning, when the patient died, the tired doctor arose, pulled the sheet over the man's head and went wearily up to his own room. As he did so, he noticed this small girl, wide-eyed, shrinking back into the shadows as he passed.

Later in the day, the doctor caught sight of her again, and turned to look more closely but she gave a sudden shriek, and went dashing away from him in terror shouting, "He's a white leopard man who stabs people to death!" Her family could not change her mind as she continued to whisper to her playmates, "He is a white human leopard who is allowed to go about freely while they shut up the black ones in prison."[10]

Thus the doctor learned almost immediately upon his return to Africa that the leopard bands were still active and aggressively causing tensions in the jungle community. As secret organizations attempting to enforce the customs and folkways of the tribes, their purpose was to halt the transition to white man's culture via a reign of terror, including instant reprisals against those individuals who drew away from native customs. The "Westernization" taking place had been temporarily stopped by the wartime disintegration of the white community. Tribal authority had just begun to make a comeback when the white man returned. To thwart the recovery of European influence, as well as the continued Christianization which it was felt brought discredit to native ways, the old-line African reactionaries continued to employ the leopard band as a vigilante group.

Overall, the evidence of the breakdown of native community solidity (accelerated by the war and the increasing economic pressures) was noticeable in terms of the diversity of the population in the hospital area. Rapid social change had come to the area, beyond the control of existing individual tribal government. Before the war there had been two primary tribes in the Lambaréné area: Pahouins and Galoas. Now there were many. The Bendjabis had become a problem while Dr. Schweitzer was a prisoner of war. Now there were additional tribes at the hospital. Notable were the Bapunus and the Bakeles. Once Schweitzer said to a native who had brought in his injured brother, "Remove this patient from the surgical table so that I may examine your brother." The native refused, answering a further request by Dr. Schweitzer, who had tried explaining that emergency treatment could only be given after an examination, by saying, "No. The man on the operating table is of the Bakele tribe. I am a Bapunu." Some of the pre-World War I enmities were still alive.[11]

Daily the rebuilding of the hospital went forward in spite of difficult relationships, social change and general confusion. While administering to the sick and disturbed, Schweitzer had to construct, repair and enlarge his facilities. When the gathering together of a sufficient work force seemed almost hopeless, help came from an unexpected source. One of the black timbermen, Emil Ogouma, loaned the doctor the services of a labor gang that had a short time remaining before its contract expired. The gang had a foreman and five laborers. They were able to tackle the most urgent repairs, while Schweitzer and Noel continued their search for roofing material. With the additional help of the crew, the doctor was also free to unpack drugs and supplies. The roof of the large ward was completed and another was near completion. Before this came to pass, however, the contract expired. It was useless to try hiring any of the local Africans to help, for they were all occupied in the timber trade.[12]

Now Schweitzer had to depend on the families of his patients for assistance. Unfortunately, they proved to be neither helpful nor productive. They needed constant supervision. Some days they would just disappear to go fishing, palaver, or search for food. Finally, he allowed his helpers to spread a rumor that his fee for medical services rendered would be a supply of roof tiles. While he did not intend to hold the poor to this, it did produce some extra roofing material for the hospital.[13]

Gradually, the hospital was rebuilt. But still more buildings were needed, one for contagious patients, another for mental patients. Noel built a cell for one mental patient, N'Gonde, who had been a victim of sleeping sickness. When N'Gonde became cured, he turned out to be a fair carpenter, and was hired immediately as roof mender.[14]

Then, Dr. Schweitzer received the exciting news that his first registered nurse had arrived from Strasbourg, Mlle. Mathilde Kottmann. She was a slender, solemn girl who did not know the meaning of fatigue or impatience and would work thoroughly at every task. She was assigned to the doctor's house where the white patients were treated. With complete confidence, she took over the supervision of the household, filling lamps, gathering eggs, boiling water and caring for the washing, all of which chores had fallen heretofore to Noel and the doctor. As soon as she had the house in order and the patients cared for each day, she went down to the hospital to provide extra help.[15]

In August, Noel returned to England.[16] Dr. Schweitzer missed him greatly; he had been doctor's assistant, carpenter, foreman, janitor and typist. Noel wrote in his notebook on his return trip that he felt sorry "for poor Dr. Schweitzer, who tried so hard but was doomed to failure."[17]

But a new staff member was on the way to Lambaréné.

A few months later, the first medical doctor to join the staff arrived from Alsace. He was Victor Nessman, M.D.[18]

This staff of two doctors and one registered nurse carried on with effectiveness during the epidemic and famine which struck the Ogowe valley in the winter of 1924–25. Rain had continued during the entire dry season, disrupting food growth and health.

Just before Dr. Nessman arrived and before Noel left, Dr. Schweitzer himself went through an extended period of fatigue and loss of energy. He had unknowingly suffered a series of sunstrokes and became weak and tired easily. The doctor had not noticed that a hole had opened in the roof of his office due to the shifting of the roof tiles. A tiny shaft of sunlight focused on his head constantly while he sat at his desk. Gradually, he diagnosed the symptoms of his fatigue as sunstroke, although he could not imagine how it had happened. Then Noel noticed the sunbeam on his head. When it was pointed out to Schweitzer, he commented ironically that one could never be too careful in this tropical climate.

With the new year, all three of the staff became ill. Nevertheless, they doggedly continued with their daily work. A few weeks into the new year, they received word that a third doctor from Berne, Mark Lauterburg, would arrive soon.[19] He was very much needed to assist in surgery. Dr. Schweitzer and Dr. Nessman were exhausted by doing most of the orderly chores and nursing care. Accordingly, operations were being drastically curtailed.

With the arrival of Dr. Lauterburg, one doctor could be spared at times to travel to the villages. This was the beginning of an out-service program to the area surrounding Lambaréné. Dr. Schweitzer wrote that he felt this to be a very important function of the hospital, but no really comprehensive program ever developed.

In the spring, the hospital received a gift from Sweden, a motorboat, which enabled the doctors to penetrate the jungle rivers, the lumber camp areas and go down to the coast to treat patients with dysentery. The boat saved many days of their valuable time as they were no longer dependent on the whims of the natives who travel the river.[20]

With the increase of the patient load from the original forty to one hundred and twenty, more and more land was needed for construction. But the mission could not provide it. Because of the existing famine, Dr. Schweitzer felt it was imperative to plant at least part of the food they consumed; because of the crowding, he felt there was a great danger of fire destroying the hospital. Something had to be done. And soon.[21]

A second nurse, Mlle. Emma Hausknecht joined the staff, and Mlle. Kottmann became the chief foreman, palaver judge, and taskmaster. She directed the nursing activities among the Africans as well. Mlle. Hausknecht worked with the ever-increasing number of white patients and did the housekeeping. The doctors could not concentrate solely on medicine. Schweitzer found that the Africans, used to a matriarchal type of domestic control, responded well to taking work orders from the women. Now, things began to function more normally with the additional staff, but this created an even greater pressure for more room, light and air. Without this, the hospital could not make maximum use of their services.[22]

When Dr. Schweitzer had first arrived in Africa, M. Morel had taken him to a site opposite the island of Lambaréné. When he returned in 1924, he had again visited the same place, thinking it was a spot ideally suited for his hospital. However, before he had not had the time or money to spend clearing the land. After making many solitary trips, he decided now to build a new hospital there, knowing it would still cost him dearly in funds and energy. He visited with the district commissioner and made out an application for a land grant. Upon his return he called a staff meeting.[23]

After supper was over, the three doctors and the two nurses remained seated at the table. Dr. Schweitzer explained the relocation problem with which he had been wrestling for weeks, and requested that the staff discuss the advantages and disadvantages of the hospital's present location. First, the site's advantages were taken up.

Andende was accessible. The personnel there were most helpful. The river was a wonderful highway. The natives did not hesitate to come to the present site. The white people on the island, as well as those in the logging camps and up and down the coast, could get there easily. There were many more advantages to the present hospital location as well.

Next, the disadvantages were discussed. First, there was a pressing need for more room because of the epidemics of dysentery and famine. There was no space left for buildings or a garden at the mission. The hospital was congested and so heavily populated with contagious patients and their families that epidemics were often fed rather than controlled. There was insufficient housing for the staff and no place for them to be alone when off duty. "There was no room for special buildings desperately needed for disturbed patients, lepers, and the critically ill who needed to be separated for their sake and the sake of others," Mlle. Hausknecht added.

Dr. Schweitzer was in complete agreement with his staff's comments. "The missionaries have helped us for many years whatever our needs—food, transportation, or native help. We are grateful to those at Samkita and here at Lambaréné, and to the Catholics. But," he added, "the Paris Society, kind as its members are, never really helped us. They have never sent any doctors, nurses or drugs. We have been dependent on ourselves except for part of the cost of the original buildings. What I borrowed, I paid back. We have become a nuisance to the Society in many ways. The natives encroach on its property, cluttering it up, stealing from it and leaving their sick and dying there. They would like to have a chapel, since they are the only mission without one. They would no longer be deprived of one if they once again could have the hospital grounds for the mission's use."

Then he told the staff about the decision he had made. "It would be a wonderful site for the hospital." The land lay less than two miles upstream, just below the Catholic mission, on the Lambaréné side of the river. It was in a valley with the hills in back forming a perfect location for the houses. The name of Adolinanongo means 'looking out over the peoples.' It covers 172 acres, an area greater than the entire mission owns." It had been inhabited in the past, Dr. Schweitzer said, so that there was a clearing, and oil-palm trees which would make it easier to clear the land and provide shade.

When the doctor finished, the staff members sat for a moment as if stunned, and then suddenly felt elated. No longer would they have to work with makeshift arrangements; they would have a hospital planned and built as it should be.

This decision meant a sacrifice for Schweitzer. He would not be able to go home to Europe that winter as he had hoped. This was a big project for him to undertake, and it would require all his experience, energies and supervision if it were to be done properly. There would be difficulties in building the new hospital while carrying on his practice at the old mission hospital. But he knew he must try to perform both tasks.

In spite of the great effort, he would at last have an independent hospital. He would be released from the limitations set by the Paris Mission Society and would be his own master. No longer *"muet comme une carpe,"* he would be his own man.

The hardships of building a new hospital in the jungle would have stopped many men, but Dr. Schweitzer saw it through with the help of his staff. He wanted to get the hospital walls completed so the patients could move before the dry season ended. The interior finish and trim could be done by the others when he went on leave to Europe, to visit his wife and child. When there, he could tell his friends and supporters about the new independent, self-supporting hospital, appealing to all people for help. This appeal would be true to his beliefs about charity. "It was, and is still, my conviction that the humanitarian work to be done in the world should, for its accomplishment, call unto us as men, not as members of any particular nation or religious body."[24]

The following January, in 1927, the buildings were ready for removal from the old site, and a great flotilla began to move up the river, transporting the patients to their new hospital. All Schweitzer's friends with boats offered their help. In one day, they were finished. The hospital had been fully relocated.

It was not until July that the hospital was completely furnished and occupied. But when this happened, a new era for Dr. Schweitzer began in Africa. The world at the time was hardly aware of it but from that moment on, the Albert Schweitzer-Bresslau Hospital would grow in stature and importance.[25] Both he and the new hospital were becoming firmly established in the African world.

15

Between the World Wars

"The poetry of Africa has got hold of me, and it will take a long time before it releases its grip," wrote Dr. Schweitzer after his return to Africa. Now, he was settled in his own hospital. His venture had always been personally independent, but now it was independent institutionally as well. He was free to expand facilities further, but the financial liability for such building would be his also. The new buildings he had were the best that could presently be built in Africa, using native materials and a few scarce imports.[1]

All the buildings, for example, had corrugated iron for their roofs instead of the unsatisfactory leaf tiles. There were no more bamboo buildings such as those still found at the mission. The new structures were of mahogany from trees in the immediate area, a wood grain so hard that even giant termites and carpenter ants could not attack it. The new complex was set on piles so that when the floods came during the rainy season, the waters could flow beneath the raised buildings. "So I shall be a modern prehistoric man, and build my hospital like a lake-dwellers' village," Schweitzer commented at the time of construction.[2]

He could contemplate the completed buildings and new facilities with genuine satisfaction. There was a special ward for lepers, one for mental patients, separate wards for the different tribes now using the hospital, another ward for Europeans, and, most important, there were adequate quarters for the staff. During the past year, 1927, his staff had increased with the arrival of Dr. Fritz Trenz and Dr. Lauterburg's sister, Martha, who had come to serve as a nurse. Others were on the way. The corps of the future large medi-

cal staff began to form. Never again would the hospital lack
for an adequate supply of medically trained personnel.[3]

The site on which the new hospital stood had a romantic
past. From here, many years before, one of the most legendary figures in African history had begun his fabulous
journeys. After 1875, Trader Horn had worked at the English
trading firm of Hatton and Cookson. (Their store is still an
impressive enterprise on the island of Lambaréné.) Trader
Horn built a house on Adolinanongo (now Hospital Hill),
and from here set out on the trips which made his name
synonymous with a type of seedy, careless, hard-bargaining,
drifting barterer who plies his trade in underdeveloped
countries.

Adolinanongo had also been the site of the large village
of the King of the Galoas, the Sun King, N'Kombe, who
ruled the territory when the English, French and Germans
first arrived in the mid-nineteenth century. N'Kombe gave
protection and housing to the English traders, Hatton and
Cookson, and in turn, to their employee, Trader Horn.[4]
Horn's house was on this slope until 1884, the time of his
final trip along the Ogowe, from which he never returned.

He wrote his autobiography in his last years, told to a
South African writer, Mrs. Ethelreda Lewis. When published
in 1927, with a foreword by John Galsworthy, it created
considerable interest and controversy. Dr. Schweitzer was
among those who exposed the semifictitious nature of his
recollections and sifted out the truth, checking Horn's narrative against existing recollections of people and the public
records of the area.

Trader Horn did help to open up commerce along the
river, and with the inland tribes. But his insistence on free
trade also led to the spread of new diseases into the valley.
In the old tribal pattern of trade, boundaries of tribal territory were absolute, and porters from one tribe passed along
goods to the next, who in turn passed them on, each chief
receiving his bounty. This system cut down much personal
contact. Traders such as Horn, however (with their carriers),

passed through the former boundaries, and recruited porters as they went to return goods, in the process crossing over still more tribal boundaries. Diseases were transported with the men and goods. After one of Trader Horn's excursions, for example, half the population of the lower Ogowe valley was wiped out by a single epidemic of smallpox. In the same manner, another trader from the Congo region introduced sleeping sickness into the Ogowe valley.

Count de Brazza also had explored this area for France in the nineteenth century, and his records and claims helped establish this territory for France. He sought the Ogowe connection with the Congo, and actually succeeded in portaging between the headwaters of the two rivers, going up the Ogowe and returning along the Congo. However, as he pointed out, this journey was impractical and was never developed as a normal trade route.

The Ogowe and surrounding jungle abounded in elephants, gorillas, leopards, hippopotami, crocodiles and many other fierce, large animals. The lion was the only animal seldom found here. There was an abundance of birds in the area as well.

One of the larger birds along the Ogowe is the pelican, and until his death, Dr. Schweitzer always had one or more such birds as pets, hovering conspicuously about the hospital grounds, waiting to be fed. Trader Horn related that on one trip he shot a pelican, and found its huge bill filled with two large trout which he fried over an open fire. He roasted the pelican for the same meal, and found the plump breast was "red, grainy meat, like the finest beefsteak," while the wings were choice fowl. Thus, he reported, that with one shot he had secured meat, fish and fowl for one meal.

Many times Dr. Schweitzer was called upon to treat patients who had the misfortune to confront a leopard, and the good fortune to escape alive. Most do not. One European accompanied by a hunting party wounded a leopard with one shot and followed the bloody tracks. Just as he again sighted the leopard and was about to shoot, the native bearers coming up from the rear saw the animal and cried out to warn him. The angry leopard sprang. The man struck at the beast with the butt of his rifle, but it seized his arm and held on until the natives dispatched it with their spears. After being carried ten days through the jungle, the man recovered with good care at the hospital. But usually the lethal germs on the leopard's claws are fatal if the skin is gashed. They pierce deeply into the flesh, often into the bone.

"Just at present, we have to call up daily at bandaging-time 'the leopard man,'" Dr. Schweitzer wrote, "this is a quiet young fellow who was attacked by a leopard while asleep in his hut. The animal seized his right arm with its paw, but released him as people hurried to the site with a light. As the natives know by experience what terrible infection is caused by a leopard's claws, they put the man into a canoe at once to bring him to me. On his arrival twelve hours later, the arm was already swollen and hard to the touch and extremely painful. Fever had set in too. In the skin itself, no sign of injury could be seen except four tiny marks which might have been made with a needle. But when the place was opened with a lancet, it could be seen that the claws had torn the flesh right down to the bone. Our leopard victim will very soon be fit to return home, and meanwhile he makes himself useful by helping to iron the linen."[5]

Some of the most serious bites the doctor had to treat were not made by animals but by humans. Joseph once noted, "The worst bite is that of the leopard; worse still is that of a poisonous snake; worse still a monkey's bite; but quite the worse of all, that of a man."[6] Symptoms of serious infections occur, and in some cases a general blood poisoning sets in, Dr. Schweitzer reported.

Among the patients, there were some who demanded payment for their recovery. One N'Gonde had a severe case of sleeping sickness, running a high fever and becoming so disturbed mentally that he had to be physically restrained. On being cured, and returned to a normal state of mind, he charged the doctor: "Now that you have cured me, buy me a wife."[7] Schweitzer, throughout his medical career in Lambaréné, had similar extraordinary experiences with his patients.

The ways of Africa ate deeply into the spirit of Dr. Schweitzer. He felt it in many ways, often in terms of his own experiences. Once he tried to express it in terms of music. He wrote of a typical work party, describing its mood in clearing brush from the hospital grounds:

"A day with these people moves like a symphony. Lento: They take very grumpily the axes and bush-knives that I distribute to them on the landing. In snail-tempo the procession goes to the spot where bush and tree are to be cut down. At last everyone is in his place. With great caution the first blows are struck. Moderato: Axes and bush-knives move in extremely moderate time, which the conductor tried in vain to quicken. The midday break puts an end to the tedious movement. Adagio: With much trouble I have brought the people back to the workplace in the stifling forest. Not a breath of wind is stirring. One hears from time to time the stroke of an axe. Scherzo: A few jokes, to which in my despair I tune myself up, are successful. The mental atmosphere gets livelier, merry words fly here and there, and a few begin to sing. It is now getting a little cooler, too. A tiny gust of wind steals up from the river into the thick undergrowth. Finale: All are jolly now. The wicked forest, on account of which they have to stand here instead of sitting comfortably in the hospital, shall have a bad time of it. Wild imprecations are hurled at it. Howling and yelling they attack it, axes and bush-knives vie with each other in battering it. But—no bird must fly up, no squirrel show itself, no question must be asked, no command given. With the very slightest distraction the spell would be broken. Then the axes and knives would come to rest, everybody would begin talking about what had happened or what they had heard, and there would be no getting them again into the spirit of work.

"Happily, no distraction comes. The music gets louder and faster. If this finale lasts even a good half-hour the day has not been wasted. And it continues till I shout 'Amani! Amani!' ('Enough! Enough!') and put an end to work for the day."[8]

Schweitzer's view of the complexity of the African personality stands out in all his recollections. Once when talking about magic, Dr. Schweitzer recalled the story of the one-eyed European lumberman at Port Gentil. Needing to go away for a short time and with no one to leave in charge of the Africans, he took out his glass eye, laid it on his desk, called in the Africans, and told them that he would be gone for a while but would leave his eye to look after things so that they would be watched while he was gone. Upon returning he found to his delight that work had gone forward just as though constant supervision had been maintained. He was gratified for this meant that he had solved the problem of absentee supervision of his crew. Accordingly, he took a longer trip again leaving his eye lying conspicuously on the desk. Two weeks later, he returned to find work piled high with little—if anything—done during his absence. Dismayed, he rushed into his office to see what had happened. In the center of the desk was a large hat which, upon being lifted, disclosed his glass eye beneath. Thus he learned a lesson from the natives: every magic has its countermagic.[9]

Once in his very early days in Lambaréné, Dr. Schweitzer was talking with a European about the Pahouins. "Aren't you afraid that you might end up in a cannibal's pot?" he was asked. "If I do," he laughingly replied, "I hope they will say, 'Dr. Schweitzer was good to the end.'"[10] At this stage of hospital development, Schweitzer might have thought an end of a different sort was in sight, that he had developed the most adequate hospital needed to meet the needs of the Africans. But forces were already at work to change, enlarge and challenge the scope of his idyllic communal medical center.

The treatment now rendered was varied and difficult. One of the advantages of having a larger staff was that now research on the more puzzling aspects of tropical medicine could be carried on. Dr. Trenz was the first staff member to become noted for research in tropical disease and for many years served as a professor of tropical medicine at the University of Strasbourg. While in Lambaréné, Trenz isolated a vibrion which he identified as a member of the cholera bacteria. His problem was studying it under laboratory conditions. At the time of his discovery, it was not possible to set up the controls necessary for laboratory research in Lambaréné; Dr. Trenz realized that he must take the bacteria to Europe. But the means to transport it was a problem, which the doctor finally resolved by inducing it into the human body—his own. It had occurred to the staff that if he could take a creature infected with the bacteria along, he could then extract a fresh specimen for study once safely back in Europe. However, they realized that it would be illegal, and understandably so, to transport an infected animal and take it through quarantine. Thus, he took the vial containing the vibrion and drank it himself before boarding the ship for Europe. Sick with a fever and suffering from dysentery, the doctor finally arrived back in Strasbourg in early 1927 after the slow boat trip, and there extracted fresh, healthy specimens of the bacteria from his own body to carry on his research. This first dramatic example of tropical-disease research was not to be repeated, but it became ingrained in the tradition of Lambaréné that, at all costs, and as a part of regular medical practice, continued research should go hand in hand with the healing function of the hospital. In time, the hospital began to receive experimental drugs and equipment for testing from European pharmaceutical foundations. Accordingly, as the hospital moved toward its destiny in World War II, it was fast changing from a backwoods establishment to a modern facility. Other developments were paving the way for the emergence of the postwar hospital as a focal point of world opinion.

Small groups of outside specialists began to visit the hospital, giving of their skills in the heart of the jungle, and in turn learning from the specialized talents of its doctors on a unique medical frontier.[11]

Yet this remained primarily an Alsatian-staffed jungle-outpost hospital. The new facilities did create something unique among hospitals. A full African village emerged, composed of many tribal units, a commissary, plantations, a landing, barns, pens, groves, roads and a well. It grew into a pulsating community where one could find on any day several hundred African patients, with many more family members awaiting them. Dozens of buildings, often with cement foundations, spread over the area. Bananas, manioc and rice were grown in quantity and distributed each week to Africans who came to the Schweitzer Hospital.

The expenses of the hospital meanwhile were being sustained by overseas friends, contributions from religious and humanitarian organizations and by royalties from the extensive writings of Schweitzer. His books were translated into English, French and German. *Out of My Life and Thought* (Henry Holt, N.Y.), 1933, was to approach nearly a half million copies in print.[12]

Prior to World War II, visitors did not expect to find a modern hospital in Lambaréné. But following the war, many Americans and Europeans were surprised at what they saw. The unique character of the hospital had been cemented even more rapidly than had the physical hospital itself. There are no "Quiet zone" signs in Lambaréné, no "Hush, Please" posters. This is not a silent hospital where employees in nylon uniforms move quietly through isolated halls, but a bustling village of Africans, farm animals and land for crops. Albert Schweitzer had created a unique and amazing hospital—a village where a patient can feel completely at home. There was probably no other place like it in Africa or in all the world. By the time World War II arrived, its unusual mold was already cast.[13]

At Schweitzer's hospital, blacks and whites mingle. There are many languages heard: Galoa, Fang and other tribal tongues; French, German and English. Seldom is one out of hearing of a confusion of tongues in this international settlement.

In time, the doctors and nurses also came to represent a heterogeneous background, but as late as World War II the staff was composed solely of Alsatians and Swiss. After the war, this was to change and there would be five or six permanent doctors on the staff, coming from three continents: Europe, Asia and America. The dozen or more registered nurses would come mainly from Europe with some from the United States, Japan and Korea. Through the years, they have been under the supervision of Mlle. Mathilde Kottmann, Mlle. Emma Hausknecht, and in Schweitzer's final years, under Mlle. Ali Silver. All three of these women had been with Dr. Schweitzer since his early days. There are also paraprofessional practical nurses at the hospital who are locally trained Africans. There are usually two dozen or so on duty. These nurses are mostly males and are usually married men. They have plantation sites allotted to them which their wives manage. Those who have more than one wife have larger plantations so that they can raise more fruits and vegetables from the sale of which they augment the salary paid them by the hospital.

The Schweitzer Hospital moved toward World War II as a jungle hospital, more or less isolated, serving Africans who lived in the virgin jungle, and the few white people in the area. The world had become conscious of the hospital mostly because of the greatness of Dr. Schweitzer in other fields. It knew little of the hospital itself in those days, however, except for his books about the hospital's beginnings. Travelers to the hospital were few; reporters and correspondents never penetrated the deep jungle or traveled the sluggish flowing river; means of transportation were simply too primitive. And Dr. Schweitzer, like any country doctor, was content to be left alone to do his work. But just as a country doctor goes to a big city for supplies, relaxation and intellectual stimulation from colleagues, so Dr. Schweitzer went to Europe. But his life remained solidly anchored in the African jungle hospital.

The two nearby mission stations run colleges which, after

the French tradition, are secondary schools rather than American colleges. One bright man who worked as an orderly at the hospital attracted Dr. Schweitzer's attention, and was encouraged to go to Paris to study medicine at the Sorbonne. Great was the dismay and disappointment at the hospital when, years later, he returned for a visit, a doctor of medicine, only to report that he had decided to stay in Paris and set up practice there. This experience reoccurred far too frequently. Africa lost most of its capable young men when they went off to universities in Europe or the United States. During the colonial period, they seldom returned to Africa, after tasting the more sophisticated life of highly developed countries. In response to this, Dr. Schweitzer, who had come to value the native culture highly as sufficient unto the ends the hospital required, came to accept the fact that bright natives, locally trained, could serve their country and the hospital with excellence even though they lacked a formal, successful European education. Consequently, he began to encourage competent young men to join the hospital staff as male nurses, to be trained by his doctors and registered nurses. Thus, the male-nurse program evolved at the Schweitzer Hospital.[14]

Some thought Dr. Schweitzer was shortsighted in this decision. Yet it was in fact farsighted to keep intelligent Africans on the continent until such time as African culture, or the zeal for country which is an end product of independence, could instill the desire to return or remain there. (New universities in Africa, aided by foreign countries, with faculties composed of visiting professors from Europe and the United States, may create the conditions for an even larger percentage of natives who stay in Africa.) Dr. Schweitzer stood stalwartly by his decision—never objecting to those who wished to go to Europe or the United States, but no longer encouraging them to do so. Instead, he offered opportunities to those who met the rigid requirements to join his staff.

Schweitzer also encouraged these young men to retain their tribal and cultural ties after becoming professional members of his staff. He had seen too many self-styled, Westernized "intellectuals" who had cut themselves off from the roots of their culture, and become unacceptable in a native society which they also chose to no longer accept themselves. Accordingly, Dr. Schweitzer offered native staff members plantations, an opportunity to create their own family compound, and adjustable schedules to fit family and planting needs. Many of the African male nurses followed the native custom of polygamy. Thus they never became wholly assimilated into the white staff, and this, in time, became a subject of discussion among visitors. Yet in Dr. Schweitzer's eyes, his system was simply a matter of helping his African colleagues maintain dignity and status as Africans among Africans, thus fulfilling very basic psychological needs.

Many great pragmatic decisions evolved during the years of the late 1920s and early 1930s. This was a hospital to meet local conditions, and Schweitzer had a deeper understanding of the needs of the people. In time, others would challenge the doctor's insights and procedures. But the wisdom of many decades of close association with African culture, and the great popularity of the hospital, suggest the validity and success of Dr. Schweitzer's ideas and methods. But Schweitzer never sacrificed the ideal he had enunciated in his early years: "My hospital is open to all sufferers. Even if I cannot save them from death I can at least show them love, and perhaps make their end easier."[15]

Albert Schweitzer's Ethics

Schweitzer first presented the ethic of Reverence for Life in *Philosophy of Civilization*, the first volume of which he wrote during his World War I internment in Lambaréné. After his ultimate release from a camp in Europe in a prisoner exchange, he returned to Alsace, but had no knowledge of the whereabouts of his manuscript. Then came the invitation from Bishop Söderblom to lecture at Uppsala on the theme of "the decay and restoration of civilization," not counting one sermon on "Reverence for Life" preached on February 16, 1919 in Strasbourg, it was here that he made the first, full public pronouncement of the ethical norm he was developing. Later, he miraculously received his manuscript through the mail, without note or comment from the American missionary.

Schweitzer gave the Dale Lectures at Oxford in 1922 where he presented a second portion of the Reverence for Life philosophy, *Civilization and Ethics*, and the following January lectured on this subject at the University of Prague. In 1923 the *Philosophy of Civilization* was published, provoking wide discussion, and both agreement and dissent from among intellectuals everywhere. No matter what other subject Schweitzer discussed, Christian theology, comparative religions, Oriental civilization, or the need for African service, the particular subject's relationship to the Reverence for Life theme always emerged in his speech. He was almost obsessed with the concept as a guideline for mankind on his journey toward the perfecting of civilization and the self-realization of his life.

Years later, he was to tell Norman Cousins:

Christian theology has found it difficult to come to terms with my thought, though Christians have not. I have a feeling that the Christian theologians are reluctant to come in through the door I have tried to open. I have tried to relate Christianity to the sacredness of life. . . . But the Christian theologians confine Christianity to the human form of life.[1]

Consequently, when Schweitzer found that his philosophy met with official resistance from the religious establishment, he pressed all the harder to make his point known to the people themselves. He thrived on every new challenge, and the proselytizing of this philosophy was one of the major ones of his life.

The years between the two wars were fruitful ones for Schweitzer. The work of the hospital progressed; not spectacularly, but continuing to provide worthwhile services to all who appeared: the indigenes (Africans from the tribal villages); the Evolues (Africans influenced by European culture); and Europeans—foresters, planters, traders, administrators and missionaries. The hospital grew, the staff became well established and somewhat larger. Efforts were made to send physicians on regularly scheduled visits to outlying tribes and villages. All in all, the jungle hospital became a steady factor in the life of its section of equatorial West Africa.

Dr. Schweitzer explored the possibility, in 1924, of establishing a branch hospital in the Cameroons. He traveled to Douala, a throbbing native city in the Cameroons, populated by a mixture of Africans who were Moslem, Christian and native. It had a well-known market which drew craftsmen from afar with their wares. Schweitzer found this city exciting, stopped briefly with his guides, and then journeyed inland to the abandoned mission station at Nyasoso. Pushing northward, they crossed the French border into the British Cameroons, and reached a deserted station originally occupied by Swiss missionaries.

After looking the site over, and making copious notes and diagrams, Dr. Schweitzer and his guides ascended the steep incline leading to the city of Buca, 3200 feet above sea level, in the Cameroon Mountains. Here he stayed for a few days as the guest of Major Ruxton, the British resident who administered British law. The two men discussed at length what Dr. Schweitzer refers to as "my nebulous plans which had not yet jelled" and the doctor enjoyed the hospitality of the major and his wife.

With continued hope and expectation for a branch hospital, Dr. Schweitzer returned to Lambaréné only to realize that so much was required of him there that it was impractical to pursue a new undertaking immediately. He plunged into the rebuilding program at Lambaréné and put the other plans out of his mind. New developments at Lambaréné, including site changes, constantly postponed the opportunity of a second hospital over the years. In time, the idea was dismissed entirely and the Schweitzer Hospital remained solely a Lambaréné operation.

During the period between the two wars, Schweitzer traveled to Europe four times, returning there constantly for the purpose of fund-raising, and to see his wife and daughter, Rhena, who was growing into a lovely young woman. In Europe his lectures and concerts took him to Czechoslovakia, Sweden, Denmark, Holland, Germany, Switzerland, France, Spain and Great Britain. His native Alsace had become a part of France, and he was now regarded as a Frenchman. Nevertheless, Germany continued to honor him during the days of the Weimar Republic. On August 28, 1928, he received the Goethe Prize from the City of Frankfurt. In England he gave the Hibbert Lectures at Manchester College, Oxford, and the Gifford Lectures at Edinburgh. He also continued to write.

In the late nineteen-twenties, Dr. Schweitzer agreed to write a brief self-portrait. But Felix Meiner, the publisher, decided it was too important to be simply one of the book's chapters and reissued it as a single volume. Dr. Schweitzer felt immediately that this presentation might mislead people for he had not thought of it as his definitive statement, but merely as a brief, rough sketch of his philosophy of life.

The publisher agreed to withdraw the book from circulation if Dr. Schweitzer would write an autobiography.

This did not appeal to Schweitzer. Fifty-four years did not seem to him the full course of his existence; he felt that important changes of outlook and many new activities were still to come. He wrote to Meiner from Lambaréné and told him this. Meiner countered by saying that people were interested in an account of his life and if he didn't write one, others would. Helene suggested that he at least write on the development of his thought up to the present time, a possible solution to their dilemma with Meiner.

Schweitzer grumbled about the difficulty of owing a favor which had to be paid back, but he went almost immediately to his desk and began writing on a vigorous schedule. He slept two hours, left his study only for meals and spent the rest of the day at his desk while the staff carried on the hospital's work. He kept this pace for days, often completing a chapter in twenty-four hours. The manuscript was finished in a month's time.

Out of My Life and Thought, published in Leipzig in 1931, in England in 1932, and the United States in 1933, has been the standard volume that gives Schweitzer's interpretation of his life "although I do not know the issue of my life at this time."

The world will remain indebted to Felix Meiner for insisting that this reluctant author produce this work. It provided recollections of many of Schweitzer's activities before the passing years had time to dim his memory, and offers great insights into the mind of its author. In it, for example, Schweitzer gives the imperishable account of his discovery of the ethical premise which made life meaningful to him: Reverence for Life. It happened on a journey up the Ogowe to N'Gomo on an errand of mercy in 1915. Recalling that trip, he wrote:

Slowly we crept upstream, laboriously feeling—it was the dry season—for the channels between the sandbanks. Lost in thought

I sat on the deck of the barge, struggling to find the elementary and universal conception of the ethical which I had not discovered in any philosophy. Late on the third day, at the very moment when, at sunset, we were making our way through a herd of hippopotami, there flashed upon my mind, unforeseen, and unsought, the phrase, "Reverence for Life." The iron door had yielded: the path in the thicket had become visible. Now I had found my way to the ideas in which world-and-life-affirmations and ethics are contained side by side! Now I knew that the world-view of ethical world-and-life-affirmation, together with its ideals of civilization, is founded in thought.[2]

Schweitzer had carried this basic idea throughout the long, trying period of internment during World War I. In the twenties and thirties, he tried to give substance to it so that others could understand, as did he, that ethics could be grounded in a rationalism that was consistent and made sense. His *Philosophy of Civilization*, written in two volumes before his internment in Europe and left behind in Africa in 1917, had been his first formal discussion of this concept.

Pierre Teilhard de Chardin never used the phrase "Reverence for Life." But he understood it and, like Schweitzer, sensed that "Mother Nature" was not a large enough term to embrace the whole universe of life. After visiting along the coast of Jersey in 1919, he wrote in the *Spiritual Power of Matter*:

Blessed be you, harsh matter, barren soil, stubborn rock: you would yield only to violence, you who force us to work if we would eat. Blessed be you, perilous matter, violent sea, untamable passion: you unless we fetter you will devour us.

Blessed be you, mighty matter, irresistible march of evolution, reality ever new born: you who by constantly shattering our mental categories, force us to go ever further and further in our pursuit of the truth. Blessed be you, universal matter, immeasurable time, boundless ether, triple abyss of stars and atoms and generations: you who by overflowing and dissolving our narrow standard of measurement reveal to us the dimensions of God.[3]

Again the common denominators of these two great men are visible.

Schweitzer's lectures at the University of Uppsala, presented at the request of Bishop Söderblom, were the first publicly recognized expression of the developing ethic which was to become the concept most frequently associated with him. At Uppsala, he said that Reverence for Life grew out of the world negation and life affirmation which was the truly philosophical position. Man, he said, must not limit life to the affirmation of man alone. Man's ethics must not end with man, but should extend to the universe. He must regain the consciousness of the great chain of life from which he cannot be separated. He must understand that all creation has its value, and requires of man the same reverence one feels so personally toward loved ones. The will to live motivates all life, he went on, and life should only be negated when it is for a higher value and purpose—not in merely selfish or thoughtless actions. What then results for man is not only a deepening of relationships, but a widening of relationships. Life, he had said, itself becomes sacred:

He tears no leaf from a tree, he plucks no flower, and takes care to crush no insect . . . If he walks on the road after a shower, and sees an earthworm which has strayed onto it, he bethinks himself that it must get dried in the sun, if it does not return soon enough to ground into which it can burrow, and so he lifts it from the deadly stone surface, and puts it on the grass. If he comes across an insect which has fallen into a puddle, he stops a moment in order to hold out a leaf or a stalk on which it can save itself.[4]

Now Schweitzer went on to develop his thoughts on this subject further in *Out of My Life and Thought*.

Aside from his philosophical pursuits, Schweitzer was attending to other projects that required his leadership between the wars.

He was kept busy by both administering the hospital and raising funds to support it, which, during the economic de-

pression in postwar Europe, required a greater dependence
on income from lectures, recitals and book royalties and less
on the benevolence and charity of donors. Consequently, he
visited Europe in 1927, 1932, 1936, and again in 1939, at
which time, feeling that war was imminent, he returned to
Lambaréné after a relatively brief visit.

On his trips he spoke on the theme, Reverence for Life,
as well as outlining in an extended series of lectures the other
ideas and arguments he was preparing for publication. Of
special joy to him were the opportunities he had to discuss
African life and culture as a simple country doctor, but his
greatest happiness of all came when he sat down at a good
organ.

Pierre van Paassen, the foreign correspondent, recalled an
incident in 1934 that happened while he was a guest at the
parsonage of the village church of Zutphen, Holland. Albert
Schweitzer was to preach the Christmas sermon. The correspondents knew Dr. Schweitzer had arrived on December
20 although he was not to preach until December 25. All
week he seemed to be in seclusion, and they failed to locate
him, until van Paassen and the others, while walking past
the cathedral, heard the sound of the organ through the open
door. Entering, they found Dr. Schweitzer, covered with dust
and sweat, cleaning and tuning the huge organ. On Christmas
Day, he not only preached the sermon, but played the organ
as well, and as the churchgoers entered, and the processional
sounded forth, they whispered to each other their disbelief
that this was their old organ.[5]

The pastor of the church, thrilled with the service, told
Dr. Schweitzer that the service was a divine inspiration. The
doctor, with the famous twinkle showing in his eye, replied,
"It is customary to say, the sermon should be divinely inspired, a gift of God, although I work so hard for the right
words, I can't consider it a gift from on high; but the music—
that was my Christmas gift to the people."

His interest in Bach always remained high. Schweitzer loved
such occasions on which two of his great joys, the Church

and its music, combined and he could preach the simple faith to simple people. Most of his speaking, however, was to learned audiences, when he dealt with the ethics of Reverence for Life and the large issues of civilization. He was asked to speak at seminaries, church or missionary conferences, universities, medical societies, and memorial celebrations every time he returned to Europe. He enjoyed the theological discussions and encounters with churchmen. But his increasing interest was Reverence for Life. This, of course, was being expressed as much in his life as in his lectures, especially in his self-sacrifice of going to the African jungle to help natives so long oppressed and without a champion. The African generally continued to be regarded as a utility to be exploited by the colonial governments or as a potential convert to add to the mission churches' rolls. He was both a laborer and a consumer, but was often regarded as less than a human being.

Schweitzer's friend, Martin Buber, also pioneered in concepts of human rights. He was excited by the formation of a group of agricultural workers who went to Palestine to become a new community. Their intention, under the leadership of A. C. Gordon, was to establish living and working arrangements with the Arabs. For Buber, this was the final test for those who truly grasped the spiritual realities of the Zionist movement. Buber himself was to live with an Arab family in the Moslem section of Jerusalem.

This peaceful coexistence was the only possibility Buber saw of building an enduring community. But the tensions and discord that followed were not to advance his cause. In 1927 he wrote:

The watchword is service to the foreign peoples living in the land, for the sake of the community which must be brought to birth here; there must be created a link between their interests and ours—but also the furtherance of their distinctive interests in order to make them realize that their standing and working together with us is not only desirable but also possible. For their well-being must also be our concern. They are part and parcel of the community which must come into being here![6]

Whenever he was in Europe, Schweitzer consistently took advantage of every opportunity to discuss the optimum relationships of the civilized nations with native peoples. Farsighted in most things, and with a broad understanding of the shortcomings of colonialism, Schweitzer was faulted for a blindness to African aspirations for self-government. During the 1920s and 1930s, he pronounced colonialism as unethical if it did not advance African maturity. He said that Africans were entitled to basic human rights which should be guaranteed and, if need be, protected by the common moral tone of civilized nations. He felt that the League of Nations should protect the rights of the colonial people.[7]

Hindsight is often the better part of wisdom, and today it is clear that Africans even at that time were moving swiftly toward freedom. Dr. Schweitzer, so often the pioneer, had, in his advocacy, approached the door of freedom, but stopped at the threshold. Consequently, it was said that he failed to champion African independence. In his defense, all that can be said is that few people in the 1920s and 1930s really expected African freedom to come in the next half century, let alone quarter century. Yet, Dr. Schweitzer in his high regard for the native personality, in his support of their full human rights and in his acceptance of their tribal culture as eminently respectable, helped give dignity to the African. Schweitzer once said, "I expect I am not the only white man who feels himself put to shame by the natives."[8]

As he summarized his first stay in Africa, he wrote:

If a record could be compiled of all that has happened between the white and colored races, it would make a book containing numbers of pages, referring to recent as well as early times, which the reader would have to turn over unread, because their contents would be too horrible. We and our civilization are burdened, really, with a great debt. We are not free to confer benefits on these men, or not, as we please; it is our duty. Anything we give them is not benevolence, but atonement. For every one who has scattered injury, someone ought to go out and bring help, and when we have done all that is in our power, we shall not have atoned for the thousandth part of our guilt. . . . So again we see the real burden of the humanitarian work must fall on society and its individual members.[9]

During his European visits, he preached the necessity of aid to the Africans, not as benevolence but as a duty. Reverence for Life explained his service—and that of others who through medicine or some other means of humanitarian service gave of their lives in careers of self-sacrifice. But to Schweitzer his life in Africa represented not self-sacrifice but self-realization and joy—and the natural consequence of his philosophy of life.

For him, a man to whom everything of importance lay primarily in the intellectual and rational, the proof of his ethic was found in philosophy, and secondarily in practicality. And in his philosophy he cut through the accretion of ages of Western thought to see world negation (i.e., freedom from the world and worldly goals and desires) as essential in order to move forward to a higher, philosophical life affirmation. This view, he felt, was best presented in Eastern thought, and so his Gifford Lectures of 1934 touched upon the idea which he hoped to develop into a separate book. Schweitzer's *Indian Thought and Its Development* is a profitable study of the mainstreams of Indian religious philosophy, which helps clarify his *Philosophy of Civilization* and his ethical insight, Reverence for Life. In the book he discussed the concept of Reverence for Life as it appears in the various Hindu and other Indian systems of thought and related it to his own. Also, in seeming response to some of the critics who called Reverence for Life an absurd extreme, he wrote:

However seriously man undertakes to abstain from killing and damaging, he cannot entirely avoid it. He is under the law of necessity, which compels him to kill and to damage both with and without his knowledge. In many ways it may happen that by slavish adherence to the commandment not to kill, compassion is less served than by breaking it. When the suffering of a living creature cannot be alleviated, it is more ethical to end its life by killing it mercifully than it is to stand aloof. It is more cruel to let domestic animals which one can no longer feed die a painful death by starvation than to give them a quick and painless end by violence. Again and again we see ourselves placed under the necessity of saving one living creature by destroying or damaging another. The principle of not-killing and not-harming must not aim at being independent but must be the servant of, and subordinate itself to, compassion. It must, therefore, enter into practical discussion with reality. True reverence for morality is shown by readiness to face the difficulties contained in it.[10]

Schweitzer saw Reverence for Life as operative on several different planes, and took cognizance of them all. Still another level is that which he touched upon as a physician. He wrote:

To the man who is truly ethical, all life is sacred including that which from the human point of view seems lower in the scale. He makes distinctions only as each case comes before him, and under the pressure of necessity as, for example, when it falls on him to decide which of two lives must be sacrificed in order to preserve the other.[11]

More specifically, he saw such a decision as often the choice between a person or an animal; higher or lower life. He wrote:

I rejoice over the new remedies for sleeping sickness, which enable me to preserve life, whereas I had previously to watch a painful disease. But every time I have under the microscope the germs which cause this disease, I cannot but reflect that I have to sacrifice this life to save another.[12] If he (man) has been touched by the ethic (of) Reverence for Life, he injures and destroys life only under a necessity which he cannot avoid and never from thoughtlessness.[13]

Thus, Schweitzer's ethic is far from absolute, and always has within it the condition of the intelligent decision-making of an ethical mind. In other words, one is compelled to make decisions to kill at times; life must be sacrificed for other life, Schweitzer was saying, *but never without the realization that there is a great chain of life from which we are not separate, and that in the death of any life, we too suffer a loss.*

Admittedly, even the friends of Dr. Schweitzer like to join in the humor that comes from carrying Reverence for Life to its extreme expression. The story has often been told of Adlai Stevenson slapping a mosquito on Schweitzer's neck, to which Schweitzer responded, "That was *my* mosquito." But all humor aside, the high morality of Schweitzer's principle is incontestable.

17

The Challenge of Europe

To many observers, Albert Schweitzer was a European who happened somehow to be strangely challenged by Africa. Such is the paradox of the man, however, that he may best be understood viewed as an inhabitant of Africa who was challenged, even tortured by the decay and disintegration of European civilization. At a reception once, during one of his European trips, an admirer asked, "Now that you have been in Africa for several years, Dr. Schweitzer, what do you think of European civilization and Western culture?"

"It would be a wonderful idea!" the doctor exclaimed.[1]

To a highly ethical person, sensitive as was Schweitzer to the suffering and the longings of people, what was happening to the Western world was disastrous.

Throughout the period following the end of World War I, with the drafting of the Versailles Peace Treaty, the transfer of Alsace-Lorraine from Germany to France, the establishment of the League of Nations, and the birth of the Weimar Republic, Dr. Schweitzer remained true to the German academic heritage of his youth—political non-involvement to the point of complete neutrality. In personal letters and in remarks during lectures, he hailed the League of Nations. But although he hoped for the success of the League (and feared it might fail), he personally remained basically non-political. During this period of his life, Schweitzer stood, as a man, above the political storms; a Herr Professor of the German tradition; an intellectual concerned with things of the mind, desirous of leaving the practical matters of state management to political guardians.

No one in Europe questioned this stance. Indeed, during the

1920s and early 1930s, only Socialists, Bolsheviks and extremists among the intelligentsia became involved in politics. It would have been shocking to the public for Dr. Schweitzer to become active, politically. In addition, there were other complications to explain his position. Until the Armistice, he had been regarded as a German national. Now he found himself a French citizen. Outside of the province of Alsace-Lorraine, there was no place, in the decade immediately following Versailles, where an Alsatian would be accepted let alone welcomed as a political participant. Political isolation was virtually forced upon him. But in all fairness, it must be said that he did not fight it.

In Schweitzer's view, it was the destiny of men to influence states, societies and political circumstances by personal action rather than by group participation. His attitude was to let others be involved as institutionalists; he would remain what he had always been, a concerned person exerting pressure on civilization at the place where he thought it would be most deeply felt, where his own life touched others. This might happen in the jungle hospital, on a lecture platform, in a publisher's folio, or on a concert podium. Schweitzer had many opportunities to exert pressure to help form opinions on world events and problems. Given this fact, it seems strange that so little material on such subjects is evident among his work. One searches almost in vain to find great pronouncements by him on the concerns of war and peace, or on the economic and social problems of the post-World War I era.

Of course, in a broad sense, he talked about the problems of society in his two volumes on civilization. In the *Decay and Restoration of Civilization,* he wrote that modern man was lost in the mass, in a way which had no parallel in past history. Diminished by the size of his society, and the enormousness of the problems he faced, modern man was not becoming the master of his own destiny but humbled to "an extent that is almost pathological." He then went on to show that civilization, in the form of the organized state, "has become a power of yet unknown strength in the spiritual life." Schweitzer felt that in addition the increasing loss of personal independence forced men into well-defined ruts, most apparent where man ceased to claim a spiritual existence of his own.

He is like a rubber ball that has lost its elasticity, and preserves indefinitely every impression that is made on it. He is under the thumb of the mass and he draws from it the opinions on which he lives, whether the question at issue is national or political or one of his own belief or unbelief.[2]

In this paragraph alone, Schweitzer forecast the direction that would be taken forty years later by modern social scientists in assessing man. David Riesman in *The Lonely Crowd*, William H. Whyte in the *Organization Man*, and Herbert Marcuse in *One Dimensional Man* are only a few of the social analysts for whom Schweitzer helped pave the way. Many found Dr. Schweitzer's point of view helpful during the 1930s in understanding the rise of Adolf Hitler's Nazi state with its nation of sheep. Among those responding to his analysis was Albert Einstein, who entered into correspondence with Schweitzer. And there were further indications of Schweitzer's growing influence.

The *Christian Century*, in its issue of November 21, 1934, gave a summary of the Hibbert Lectures delivered at Manchester College, England, where he spoke on "Religion in Modern Civilization." The opening paragraph read as follows:

I am going to discuss religion in the spiritual life and civilization of our time. The first question to be faced, therefore, is: Is religion a force in the spiritual life of our age? I answer in your name and mine, "No!" . . . There is (however) a longing for religion among many who no longer belong to the churches. I rejoice to concede this. And yet we must hold fast to the fact that religion is not a force. The proof? The war . . .[3]

This paragraph accurately portrays the pessimism Dr. Schweitzer felt as the storm clouds of World War II were gathering. To him, one could not go serenely along uncommitted to the necessity of removing war from human society.

Based on this and other attitudes he held, it may be presumed that Dr. Schweitzer was political in a far more important way than even he realized. In time, the need to address himself to imminent issues in concrete terms emerged. His first specific involvement came in Frankfurt, Germany, on the eve of Hitler's thrust for power. Nazi storm troopers could already be heard in the streets, and the movement begun in a Munich beer hall was threatening the weak Weimar Republic. Schweitzer used the occasion of the centennial celebration of Goethe's death in Frankfurt am Main—March 22, 1932—to articulate his concern and issue a call for a reversal of direction.[4] He told his audience, and all Germany, that:

. . . the great problem in the coming evolution of things will be this: how the individual can assert himself in the face of the multitude.

He told them he was speaking of Goethe's message which he pointed out was relevant to the present:

Goethe's message to the men of today is the same as to the men of his time and to the men of all times: "Strive for true humanity. Become yourself a man who is true to his inner nature, a man whose deed is in tune with his character."

He went on to ask his audience,

Can we still achieve such humanity in the midst of the frightful circumstances of our day?

Goethe wanted freedom for the people, but the manifestation of the mass mind created a real hazard. Having himself witnessed the French Revolution and the wars for freedom, he came to feel that:

. . . the revolutionary is for him the will of the masses bent on overthrowing the will of the individual . . . Goethe is the first who feels something like a concern for man.

And now, a hundred years after his death it has come to pass, through a calamitous development determined by events . . . that the material and spiritual independence of the individual, so far as it is not already destroyed, is most seriously threatened.

Recalling Goethe, he continued to speak of the precarious position of the individual in the 1930s:

He is summoned as no other poet or thinker to speak to us in this hour . . . he comes with the most timely counsel . . . He says to postwar Europe that the frightful drama that is being enacted in it can come to an end only when it sets aside the economic and social magic in which it has trusted, when it forgets the magic formulas with which it deludes itself, when it resolves to return at any cost to a natural relationship with reality. To the individual he says: Do not abandon the ideal of personality even when it runs counter to developing circumstances . . . Remain men, in possession of your own souls. Do not become human beings which have offered hospitality to souls which conform to the will of the masses and beat in time with it.

Then with a look forward, he noted that in less than another two decades (1949), there would be an occasion to honor the two hundredth anniversary of Goethe's birthday. Schweitzer observed,

May it be that he who gives the memorial address at that new festival may be able to state that the deep darkness which surrounds this one has already begun to lighten . . .[5]

The Nazis were incensed by the speech and many friends feared for Schweitzer's life. The darkness was deeper than ever, and yet he had courageously spoken out for a return to reason and humanity before it was too late. Unfortunately, the times were out of control, and though the expected seizure of power in the fall did not take place, it came the following January, in 1933. After the Reichstag fire, aging President von Hindenburg called on Hitler to become chancellor.

It was clear that Schweitzer was now a *persona non grata* to the government, and would eventually have to leave the country. Yet many who remained in Germany found comfort in his words and position. One such person was a young minister, a former pacifist, Dietrich Bonhoeffer, who, upon the assumption of power by the Nazis, accepted an invitation to become minister of the German congregations of St. Paul and

Sydenham, London. He remained there until 1935, departing only for brief visits to America, when he realized the need to make an unequivocal statement of protest against the German Christian community that had bowed silently before the totalitarian regime of Hitler. He returned to Germany to lead an emergency seminary for young ministers, and it was there that the *Philosophy of Civilization* by Dr. Schweitzer served the students as a description of the mass conformity and loss of individuality that was being witnessed in Germany on every hand. Almost alone, it seemed, Bonhoeffer tried to arouse the German religious community to withstand the restrictions and threats of Nazism. During this period, Bonhoeffer wrote *The Cost of Discipleship*, dealing with the developing crisis in Germany's cultural life and its Church. Unlike Schweitzer, he renounced his pacifism, and declared all out resistance to the course of events. The world knows the tragic cost of his discipleship, his hanging by the SS, set forth vividly in the surviving material published in English as *Letters from Prison*.

Schweitzer, however, was no longer a German national, and with a Jewish wife, could not safely re-enter Germany. His articles, lectures and books had to be his spokesmen. In addition, he had many close ties with German churchmen, whose difficult position he was forced to respect. In 1934, when both Schweitzer and Bonhoeffer were in London, they discussed common problems. Schweitzer, too, was committed to peace. He had long ago cast his lot with the free world against the Nazi menace. While in England, he decided never again to enter Nazi Germany. Hitler represented the exact kind of glorified war spirit to which Schweitzer was morally opposed. While lecturing in England, Schweitzer began to receive letters from German friends who pleaded that he not visit them if he came to Germany. They said they dared not speak out or take sides, and could not afford to risk their political neutralism or bring their thought under question by association with Schweitzer. Particularly dismaying to Schweitzer was the increasing number of religious leaders and pastors in the German State Church who wrote to him in this vein. He concluded that a state-connected Church simply could not be "the plumb line to God" (Amos 7) in an hour of national, social, political and moral failure. Accordingly, Dr. Schweitzer canceled his scheduled speaking dates and concerts in Germany and, true to his word, was never to return to Germany as long as Hitler was alive.[6]

In June 1963, Dr. Schweitzer recalled this era when the Hamburg publisher, Rowohlt Verlag, sent him a copy of Rolf Hochhuth's play, *The Deputy*. Schweitzer wrote to Rowohlt:

I was an active witness of the failure which took place in those days, and I believe we must concern ourselves with this great problem of the events of history. We owe this to ourselves, for our failure made us all participants in the guilt of those days. After all, the failure was not that of the Catholic Church alone, but that of the Protestant Church as well. The Catholic Church bears the greater guilt for it was an organized, supra-national power in a position to do something, whereas the Protestant Church was an unorganized, impotent, national power. But it, too, became guilty, by simply accepting the terrible, inhuman fact of the persecution of the Jews. For in those days we lived in a time of inhumanity of culture, the beginning of which dates back to Friedrich Nietzsche at the end of the preceding century. The failure was that of philosophy, of free thought, as well.[7]

The two attitudes of Schweitzer which stand out are clear: First, that his own Protestant Church had shown itself to be "an unorganized, impotent national power," and the second that the guilt of silence—of not speaking up—had to be shared by all. The crime of silence should never again be allowed to be our lot, he said. People must speak out.

Crime, atrocity, shame, guilt and forgiveness are the recurring themes in the thought of Albert Schweitzer. And so they were as well with Martin Buber, who watched the massive guilt of a nation grow and dramatically isolated the main issues involved when he delivered a lecture at Frankfurt, Germany, a meeting sponsored by the German Book Trade in 1953.

When I think of the German people of the days of Auschwitz and Treblinka, I behold, first of all, the great many who knew that the monstrous event was taking place and did not oppose it. But my heart, which is acquainted with the weakness of men, refuses to condemn my neighbor for not prevailing upon himself to become a martyr.

Next there emerges before me the mass of those who remained ignorant of what was withheld from the German public, and who did not try to discover what reality lay behind the rumors which were circulating. When I have these men in mind, I am gripped by the thought of the anxiety, likewise well known to me, of the human creature before a truth which he fears he cannot face.

But finally there appears before me, from reliable reports, some who have become as familiar to me by sight, action and voice as if they were friends, those who refused to carry out the orders and suffered death or put themselves to death, and those who learned what was taking place and opposed it and were put to death or those who learned what was taking place and because they could do nothing to stop it killed themselves. I see these men very near before me in that special intimacy which binds us at times to the dead and to them alone. Reverence and love for these Germans now fills my heart.[8]

Yet the churches were in fact silent. The churches of Europe which are supported by the state became agencies of the state—and they lost their ethical tongues. They had neither the will nor the courage to resist the popular opinion created by national propaganda. Churches supposedly committed to following the ethics of Jesus became the marshaling agencies for the war spirit. They earned their state subsidies, but they lost their integrity in the process.

Recalling the trying events of this era, Schweitzer later told a group in Lambaréné,

. . . from the days of my Confirmation classes, I was unhappy with the tendency of many Christians to evade the issues of the ethical application of the teachings of Jesus. This issue haunted me as a university student, and later when I was a teacher and a preacher. Always, I tried in those early days to find some means of making the ethics of Christianity live. It hurt me that people could not understand why I tried to help prisoners, and later why I decided to come to Africa. I was almost denied ordination by the synod because of my views, and indeed was told, "Because of the heresies you have already put into print, there is probably not another synod of the Lutheran Church in the world that would ordain you, but we know your father and your teachers and so we are willing to take a chance on you." Well, I was willing to take a chance on them too, but with the rise of Hitler, and the silence of the churchmen, with only a few notable exceptions, I came to realize that the Church could not be counted upon to withstand the state or the culture in which it held a privileged position. I had always wondered that after two thousand years, a Church dedicated to following the Prince of Peace had not found a means of resisting and overcoming the war spirit and the military machines. When, after the rise of Hitler, good, conscientious churchmen began writing me to stop communication with them, and pleading "if you come to Europe, please do not visit me," I understood that the Church which is supported by the state cannot withstand the state, but becomes a tool of it. The great churches could not be relied upon. Something within me died, and I thought, "What is left?" As I looked about me, I realized only a few small sects, the historically grounded heretical, or dissenting sects, like the Unitarians and the Quakers were the only real hope—they and the new modern spirit of humanism which might rekindle the true spirit of Jesus.[9]

Thus did Schweitzer, now a man of Africa, finally conclude that little of European culture endured. In lectures given in England and Scotland during 1934, he echoed this pessimism, calling for an assertion of a new ethical imperative in man as well as within the churches.

Like Schweitzer, Teilhard de Chardin spent an enormous amount of time with those who did not share his special convictions about God, the Church, and the world. Yet everywhere, also like Schweitzer, he was at home, not alienated—a citizen of the world. On New Year's Day, 1932, he paused with one of the Yellow Expeditions (sponsored by André Citroën, who hoped to rediscover the ancient "silk road" through China) to offer Mass at the Chinese mission of Liang-

Chow. There near the beginning of the Gobi Desert, close to the lands traveled by Marco Polo, De Chardin, the geologist-priest, addressed his friends:

My dear friends, we have met this morning, in this little church, in the heart of China, in order to come before God at the beginning of this new year. Of course, probably for not one of us here does God mean, or seem, the same thing as for any other of us. And yet, because we are all intelligent beings, not one of us can escape the feeling or reflection, that above and beyond ourselves there exists some superior force and that since it is superior to ourselves, it must possess some superior form of our own intelligence and our own will.

It is in this mighty presence that we should recollect ourselves for a moment at the beginning of this new year. What we ask of that universal presence which envelops us all, is first to reunite us, as in a shared, living, centre with those of whom we love, those who, so far away from us here, are themselves beginning this same new year.

Then considering what must be the boundless power of this force, we beseech it to take a favourable hand for us and for our friends and families in the tangled and seemingly uncontrollable web of events that await us in the months ahead. So may success crown our enterprises. So may joy dwell in our hearts and all around us. So may what sorrow cannot be spared us be transfigured into a finer joy, the joy of knowing that we have occupied each his own station in the universe, and that, in that station, we have done as we ought. Around us and in us, God, through his deep-reaching power, brings all this about. And it is in order that he may indeed do so that, for all of you, I am about to offer him this Mass, the highest form of Christian prayer.[10]

De Chardin shared with Schweitzer the same prayers and hopes for a troubled world.

Following his fifth tour in Africa (the greater part of 1935), Schweitzer returned to Europe again for eighteen months. He gave a second series of Gifford Lectures as well as organ recitals to raise funds to carry on his work in Africa. The main source of funds in Germany had now been cut off be-

cause of the nation's political upheaval. It was during this
period that he and Dr. Wilfred Grenfell met twice. Grenfell
had established the Labrador Medical Mission and was renowned for his work among English fishermen and Eskimos.
He spent forty years of sacrificial service in Newfoundland,
where much of his work was conducted on board a hospital
steamer. Schweitzer reported of their meeting,

We began at once to question each other about the management of our hospitals. His chief trouble was the disappearance of
reindeer for the periodic migrations; mine the loss of goats from
theft and snakebite. Then we burst out laughing: we were talking
not as doctors concerned with patients, but as farmers concerned
with livestock.

The second time they met, they were asked to sign a guest
book, and Dr. Schweitzer watching the trim, small doctor
from Labrador sign the register was struck with the humor of
their contrasting physical shapes. He wrote under his name,
L'Hippopotame est heureux de rencontrer l'Ours Blanc.[11]

During the 1930s Schweitzer's wife and daughter had been
living in the Black Forest town of Königsfeld, where Helene
found the climate more tolerable than in Alsace. However,
the reaction of German nationalist cliques to her husband's
Frankfurt address made it safer for her to move beyond the
borders of Germany, so Helene took up residence in Lausanne,
Switzerland. Here, in a traditionally neutral country, high in
the mountains, Dr. Schweitzer spent as much time as possible
with his wife and young daughter. From there, he went frequently to Günsbach, (now French) and played the organ in
concerts in the Low Countries, the British Isles and the
Scandinavian countries.

Professor Ernest Bueding of Western Reserve University
in Cleveland, Ohio, was working in Paris during this time on
a research project at the Pasteur Institute. He described how
a group of research workers were carrying on an experiment
involving the use of a vaccine against yellow fever. They succeeded in establishing some initial immunity, and a news

account of this new development appeared in a Paris paper. Shortly thereafter, a doctor from Alsace telephoned requesting information about the vaccine. The person answering the phone did not get the name of the inquirer, but gave the requested information. The doctor then said he would like to take some of the vaccine back to Africa to use in vaccinating patients in his hospital as well as other natives.

When he was informed that it had not yet been determined whether or not the vaccine would bring on any serious side effects, the doctor replied that he would naturally consider using it on a large scale only after he had tried it on himself. He was asked about his age, and he replied he was about sixty. The person in charge then strongly advised against his taking it. However, "the doctor from Colmar" insisted he would come in the next day to discuss the matter further. He said that if the vaccine was considered safe enough for the natives of Africa, it would be safe enough for him.

Dr. Bueding was in the laboratory at the time, and wondered if the "doctor from Colmar" might not be Schweitzer, who was at the time in Europe preparing the Gifford Lectures to be given later in Scotland. His guess proved to be correct as he greeted the doctor the next day. Schweitzer would not listen to the warnings that it was unwise for him to try the vaccine on himself. He would give the Africans nothing he could not take himself; on this point he was adamant. The research doctor ultimately gave in, but insisted that Dr. Schweitzer be admitted for two days to the Pasteur Hospital. There were no serious reactions from the injection. However, Dr. Bueding reported, "He was a very 'bad patient' because he could not see why these precautions of keeping him inactive in the hospital for two days should be taken."[12] As always, Schweitzer was impatient to continue his full schedule of work.

In the meantime, the hospital in Lambaréné was moving forward. In this period of European turmoil following the First World War, and the ensuing upheaval of economic and political trauma, Dr. Schweitzer was almost commuting be-

tween continents. Travel was still difficult. The tiny trans-
continental packet ships were far from pleasure craft and yet
the desire to see his growing daughter and to be reunited
with Helene, even if for only a short time each year, or every
other year, made the trips worthwhile. Her health had never
recovered from the awful war years. Schweitzer, on the other
hand, was a man of boundless energy, able to work steadily
eighteen hours at a stretch and requiring only a few hours
sleep. He joined the select company of such persons—Thomas
Edison was another—who could carry on effectively with minimal rest. Perhaps this explained the great contributions
such men made—while others slept, they worked. And the
influence of Schweitzer was reaching across oceans.

His impact in Europe had been significant since the early
years of the century, and his writings were published with
increasing rapidity after 1910. But he was not widely read or
followed in the United States until his personal contact with
a New England professor. Schweitzer had, on several occasions, referred to the former Harvard University psychologist,
Dr. A. A. Roback as "my first friend in America." Dr. Roback
recounted that in 1924 he read an article on Dr. Schweitzer
in *Neue Züricher Zeitung* which began with the words, "Albert Schweitzer is like the rainbow, which gleams in every
color and yet remains a magnificently complete unity. No
other man living has given significant literary expression to
such a variety of talents."[13] A correspondence began between
the two men which lasted until both died in 1965.

Encouraged by Professor Roback, President Lowell of Harvard University asked the Divinity School's professor of theology, Dr. J. Seelye Bixler, to call on Schweitzer on his trip to
Europe to invite him to give the famed Lowell Lectures. Dr.
Schweitzer in turn invited Professor Bixler to his home in the
Black Forest in the summer of 1928. Dr. Bixler, later president
and president emeritus of Colby College, gave the following
recollections:

The two visits I had with Dr. Schweitzer at that time mark one
of the high points of my life. Three impressions stand out . . .

First I remember being upset when he asked me if it was not time for what sounded like "Yotz." I could not remember ever hearing the word, but when he sat down at the piano and started to drum away in syncopated time, I realized it was "Jazz" he was talking about.

The second has to do with the large bundle of mail wrapped up with a strap which he threw into a far corner of the room, showing his impatience with the vast volume of correspondence he had to keep up with, yet he had plenty of time and patience for this completely unknown American who had come in to see him.

The third and strongest impression of all is based on a remark he made. He said, "I think the most important quality in a person concerned with religion is absolute devotion to the truth." I have often thought back on that remark and connected it with his scholarly passion for fact in *The Quest of the Historical Jesus*. A few days later, when he gave a Bach recital at Freiburg, he showed the same responsiveness to the claim of the abstract idea. And when later he said that he had gone to Africa in the name of common justice, it seemed as if the picture were complete.

For Dr. Schweitzer, devotion to truth, beauty, and justice is a means of following through the religious desire "Not my will but Thine be done."[14]

In the 1930s, a number of other Americans became acquainted with Schweitzer in either Africa or Europe, including the missionary, Dr. Emory Ross, Professor Edwin Prince Booth of Boston University, Professor Everett Skillings of Middlebury College and others. Gradually, the global reputation of Schweitzer had begun to bloom through his personal contacts and associations, just as the printed word was bringing his writings and thoughts to an increasingly larger audience. His works of theology, philosophy and African commentary were rapidly translated into English and printed on both sides of the Atlantic. In 1931 the first English language biography of Schweitzer appeared, written by John Regester of Puget Sound University, Washington, based on research he had done for his doctoral dissertation at Boston University entitled, *Albert Schweitzer—The Man and His Work*. It was published by Abingdon Press and went through two printings but has long been out of print. In 1935 Magnus Ratter, a

British Unitarian minister serving in Africa, wrote the first truly comprehensive biography in English, *Albert Schweitzer, A Biography and Analysis,* published by Allenson & Co., London. It appeared in the United States in a revised edition as *Albert Schweitzer: Life and Message,* published by Beacon Press. George Seaver's *Albert Schweitzer, the Man and His Mind* followed. Thus, interpretation of Schweitzer was underway. It was also during the 1930s that many people in the peace movement in the United States—Clarence Russell Skinner of Tufts College; John Haynes Holmes, Harry Emerson Fosdick and John Muzzey of New York; and Charles Clayton Morrison of Chicago began quoting Schweitzer's ethical position as supportive of their own absolute ethics regarding pacifism. Dr. Schweitzer had not yet visited America but in 1937 and 1938 Helene and Rhena came, with Mrs. Schweitzer lecturing on the work and needs of her husband's hospital.

In spite of the growing emphasis being placed on his ideas and his achievements around the world, the secret of Schweitzer's triumphs still remained in his thorough naturalness and energy. He could yield to human situations with ease—with his sense of humor about himself, and his ability to enjoy the simple pleasures whether playing jazz, matching wits with friends, or turning extremely provincial in the face of sophisticated expectations of him. These aspects of his behavior were not an act, but came simply from his sense of joy about the richness of life, an attitude which he described as an expression of gratitude for benefits he felt had been bestowed on him rather than earned by him. Throughout the 1920s and 1930s the tensions arising from the two spheres of his activity—Africa and Europe—kept him constantly alert and active. In the constructive activity of the African hospital, he found solace from the disintegration of culture he witnessed in Europe; and in the creative work of writing, lecturing and performing in Europe, he found equal relief from the traumatic effects of working with the ill and diseased in Lambaréné.

While Dr. Schweitzer's intellectual stature continued to be enhanced in Europe by his presence there, he spent much more time in Africa where marked changes were underway. The natives—now called the indigenes—were undergoing the struggles of tribal and territorial, social and cultural transitions, and were disturbed by further vanishing economic growth and new European ways of life being introduced. The indigene became a split personality—still part African, but increasingly caught up in Western civilization. When the doctor had written his thoughts on the natives in 1929, he had said,

Have we white people the right to impose our rule on primitive and semi-primitive peoples—my experience has been gathered among such only? No, if we only want to rule over them and draw material advantages from their country. Yes, if we seriously desire to educate them and help them to attain a condition of well-being . . . The tragic fact is that the interests of colonization and those of civilization do not always run parallel, but are often in direct opposition to each other.[15]

He went on to show that the development of world trade now made impossible the return of the African to a precivilized state; his transformation into a "civilized person" was underway, and indeed inevitable. In his view it was even necessary to protect the native from his own unscrupulous chiefs whose weapons and money, achieved through commerce, virtually reduced the populace "to servitude and turned them into slaves who had to work for the export trade to make a few select people rich." Consequently, Dr. Schweitzer saw the inevitable choice to be faced: "In view of the state of things produced by world trade, there can be no question with these people of real independence, but only whether it is better for them to be delivered over to the mercies, tender or otherwise, of rapacious native tyrants or to be governed by officials of European states."[16]

Obviously, at this time—the 1920s—Dr. Schweitzer felt that the European colonial administrator was the lesser of two evils, but he did not feel that he offered the optimum answer for the African and his future. The ideal solution, in his opinion, would be freedom for the natives—freedom from what Schweitzer later called "both White Colonialism and Black Colonialism." He was dead-set against native exploitation, whether external or from within their own or neighboring tribes. This marked the beginning of the "middle path" in the power struggle in Africa which Dr. Schweitzer was to follow all his life, a position often misunderstood by both European or African, colleague and critic alike.

18

War Comes Again

Dr. Schweitzer traveled to Europe again in early February 1939. He returned to Africa on the same ship, the *Brazza*, twelve days later.[1] He departed not to avoid the war, but to escape a struggle wherein he was not a free agent, able to act on his own moral convictions. He was no longer a German national, and was totally opposed to the Nazi regime. In addition, with a Jewish wife, Dr. Schweitzer's political options in Germany were reduced even further. Moreover, the French had dealt with him as an enemy alien in World War I, and he had no reason to have greater confidence in their treatment now. Finally, his hospital needed his leadership. This was a position in which he could serve humanity in spite of the bleak oblivion settling over his native Europe.

So Schweitzer returned to Lambaréné for the war years, and he gave a detailed account of this difficult period. His supplies were cut off. Stringent economy of operation and rationing were introduced. All but the most severely ill patients were sent home. It was a repeat of 1918 but with greater intensity.

The Vichy French were fighting against the Free French in Africa and battles raged all along the Ogowe, particularly in the air.[2] Both sides agreed to respect the sanctity of the hospital, and while it never was bombed or strafed, stray bullets hit one of the adjoining buildings facing the Ogowe. These buildings had all been reinforced with corrugated iron previously purchased and intended for new roofs.

The war injured on both sides were treated by Dr. Schweitzer. Again he experienced the irony of being far from Europe and yet close to a battle between the two frequent European adversaries, France and Germany. In this case it was the Vichy French of the Nazi puppet government of Pétain and Laval on the one side, and the Free French under General Charles de Gaulle, fighting with the aid and blessing of the Western democracies, on the other. De Gaulle's headquarters were in Brazzaville, capital of the French Republic's West Equatorial African empire, whereas the Vichy French were operating out of the French Cameroons, where the economy was still German-controlled in spite of the French political control. The Ogowe River valley became the battle line between the two forces. Dr. Schweitzer realized that even in Africa the war could not be escaped, that it was a world-wide problem—not merely that of the few participating nations.

War always retards some social processes and hastens others. This war was destined to have an abiding and wrenching effect upon Africa and its society. Brazzaville was not simply the Free French African military center, but the headquarters for all Free French people who stood united against the Pétain government in Vichy. On the northern banks of the beautiful and broad Congo River, General de Gaulle began meeting with the leaders of the free world, receiving its ambassadors and making plans for bringing together the French colonial powers to unite against the Rome-Berlin axis.

In order to accomplish this, De Gaulle issued edicts, gave speeches and signed codicils promising that in the event of a Free French victory, independence would be granted to the loyal colonial people who joined him in the war effort. African independence was to be the reward of Free French war policy, and from that moment on, equatorial Africa, indeed all of Africa, was never to be the same, either politically or in any other way. A vision of a Free Africa was being promised for the aftermath of the hoped-for Free French victory, and it became a promise which could not be postponed following the election of De Gaulle as President of the French Republic.

The *Brazza*, the packet ship on which Dr. Schweitzer sailed to and from Europe in 1939, stayed in port only a few days before beginning its return European journey carrying many white people from Gabon who were anxious to reach home before hostilities commenced in Africa. But they were too late. The *Brazza* was torpedoed at sea and sank, taking to the bottom many European friends and acquaintances whom Dr. Schweitzer had known through the years in Gabon. In only one incident, a large proportion of the white settlers of Gabon were lost outside of the harbor at Bordeaux; no passengers survived.[3]

Ultimately, the Free French were victorious in Africa and the situation there became quiescent for the duration of the European war.

Before returning to Africa as the war clouds had begun to threaten, Dr. Schweitzer had ordered immediate shipment to Lambaréné of all the drugs he could obtain. Upon his arrival in Africa, he pored over the pharmaceutical catalogues, checked inventories, and ordered all the medical supplies he could get in Africa and some more from Europe. Fortunately, most of his orders were filled before hostilities made shipment impossible, and they supported the hospital until American help arrived. In addition, when fighting began in Africa, concerned European merchants offered Schweitzer large shipments of staple commodities which he bought at favorable prices. He was thus able to store a three-year supply of food for the hospital, consisting mainly of rice. This was valuable to the natives, as rice had become the main substitute food for the Africans. In addition, the local trees and plantations continued to bear regular harvests of bananas and tapioca as well as other fruits, so that, coupled with the rice, a more or less balanced diet was made possible.[4]

During the summer of 1939, two doctors and two nurses from the hospital returned to their homes in Switzerland. The medical staff that remained was now composed, apart from Schweitzer, solely of Dr. Ladislas Goldschmid and Dr. Anna Wildikann. Mlle. Gertrud Koch, an experienced nurse, had left to visit her home also, further reducing the small group working with Dr. Schweitzer. The remaining nurses were

Mlles. Notzli and Müller from Switzerland; Mlle. Marie Lager-
dijk from Holland, and Mlle. Emma Hausknecht from Alsace, by now the second oldest person on the staff in point
of service. Mlle. Mathilde Kottmann had returned to Europe
and had been caught there in the war. In the meantime, Mrs.
Schweitzer had arrived in Lambaréné, miraculously crossing
southern Europe to Lisbon, boarding a Portuguese ship to
Angola, and traveling from the Congo to Lambaréné. She
arrived there for a happy reunion on August 2, 1941. This
was the extent of the small staff that carried on during the
war years. In addition, Dr. Goldschmid spent a considerable
amount of his time as resident at the government camp treating sleeping sickness, a program long left without medical
supervision, and he was not available for regular hospital work
for the greater part of the war.[5]

The hospital was hard pressed in other ways. Much of its
equipment had been exhausted by the war victims who had
been treated. The new supplies had been so depleted that a
long and difficult period lay ahead, if the hospital was to survive at all. Dr. Schweitzer and his nurses realized that its
"facilities" were now just about reduced to the personal skill
and attention that the staff could provide.

Naturally, with the war raging in Europe there was no
possibility of further medical supplies and equipment being
sent. In the United States, friends of Schweitzer responded
to the difficult situation, and in New York a small support
group was formed, The Albert Schweitzer Fellowship. It consisted of people Mrs. Schweitzer had met before the war in
New York: Dr. Edward H. Hume, Emory Ross, Everett
Skillings and James Seelye Bixler, the most active of the group.
Thus, it was, in the end, Helene's help that helped the hospital continue functioning during the war. The secretary of
the new group wrote to Dr. Schweitzer and asked him specifically how the group could help the hospital. Dr. Schweitzer
recorded, "At the end of the year 1940 I had a splendid surprise. Word came from America that drugs and other things
would be sent me if I would say what I needed."[6] Finally,

almost a year later, the American supplies arrived, "just in the nick of time" Schweitzer reported. There were not only drugs but many other items that could be put to good use around the hospital. Dr. Schweitzer wrote of the scene as he and his staff, Dr. Anna, Mlles. Emma and Maria and the others unpacked the shipment, "shouts of joy resounded when we came across something which we especially needed." Especially appreciated were the large-sized rubber gloves which fitted Dr. Schweitzer perfectly. He had been up to this point forced to wear tight gloves when operating. Cooking utensils, which were also badly needed, were included in the shipment. Best of all, this load was promised to be but the first of many regular shipments that would follow. The supplies of 1941 allowed the hospital to serve those patients already under treatment. But it was the new shipments of 1942 and 1943 that allowed for the admission of new patients, and enabled the scope of the hospital's services to once again expand. The receipt of shoes and eyeglasses in 1943 opened up additional opportunities for the hospital to serve the natives. Schweitzer wrote in his journal, "How grateful I am to faithful friends in the countries that have helped me, for now I can take in all the sick who are in great need. We are greatly encouraged in our work!"[7]

From the time of the war on, American interest in and support of the Schweitzer Hospital continued to grow. The Schweitzer Fellowship in New York, the Friends of Albert Schweitzer in Boston, and several Schweitzer societies on the west coast made aid to the hospital their primary work. The Unitarian Service Committee also made support of the Schweitzer Hospital a major non-sectarian, humanitarian service program during the war years. Great foundations, pharmaceutical houses, medical societies, and guilds of organists have also continued to support and assist the hospital.

The long tedious years of the war in Africa passed slowly. Dr. Schweitzer remained at his place in the consultation room, in the pharmacy and the surgery ward, caring for the sick and infirm, ministering to their many and various needs.[8]

Interesting stories of the war years, some real, some undoubtedly apocryphal, are recalled in Lambaréné by the few remaining people who lived there at the time. During the conflict, the Vichy French held the island of Lambaréné, and the Free French the mainland of Gabon. The Free French regularly strafed the island with their superior air power, though both sides had agreed not to bomb or strafe the hospital. The Vichy French garrison on the island had a number of regular army families attached to it, and their wives and children were evacuated to the hospital. Here in the evening, under cover of darkness, the husbands would cross the river to visit their families. Not only were the Vichy military wives here, but also the Free French families from the mainland garrison. Thus, French officers and men who were belligerents by day became companions by night. In fact, after visiting their families in the early evening, the men would often gather to play poker. Sometimes the games lasted until dawn at which point the Vichy men of the forces would recross the river and resume hostilities.

It was strange to have this type of part-time warfare take place. Nevertheless the time did come when the Vichy French decided to intensify the war in Lambaréné. Dr. Schweitzer, a notoriously light sleeper, working up to all hours of the night and arising to work before the crack of dawn, arose one morning in November 1942 and went down to check his vegetables in the plantation as the first rays of sunlight began to appear. To his great shock, he heard the crack of machine-gun fire, and bullets began to spray about him. Dropping instantly to the ground, he realized that he had suddenly become the target for a machine-gun nest set up at the tip of the island, and pointed directly at the hospital's garden grove between the jungle and the hospital buildings. He tried to move and the machine gun spat out more bullets. Slowly he rolled over and gingerly began to crawl toward a stone wall where he could be sheltered from the gunner who was apparently determined to keep him pinned down. It was necessary for Schweitzer to lie there by the wall until the sun was high enough in the sky to make him clearly identifiable. Finally, he was able to make his way safely back to the hospital buildings, where he called his leper oarsman and handed him a scrawled note to be delivered to the commandant at the Vichy French headquarters on the island. The oarsman paddled across in his pirogue, and delivered the message to the commandant. It read: "Your machine gun nearly killed me this morning. This is a violation of our agreement and of the Geneva Convention which neutralizes hospitals and medical personnel. If you shoot at me again I will prohibit your men from visiting the hospital."

The commandant was dismayed and horrified by the incident. He told the messenger to go back to Dr. Schweitzer and tell him to have the Free French commandant order a cease-fire at two o'clock that afternoon because he wished to come to the hospital to personally apologize to Dr. Schweitzer. At two o'clock with white flag raised, the commandant set out from the island in his boat, and crossed to the hospital, where he approached Dr. Schweitzer with profuse apologies about the shooting. During the previous night, while the commandant had been at the hospital playing cards, the duty officer on the island had received a message that a Free French ground group was moving up the river to invade the island. Thus, he had ordered the machine-gun nest set up, but, naturally, it was not intended that it fire on anyone in the hospital, most especially the doctor. The doctor gave the commandant a tongue-lashing for his thoughtless orders. As an epilogue to the story, the commandant returned from the garrison to the hospital that evening a sick man. Schweitzer ordered him to bed for two weeks and although he regained his health, his military spirit seemed to have disappeared in the aftermath of the hospital incident.[9]

As Schweitzer was sitting at his desk one day writing some urgent letters, a patient appeared at his window with the news that the war was over. The doctor wrote:

Not until evening could I begin to think and to imagine the end of hostilities. While the palms were gently rustling outside in the darkness, I took from its shelf my little book with the sayings of Lao-tse, the great Chinese thinker of the sixth century B.C. and read his impressive words on war and victory: "Weapons are disastrous implements, no tools for a noble being. Only when he cannot do otherwise, does he make use of them. Quiet and peace are for him the highest. He conquers, but he knows no joy in it. He who would rejoice in victory, would be rejoicing in murder. At the victory celebration, the general should take his place as is the custom at a funeral ceremony. The slaughter of human beings in great numbers should be lamented with tears of compassion. Therefore should he, who has conquered in battle, bear himself as if he were at a festival of mourning."[10]

With the end of the war the doctor was to begin a new chapter in his life. The war years had taken their toll. One world slipped into oblivion during those years, and a new one emerged. Old ways became obsolete, and old virtues suddenly seemed amazingly out of date. Time took the lives of loyal and long-standing friends. The older generation of African leaders with whom Dr. Schweitzer had communicated, but from whom he had been separated by the war, died one by one, so that the doctor now found new, younger, unknown spokesmen representing the Africans to deal with. With a few notable exceptions, such as Léon Mba in Gabon, the new leaders were not personal friends. Yet all members of the first independent Gabonese cabinet, except for two, had been born at the Schweitzer Hospital.

With the cessation of hostilities, Dr. Schweitzer hoped to find new staff recruits, but wrote, "We were forced to abandon the extensive hopes which we had cherished." Mlle. Koch returned to Europe and Dr. Wildikann left for Israel, but at long last Mlle. Mathilde Kottmann arrived from Alsace. The medical staff now consisted of only Dr. and Mrs. Schweitzer and Mlle. Kottmann. Then came the near famine of 1945 when banana and tapioca crops fell off disastrously due to the continued rain during the dry season. Mere feeding of the patients became extremely difficult.[11]

Thus, the staff was depleted, the Schweitzers were weary;

the famine condition grew worse and the ultimately tragic realization came that funds were so low that the situation at the hospital had become hopeless. During the war period, medical supplies from America had saved the hospital, but no significant funds had come to Lambaréné for many years. Schweitzer counted on income from lectures and concerts to finance the hospital. But his 1939 tour was canceled and he had not been back to Europe since. Dr. Schweitzer confided to Helene and Mlle. Mathilde that he felt the hospital was in its last days. He saw no hope. As had been the case during World War I, the hospital was coming to a grinding halt. All that remained was to close it out. The doctor seemingly had given up. Sadly, Helene and Mathilde also recognized that the failure had to be faced

In a letter to Dr. Charles R. Joy, written on October 19, 1946, Dr. Schweitzer described the difficult situation which had built to a climax:

Let me tell you what happened to me last Wednesday morning, October 16, when I went in my small canoe (which we call the "Clipper") to Lambaréné in order to get the letters brought by the river boat from Port Gentil. First I opened a letter from Banque Commerciale Africane, dated October 11, and learned that the hospital owed frs. 124.752 to that bank for payments made for us. I knew that we had overdrawn, because we had made purchases in the large stores so as to take advantage of the prices before they should go up. The rise in prices was expected at the time the new shipment of merchandise arrived from Europe one of these days. But as it was, the purchases had been made by nurse Emma, who had written the orders of payment and then had had to leave in a hurry for Europe, as the boat was leaving ten days before it was expected to leave. Nurse Emma had not been able to keep me informed about our financial situation; therefore, I did not know how much we had overdrawn and was horrified by the news contained in the letter. In the other bank of Port Gentil, the Bank of Occidental Africa, (in case anything should happen we have accounts in two banks) we must have had approximately frs. 30,000, which I did not want to touch, for they were earmarked for current expenses (food for the numerous native patients, payment of the salaries of the men nurses and native workers, etc.). How could we possibly get out of such a situation? I was already composing in my head the letter to the Banque Commerciale in which I was going to ask the bank to grant us further delay for the amount which we owed. . . . In my despair I opened one letter after the other brought by the boat. The last one was a small envelope from Port Gentil and I expected that it would probably contain some request from a native for medicine to be sent to him. But to my utter surprise, I read that the director of the new bank, who is going to open an agency in Port Gentil (National Bank of Industry and Commerce) informs me that he is holding at the disposal of the hospital frs. 380,822 from the Unitarian Service Committee, United States! As this bank is not yet opened in Port Gentil, it has no letterhead paper and there was nothing to lead me to believe that this letter came from the bank and nothing had prepared me for the news that I would find news of the arrival of the important gift which you had informed me about some time ago. You can well imagine the relief brought by this news! Now I would be able to reimburse promptly to the other bank the important sum which we owed it. We could leave behind us all the difficulties which I have been expecting and which were such a cause of worry to me. On the way back towards the canoe, the manager of the large store, who was standing near his door, called me in order to say that he had just received butter from the Cameroun (for a long time it had not been possible to buy any butter). Then I entered and bought several kilos of butter and went home. At the table I announced to the doctors and nurses that I had bought butter and that gave them much pleasure. As you see, the first use we made of your gift was to buy butter. But as soon as the nurse who runs the house and handles the purchases saw that we were no longer in financial difficulties (due to you), she presented me a list of certain articles of which we were very much in need: First, material for the linen in the operating room (where since the war years it was impossible to replace things). Much of the linen was so full of holes that it could no longer be mended! I had described to you about Wednesday morning so that you should be able to realize the situation we were facing at the time of the arrival of your gift. . . .

I can find no words to express the extent of my gratitude. You are so good for my work and for myself without knowing me personally. I cannot understand the reasons for such thoughtfulness for my work and for myself. You cannot know how I feel uplifted and encouraged by your kindness. On returning last Wednesday I felt very much rested, I who had been feeling so tired after all the work I had had to do day after day. I forgot to tell you that with your help I was able to pay immediately for the 2000 kilos of cement which I had to buy to make a landing pier in front of the hospital so that the ships could dock without difficulty in all seasons—both high tide and low tide. The level of the river according to seasons varies over six metres. In August and September I became once again a mason just as I had been in 1925, 1926, 1927 at the time I was building the hospital. An old mason, who had helped me then and who is just the same age as I, and I have built a thick wall with large stones that have not been cut. The dock should have been built long ago, but I always seemed to put it off from year to year by thinking of the expense and the work. It is during the dry season this year when the water was lower than it usually is, permitting us to do the foundation work in exceptionally good conditions that I decided to undertake the work. Many years may elapse before such conditions should present themselves again. Of course what I have told you of Wednesday morning is for yourself and the members of the Committee. Pray do not have it published.* But I beg you to tell those who have contributed to that gift that it has been for me of tremendous help in these difficult times when prices are up, when the hospital is in such difficulties. I have been able to make purchases which were very necessary and which I could not have made otherwise. Let them also know how grateful I am for their great kindness!"

Later Mlle. Mathilde as well as his daughter would recall that this letter provided probably the most important moment in the life of the hospital. Schweitzer's daughter, Rhena, remembered the sense of gratitude and appreciation her father and mother always held for the Unitarians in America who had chosen this particular time to make a contribution, a time

* Not published until now when Dr. Schweitzer's daughter granted permission.

when it appeared that everyone else had forgotten the financial needs of the jungle hospital.[12]

Dr. Schweitzer then wrote a letter on December 4, 1946 to Mr. William Cary in Paris, saying:

Thank you for your letter of August 16, 1946 announcing to me the great gift of the Unitarian Service Committee for my work. The $4,375 have been credited to me . . . I have written also to the Unitarian Service Committee in Boston to thank them for their great goodness. This sum reached me *the same day* when the financial situation of the hospital was extremely critical and when I did not know how to repay the bank of the advance of $1,045 which it had made me for the purchase of provisions, rice, cement and other materials. I was also very late in payment of the modest salaries of European personnel members (doctors and nurses) and the native—orderlies and plantation workers . . . All these difficulties have now been overcome, thanks to this great gift. I was very much moved! It is the second time that the Unitarian Service Committee has come to the rescue of my work in so generous a fashion. You can imagine that the situation is not easy in these hard times.

The Unitarian Service Committee had also joined with the Congregational and Christian Churches and the Episcopal Church in a seventieth birthday gift of medical supplies, clothing, and rice to which Dr. Schweitzer responded on January 23, 1945, writing to Charles Joy:

I am deeply moved that the General Council of Congregational Churches and friends in the Protestant Episcopal Church with the Unitarian Service Committee have thought of my activity here in so touching a way, sending me such kind congratulations on the occasion of my 70th birthday. Your telegram arrived just in time for it. Alas, for what I have to do and the long time, it might be good for the hospital if I could go on directing it, I ought to be 30 and not 70 years old. But it is a great privilege, that at 70 I am still able to do the necessary. Every day I realize with profound gratitude towards God the grace, that at my age I can still do my work in the African jungle.

By the great gift, which the telegram announces me and to which your Committee has so generously contributed, I am stirred with emotion and I thank you from the depth of my heart. This magnificent present will find good use. It will help to nourish the many single sick in my hospital, who have come from afar and don't possess anything and who are a constant sorrow for me. The natives of the virgin forest here are nearly all very poor. I have not only to give them food, but also put a blanket and a mosquito net at their disposal. And very often they have to stay here for weeks, even for months. I feel so sorry, if I have to send away a patient, who has not quite fully recovered, in order to economize the food, which I am obliged to give him! Your wonderful gift frees me of much sorrow in this respect. This is a glorious feeling for me, to whom deliverance of such sorrow gives fresh courage again. . . .

It has meant much to me that in this difficult time the friends of the United States have lent much generous help to my hospital. Without it, I don't know how it could have been kept running. How delighted were we, when in 1943 several cases with medicines from the United States arrived safely. And now, for the second time a number of cases have crossed the ocean and are waiting in an African port, from where we hope they may soon be transported to the mouth of the Ogowe and up the river to Lambaréné. You will know that the mission station of Lambaréné has been founded by American missionaries in 1874—it is thus of the same age as I. With Dr. Nassau, one of the first in Lambaréné, I have in 1913 and 1914 still exchanged letters. Amongst the old Christians the memory of the first American missionaries is still alive. So it seems wonderfully providential that in the hardships of our times American Churches lend their help to the Lambaréné hospital. Once more deepest thanks for your kindness!

Please transmit the enclosed letters to the General Council of Congregational Churches and to the friends in the Protestant Episcopal Church; I don't have their addresses.

Mrs. Schweitzer joins me in sending you and the members of the Committee our kindest regards.

At about the same time, Mme. Emmy Martin wrote Charles Joy, from Günsbach, also thanking him and the Service Committee for their support. She added that until now (July 1945) the personnel of the hospital had been made up entirely of people from the vicinity of Strasbourg.

The Albert Schweitzer Fellowship of New York in sending crates of medical supplies in 1943, and again in 1945, initiated the American support of the hospital; but it was the financial contribution of the Unitarian Service Committee which was its salvation. It seems today to be a pitiably small amount—in American currency, $4375—for Dr. Schweitzer to have been so appreciative. It is startling to realize that a mere bank overdraft of $1045 virtually closed the hospital in 1946. Accordingly, while the amount of money was small, the psychological factor was great.

With these funds Schweitzer could reorganize the hospital staff, and order supplies, and building materials. Wages could be paid. They had a reprieve. The hospital could go on. After lunch, Schweitzer entered where Mathilde and Helene had been packing to tell them of the good fortune that had saved the hospital.

The specter of the war finally passed. The now-elderly doctor found himself in a new Africa. During the First World War, Schweitzer had seen the result of the withdrawal of the white administrators, teachers and developers, the vacuum created by the sudden lapse in the continuity of the two cultures. During World War II, he had observed an entirely different phenomenon. A capital of a European nation was, in effect, set up in equatorial West Africa and the continent had become a party to freedom's cause and the allied war effort. Later, Free French, the capital was moved to Algiers when De Gaulle's differences of opinion with the French Committee of National Liberation were settled. North of the Sahara, the famed Afrika Korps of Hitler was demolished by Montgomery, and the Italian control over Libya and Ethiopia was brought to a speedy end by the English. Roosevelt and Churchill met in North Africa at Casablanca in January 1943, while in West Africa the Vichy French Forces were liquidated. Thus, in fast order, the control of most of Africa (South and East Africa were already either controlled by the British or in the Commonwealth) fell into the hands of free world forces.

13. Albert Schweitzer, the musician, listening to recordings of his organ interpretation of Bach. He was respected both as organ builder as well as concert performer, and many of his funds for the Lambaréné hospital were raised by organ recitals he gave throughout Europe.

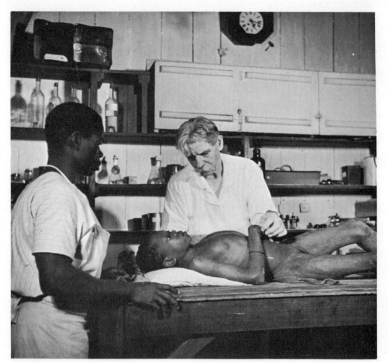

14. Schweitzer as physician, his primary role in his adult life. He treated every conceivable kind of tropical disease and trained local African natives to assist him as male nurses.

15. Schweitzer's cluttered study at Lambaréné. It was at this desk that he carried on his scholarly works including his volumes on St. Paul and *The Philosophy of Civilization.*

Schweitzer as pastor, shown here preaching at a Christmas service at Lambaréné.

17. The doctor as construction engineer. Schweitzer designed his new hospital buildings at Lambaréné, supervised their construction and took part in the actual physical labor of building them.

18. The traveler. Shown here embarking at Bordeaux, Schweitzer journeyed back and forth frequently between Europe and Africa. His family was in Europe; his lifework in Lambaréné.

19. Schweitzer with his wife, daughter, Rhena, and grandchildren in Günsbach, 1951.

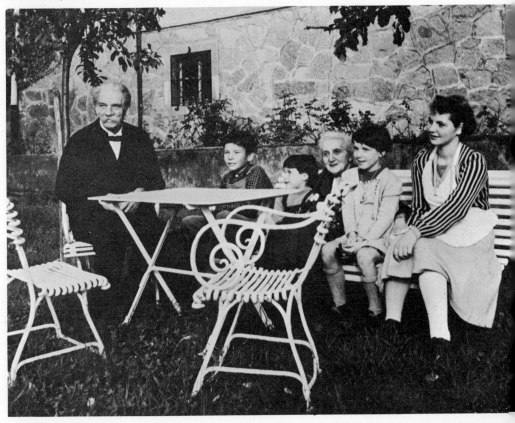

20 and 21. Wherever he was, Schweitzer devoted his attention to children. He is shown here (20) visiting his own former elementary school at Mühlhausen in Alsace and (21) at an African school at the Lambaréné hospital.

22 and 23. The world citizen. Schweitzer, shown here with Bertrand Russell (22) and conductor Charles Münch (23), numbered many of the century's great men among his friends. Albert Einstein and Pablo Casals were others, and with such friends, he was particularly anxious in his later years to share his concerns for world peace and nuclear disarmament.

24. At home in Africa. This was the last picture taken of Dr. and Mrs. Schweitzer together before she died.

25. Shown here taking one of his countless trips up Gabon's Ogowe River, Albert Schweitzer chose both to live his life and die on the continent that was, over the years, his true home.

General de Gaulle held the key to French West Equatorial Africa. He had promised freedom to those who supported the war effort, and he began to set new forces in motion to try to fulfill this promise. The war thus built up aspirations impossible to hold in check later. In the same manner, the English assurances to their colonies helped develop strong independence movements among the native populations.

Thus, beginning with the end of World War II, a bold and more determined African leadership began to speak with force and dignity of their aspirations, and it quickly became evident that the promises of Churchill, Montgomery and De Gaulle could not be dismissed. Freedom and independence were becoming inevitable. Many difficult and unhappy days followed in Africa. Colonial administrators resuming control from the military governors, found that the old political order was no longer so stable. Many of the administrators, perennial officers of a white colonial system, were not able to adjust to the times and new sentiments.

The Brazzaville Conference of 1944 made a proposal for colonial development within the French sphere of influence. Although dominated by colonial administrators, there were many Africans present at the conference. Assimilation into an international French state, and common citizenship for all Frenchmen regardless of their country of origin, including French Africans, were stressed. At the same time, suggested moves toward greater national autonomy were to feed the desire of the emancipators for total independence. In 1946, the French Constitution bent a little more, setting up the French Union which was later interpreted as granting concessions to an "evolutive" system of national self-government for member countries of the French Empire. This encouraged further the all-out efforts toward independence. By 1958, with the Fifth French Republic's inception, the final evolution of the French Community came superseding the French Union. At this time each African member nation was given the opportunity to vote, and that year a bewildered De Gaulle, during freedom demonstrations on his triumphal return to

Brazzaville, declared, "Anyone who wants independence can have it; all he need do is vote 'No.'" A majority of the states voted for self-government. Thus the drive toward independence whose fires had been fanned by De Gaulle now raced ahead of him, and political agreements with and concessions to former colonies were now forced upon France. Freedom could no longer be halted except by force, and this was no longer an option.[18]

Other political factors helped as well to transform the Africa of Albert Schweitzer. Not extremely noticeable in Africa but very influential in Paris was the strong stand consistently taken in the United Nations by the United States of America in its denunciation of colonialism. Through the United Nations, colonial powers such as France and Great Britain were placed on the defensive on this issue. The old imperialistic drive to control native populations and their aspirations was no longer viewed as ethically acceptable. People simply were not sure they had the right to deny self-determination to other peoples; colonialism had lost all vestiges of moral substance. Empires watched themselves dissolving. France, along with Great Britain, faced this situation. Adding fuel to the fire, the Soviet Union condemned capitalistic colonial policy, calling for free elections and the right of native peoples to have free political parties. It also offered opportunities for the education of students from colonies at Soviet universities. Finally, the African troops who had fought in Europe in 1939 and 1940, and had seen the collapse of France, were no longer in awe of its military might. All of these factors helped support the internal demands of African patriots. Many of them knew little or nothing of the world outside of their homeland, but educated in Africa and having a new increased sense of dignity, and a hunger for self-rule, they now pressed for independence.

A floodgate had suddenly opened. Many missionaries were bewildered by the new political developments. Merchants, traders and lumbermen were not used to working with indigenes who considered themselves freemen. Consequently, many made mistakes in human relations, some suffered economic losses, others fled as violence erupted. Schweitzer endured the entire troubled period.

He came through the turbulent times with serene confidence; of good grace moving with the growing aspirations of the people into a new African political milieu. He did not become a leader in the struggle for independence, but neither was he an obstructionist. The new African leadership was to insist that African destiny must be determined by nationals. It is difficult to determine whether Dr. Schweitzer's relative passivity on this issue was the result of his judgment that letting Africans handle the situation themselves was the only right course, or simply because of his uncertainty as to the best way to handle the situation. In any case, there were no real difficulties at any time at the Schweitzer Hospital during the period of political transition. And the hospital after all was the doctor's main concern.

West Equatorial Africa was, of course, a less turbulent place to live than most areas. Here there was no competition for the land and control of property rights as in other sections of Africa. There was no high plateau favorable for European settlement as in Kenya, no ideal farmland free of malaria and sleeping sickness as in South Africa. White residents were also few in number because of the mosquito and tsetse fly which lived in Gabon in abundance and brought disease, and generally made survival difficult. Due to all these factors, colonization and colonialism had never been major issues in the Ogowe River basin. There were white lumbermen, merchants, administrators, the military, missionaries and teachers in West Africa. But these people were all there providing services, offering employment opportunities, and supervising the affairs of government. And only a few of them, including, of course, Dr. Schweitzer, were able to survive in the unpleasant climate for longer than two contract periods or four years. Thus, in Gabon, a somewhat different temper and pace was present in the struggle for emancipation than existed elsewhere. The

development of nationalism has not been without its political
incidents, but all have been minor.

Schweitzer's approach to the African had always been a
highly personal one. It never became an abstract relationship
that could be separated from his human, personal involve-
ments. In addition, he had never been a great believer in ceremony and institutions. For both these reasons, political theory
and structure were frankly of little concern to him. Dr.
Schweitzer had become in his principal role somewhat like
the proverbial old family doctor to whom everybody could
come with whatever problems they had, certain of receiving
sound advice and a word of kindness. Literally, thousands of
families over five decades had sought him out. He was someone they could trust throughout all the heated political discussions and the new alignments being formed. He had a place
in their lives and in their country, but chose not to have one
in their politics.

Following a plebiscite, the Republic of Gabon emerged as
an independent member of the French Community in 1958.
Hospital physicians and nurses related that Africans visited
daily with the ballots and lined up at the pharmacy and dispensary to ask the staff their meaning. The staff would explain
that they were being given an opportunity to choose between
becoming an independent nation, or remaining a French colony. All indigenes had been given two slips of paper, each
headed *Referendum*. One was blue and marked "Non," and
the other was yellow and marked "Oui." They were simply
to make their decision by turning in the proper slip. Often the
puzzled natives would ask, "But how can we vote for Dr.
Schweitzer?"[14]

The coming of independence brought a whole new set of
problems to the hospital. Dr. Schweitzer dealt with the hospital's problems but continued to remain non-political in the
African situation and on the question of independence.

Now there exists two Africas, side by side and intertwined:
the Africa of the native villages and common tribal people
whom Schweitzer used to call "the children of nature"; and

the Africa of the native intellectuals. Dr. Schweitzer related a story about the time he was building his hospital years ago. While he was straining to move a heavy log, a well-dressed native clad in European clothing, stood watching him. The doctor called to the African to ask him to lend a hand. The African haughtily replied, "What? Me? I am an intellectual and don't do menial labor."

"You're lucky," Dr. Schweitzer replied, "I tried to become an intellectual but I didn't succeed."[15]

In 1960 the "Independence Election" or first general election was held when the governing officials were chosen for the new Republic. Ultimately, all contending factions joined in a coalition, with each group represented. M. Léon Mba, the respected Gabonese intellectual, was elected President. Dr. Schweitzer and his white staff members remained completely neutral during the campaign. They were embarrassed, however, by the natives who stood up at political rallies and asked again, as they had in the 1958 plebiscite, "Can we vote for M. le Grand Docteur Schweitzer?" This question was interpreted by the doctor as the seeking of reassurance that the hospital's services would still be available after independence. To some African nationalists, these sentiments about Schweitzer seemed to reflect an unseemly dependence on the white man which they felt must be discouraged. The staff reported that at the height of the election campaign, politicians appeared on the hospital grounds and made strong speeches. They claimed that the land on which the hospital stood belonged to the Africans and not to Dr. Schweitzer. But Dr. Schweitzer had no quarrel with this point. He held a grant, and the hospital existed only through the good will of the natives and their government, whatever government it might be.[16]

In an interview, Schweitzer said, "There is no problem of the Africans which they cannot solve for themselves given time, if the civilized nations of Europe and America do not blow themselves and Africa up first." This is a fair view of

Dr. Schweitzer's final appraisal of the African's ability to solve his problems.

Earlier, he had written an article which was published on January 28, 1927, in the *Contemporary Review*, entitled "Relations of the White and Colored Races." In this article, Schweitzer took for granted the continuation of colonialism, and he was sometimes called to task through the years for this assumption. However, the remarkable feature of the article was not that assumption, but the foresight of his views emphasizing the rights of the African as early as 1927. At that time the rights of colonial peoples were rarely thought of as even worthy of consideration. He listed and discussed the fundamental rights which he believed they were entitled to as human beings. These included the following: "The right to habitation; the right to free movement over the land and waterways; the right to free use of soil and subsoil; the right to freedom of labor and exchange; the right to justice; the right to live 'within a natural national organization'; and the right to education."[17] Thus, in the broadest sense, Schweitzer did have a political viewpoint about Africa and its people.

The Postwar World

After the war, Schweitzer began to find he could not remain involved solely with Africa and with medical practice. His driving ethical concern began to bring him into a world-wide role. At home in Lambaréné, the hospital needed his attention first of all, and he did concentrate mainly on its development. Because of her delicate health, Helene was again forced to leave Africa; she returned to Switzerland in 1947. In fact, since World War I she had made only brief visits to the mission and then only during one of the annual dry seasons. In October of 1948 Schweitzer departed for Europe where he rejoined Helene, his daughter, Rhena, and her family for a visit. Rhena, who later took training as a laboratory technologist, had married in 1939. Her husband, Jean Eckert, was an organ builder and engineer in Zürich. The couple settled in France where their first three children were born, but after the Nazi occupation, fled to Switzerland and lived near Zürich. Here their youngest daughter Katharine was born and all four children were educated. Schweitzer's 1948 visit marked the first time he had seen his grandchildren. In 1958 Dr. Schweitzer wrote to Rhena asking her if she could come to Lambaréné to celebrate their joint birthday on January 14. Happily, she fell in love with the area and the hospital, and from then on was anxious to spend as much time there as possible. As soon as all her children were away at school, she returned to school and studied to become a laboratory technologist in order to be of service on the staff. She was for many years a great help to her father.

The pressures and anxiety of his separation from Helene were not so apparent to outsiders, but they were an increasing burden and heartache to the Schweitzers. Almost half of their married life was to be lived apart from each other. On July 17, 1951, Mrs. Schweitzer wrote Magnus Ratter a revealing letter concerning the strain upon the couple caused by their separation. After thanking him "for the fine biography of the doctor, in his name as well as my own . . ." she continued,

Now I am on my way back to the Black Forest . . . (She wrote from aboard the M.S. *Foucauld*). When we left last October, the doctor meant to divide his time between Europe and Africa, spending six months in each of them. We stayed eight months, and at the last moment, he decided he could not come back with me, but must remain at the hospital in view of the general conditions of the world. He may be right, if complications arise, but at our age there ought not to be such separations. Yet, it would not do for me to stay on and risk becoming a burden on account of my poor health—again there is this sad alternative which has arisen so often.

She went on to wish him well, recalling the rich memories of her trip to the United States with the doctor two years before: "How present it still is with me, and yet how far away! That is because life in Lambaréné Hospital is so full of events." The letter was signed, "With thankful greetings and all good wishes, Sincerely, Helene Schweitzer."[1]

The expressed emotions in Helene's sad note, as well as her courageous acceptance of the separation because of her husband's devotion to the hospital was matched by Schweitzer's own feelings, for those who knew him at this period saw that he, too, felt the loneliness that came with the years of separation. Proverbially, distance may make the heart grow fonder, but "fondness" is not a substitute for true love and companionship. The separations had robbed the Schweitzers of these things, in particular the latter. Nevertheless, they maintained a high standard of fidelity and honesty with one another and were in constant communications. Helene knew better than anyone else that the hospital was primarily her husband's responsibility, and that if the cold war became a hot one, only his supervision at Lambaréné could maintain operation of the hospital for those who were so dependent upon its service.

Before Schweitzer's 1948 journey, he corresponded at length with Dr. Albert Einstein in Princeton, New Jersey. Over the years the two had been in touch through mutual friends, sharing ideas and hopes for a better and more peaceful world. Einstein had hoped that Schweitzer would be his guest at Princeton sometime in the near future. This was not possible on the 1948 trip planned for Europe, but Schweitzer's reply to the invitation offers a vivid account of his activity at and concern for the hospital, his view of the trend of current events in Africa, and a statement of his philosophy of life.

April 30, 1948

Dear Friend,

So often, indeed, have I written you in thought because from afar I follow your life and your work and your attitude towards the happenings of our time. But my writers cramp, an inheritance from my mother, prevents me, so that many letters planned in thought remain unwritten. But now that, through circumstances, I am obliged to forgo the opportunity to meet you in Princeton, I cannot do otherwise than to tell you in writing how sorry I am about it. And now I see in an issue of *Life* magazine, which came into my hands, pictures of the Institute which further increase my regrets about the renunciation. The picture of Dr. Oppenheimer with you is touching. And when I see a picture of you there always emerges the memory of the beautiful hours at Berlin which I spent with you . . .

Through Dr. Oppenheimer you will have heard about the reasons for my renunciation. I am no more a free man; in everything I have to consider my hospital and have to be intent always to be in a position to do the necessary for its existence. Every enterprise is nowadays burdened by all possible regulations and records and the like, that it needs a firm guidance at every instance. Therefore, I cannot be further absent from Lambaréné in any distance or time than this need of constant alertness allows. I have at this time no doctors who are thoroughly acquainted with the management. The two who are with me now will have this week finished their two years and will be replaced by two new ones whom I will have to introduce to the work. And for the whole management I have nobody who could take over the necessary decisions and responsibilities. An example: when it began to "smell" like inflation of the franc (in spite of official reassurances that this would not happen), I had to risk to convert all available money into rice, petroleum and other materials which could be had in the factories and stores, in order to exchange still in good time merchandise for the shrinking paper money. With this I risked not having later on the necessary funds to pay outstanding bills and the wages of the numerous dark personnel of the hospital. Nobody else could have risked perhaps getting the hospital into great financial difficulties, by emptying the money chest which was already in a precarious situation. I have taken this risk and saved thousands through the hurried buying which was above our means but which saved the hospital from the financial crisis in which it would have arrived if we had had to pay the prices which soared high on the day of inflation. This is just one of many examples. How could I, good theologian, ever have thought that I would become a speculator and a *hasardeur* to keep the hospital above water. However, it is worth it, that I have become a slave through the hospital.

Nonetheless, I am not giving up the hope still to be able to do other work. In one instance I do so absolutely, and that is in my practicing the piano with the organ pedal even if it is only for three-quarters of an hour, to keep in form and also to improve myself.

The Philosophy I carry with me constantly. Many chapters of the third volume of the Kultur-Philosophie are finished and others are so much completed in thought that they can be put on paper right away. I only must first get much additional work (among this, masonry work) behind me, to be able to keep at it with some degree of quietness and regularity. At the moment I am trying to eat my way through a mountain of thick gruel to reach the "Lubberland," the land of the lazy. It will be a very modest "Lubberland" but it will suffice my desires. These consist in having for myself the morning and night hours and to use the afternoons for work at the hospital. And if I can achieve that, even in a modest way, I could still be able to give to the "Philosophy of Reverence for Life" its definite form. The whole question is: will I have the efficient persons around me, capable of relieving me of as much work as possible, especially the stupid secondary work. The third volume is conceived as a symphony of thoughts—

a symphonic performance of themes. Never before in my life have I thought and felt so musically as just in these last years. In the third volume there are chapters worked in about mysticism and religion, as revolving around ethics. We are at this time three doctors and seven white nurses, among them an American. Without the material help of the U.S.A. the hospital could not be kept above water in spite of the economy with which we operate. My special field is Urology. At this time I am the Top Apothecary who works out all the orders and who keeps the large Pharmacy in order. Presently I am especially occupied with the treatment of Leprosy. We are using the new American remedies Promin and Diason, which actually achieve what the former remedies could not. At this time there are about fifty Leprous in treatment. Leprosy is widespread here.

I am enclosing a map of the hospital. A Swiss engineer, who was here in passing, has made it and given me several copies. These buildings I erected for the most part with our black carpenter. I did the masonry work, especially. Among the new generation of natives there are no good workmen as they were found among the old ones. The old ones went through the regular apprenticeship and fellowship at the Catholic and Protestant labor missions. Those of the new generation get their knowledge at the so-called Industrial Schools. They consider themselves too good to become workmen. On the whole, *what* will become of the native population in all the colonial territories when the tendency of the present generation is directed to emancipate itself from the tilling of the soil and from the trade! Nearby and observed from within, rather than from afar and from without, the colonial problems look quite different.

Now I have let myself go and imposed upon you to read many pages of my scribble. But it was a pleasure for me to be together with you in thought at my desk in the study during these night hours. When will it be granted to us really to be together? Will it ever happen?

I am reading in the *Aufbau* which I receive regularly that you will be able to play hooky, to use a good old collegiate expression. —Please remember me to Dr. Oppenheimer. I would have liked to make his acquaintance. How is your violin?

With best thoughts,

Your devoted Albert Schweitzer

The writers' cramp hand has stood up well this evening. My wife is at this time in Europe and stays in the Black Forest in Switzerland. She is relatively well. My daughter, with her husband and four children, lives in Switzerland.[2]

Einstein's reply was short and complimentary; other world events would bring them together, if only in correspondence.

September 25, 1948

Dear Mr. Schweitzer,

It goes without saying that I regret your inability of paying the projected visit to our Institute. I am convinced, however, that the work at the institution created by you is incomparably more important. You are one of the few in whom extraordinary working power and many-sidedness are combined with the desire to serve man and to lighten his lot. If there were more such personalities, we would never have fallen into such a dangerous international situation. Against blindness of the soul there is obviously still no remedy.

With sincere greetings
and wishes,

Yours,

Albert Einstein

Upon his arrival in Europe in 1948, Dr. Schweitzer, very worried about the hospital's finances, found a delightful surprise awaiting him. President Robert J. Hutchins of the University of Chicago and The Ford Foundation invited him to come to America and speak at the Goethe Bicentennial Assembly to be held in the Rocky Mountains at Aspen, Colorado. He accepted gladly. The stipend offered would contribute much toward rebuilding the hospital which was in need of many additions due to the depreciation of facilities during the war. In addition, this trip would give him an opportunity to see some of his American friends.[3]

Noel Gillespie, his first assistant, was living in Madison, Wisconsin.[4] Dr. Charles Joy, Executive Director of the Unitarian Service Committee, (the first American organization to give monetary support to the Schweitzer Hospital) was in New York and anxious to confer with Dr. Schweitzer on the translation of his works into English. There were other friends to be seen as well.

Back in May of 1947, Joy, accompanied by Melvin Arnold, editor of the Beacon Press and later president of Harper & Row, publishers, had made the slow trip northward from the Belgian Congo to Lambaréné where, on June 7, they finally met with Schweitzer and visited the hospital. Immediately, these three had found that they had much in common.

Schweitzer looked at Mr. Arnold and said that he looked sick. Admitting he was, Arnold explained that he had an ulcer which his doctors were trying to cure. The doctor led the newcomers to his pharmacy where he took down a container from the shelves and took from it a large brown pill. He gave it to Arnold. To Arnold's delight, the pill brought almost immediate relief and he credits Schweitzer with an instant cure of a stubborn ulcer which had confounded numerous doctors at home.[5]

While at Lambaréné, Dr. Joy took hundreds of photographs which were later widely printed in magazines and newspapers, including *Life* and *Time*. Arnold was at the time Director of Publications of the American Unitarian Association which was undertaking a major program to publicize the philosophy and works of Schweitzer. Thus, he found himself taking frequent notes during the course of his visit.

Schweitzer had many vivid recollections of his visit to America in 1949.

During that spring, the prolonged snowfall in the Rocky Mountains had left deep snow into early summer, and the local deer were in danger of starvation. The United States Wildlife Service, accordingly, began flying in bales of hay to be parachuted to the trapped animals. Traveling by train through the Rockies toward Aspen, the car in which Dr. Schweitzer, Dr. Ross, Dr. Joy and Mr. Arnold were passengers provided a panoramic view over a valley in which one of the mercy planes was operating. Dr. Schweitzer jumped from his seat and ran from window to window to watch the parachuting bales on their way to the waiting herds of deer below. "Who would have thought of it?" he exulted. "And in America! Reverence for Life! *Vive L'Amérique!*"[6]

While attending a banquet after his arrival in Aspen, Colorado, Dr. Schweitzer was called from the room for an interview by a newsman anxious to meet a deadline. He wanted a more detailed explanation of what Dr. Schweitzer meant by his ethical imperative, Reverence for Life. He continued to press the point, dissatisfied with Dr. Schweitzer's explanation. In the meantime, the banquet was in progress and Dr. Schweitzer was getting hungry. Finally, he said, "Reverence for Life means all life. I am a life. I am hungry. You should respect my right to eat." With that he excused himself and returned to the banquet.[7]

Another event of interest, hardly noticed by his friends, took place when Dr. Schweitzer came to the United States. A thirty-eight-year-old businessman-rancher in Arizona had read of Schweitzer's accomplishments and his philosophy and became interested in the man. He was Larimer Mellon, whose family were the founders of the Aluminum Corporation of America and the Gulf Oil Company. He had attended Princeton briefly, worked in the petroleum industry in Louisiana, and served as an intelligence officer during World War II. He had been divorced, and after World War II, had decided to spend his time doing something both physically invigorating and useful, and thus bought a ranch in Arizona. His activities there succeeded in keeping him physically occupied, but he found that he needed a greater challenge beyond that involved in ranching.

It was during a period of discontent and restlessness that he read something about Schweitzer. He had an accountant on his ranch, whose French wife was a nurse. The couple wanted to take an extended trip overseas, and Mellon suggested they go to Lambaréné and report to him their impressions of the Schweitzer Hospital. They went and were singularly unimpressed with the hospital's primitive conditions. And, Dr. Schweitzer was not even present at the hospital. Rather than accept their negative evaluation, Mellon decided to go himself. In 1948 he visited Lambaréné, but Schweitzer was then in Europe. Returning by way of Europe, the two men met in Günsbach. The next year, when Schweitzer came to America, Mellon wrote him and asked if he could talk with him about his own plans, to return to college to become a doctor and then establish a hospital like Schweitzer's. The doctor invited Mellon to see him in New York. He set a time for a meeting at Gramercy Park. When Mellon arrived, Schweitzer was with Dr. Emory Ross and a representative of an American pharmaceutical house, which was anxious to contribute supplies to the hospital. Ross excused himself, and left Schweitzer, the pharmaceutical representative and Mellon alone. Ross had been translating for the doctor as the agent spoke only English, and Schweitzer's command of the language was not adequate for full understanding. Mellon, therefore, took over the task and translated.

During the next two days Mellon had several discussions with Schweitzer and resolved his own plan of action for overseas medical missions. He enrolled at Tulane University Medical School, and with the encouragement and confidence of Schweitzer, undertook the long course of study to become a physician and surgeon in order to open a Schweitzer Hospital in a preindustrial tropical country. He explored possibilities in two South American nations and then settled on Haiti in the Caribbean. "Naturally, I called my hospital the 'Albert Schweitzer Hospital' because he was my inspiration and if it wasn't for him, I would never have done this," Mellon explained.

Mellon was thirty-eight years old when he first began seriously thinking he would like to emulate Schweitzer. He was thirty-nine when he met him, and forty when he entered medical school. His application to the Haitian government for a hospital site was granted in 1952, and the buildings for the hospital begun in 1954. He received his degree in 1953, and the hospital has been in full operation since 1956. Throughout this period, he has been helped by his second wife, the former Gwendolyn Grant, who works with him at the hospital in Deschapelles, Haiti.[8] Thus, among other things, Schweitzer's 1949 trip to America enabled him to meet a man who would be one of his major disciples.

During the 1950s, Dr. Schweitzer traveled back and forth from Africa to Europe many times. It was during this period that a firm base of financial support for the hospital was established. On his journeys he still traveled by old, familiar means, going by packet boat to Bordeaux and using the trains in Europe. He never flew in an airplane, nor did he learn to drive an automobile. His ideas and thinking were progressive, but in his personal life he often, ironically, kept old, comfortable habits.

He received a number of prizes and awards during the 1950s. On September 16, 1951, a 10,000-mark prize was awarded him in Frankfurt, Germany, by the West German Association of Book Publishers and Sellers for his efforts in promoting world peace. On February 27, 1952, King Gustav Adolf of Norway awarded the Prince Charles Medal to Schweitzer for his humanitarian achievements. On October 26, 1952, he was formally inducted into the prestigious French Academy of Moral and Political Sciences, as successor to Marshal Pétain. The subject of his acceptance address was, "The Problem of Ethics in the Evolution of Human Thought." Finally, on October 30, 1953, the ultimate tribute, the Nobel Peace prize, was awarded to Schweitzer *in absentia*, and was accepted by the French ambassador to Norway in his name. *In absentia* also, he was made a member of the American Academy of Arts and Sciences.[9]

He returned to Europe to deliver his Nobel Peace prize address on November 4, 1954, in Oslo, with King Gustav Adolf present. He spoke on "The Problem of Peace in the World of Today." Later, three addresses he gave on "Peace or Atomic War?" were broadcast over Radio Oslo, in 1957 and

1958. These addresses marked the emergence of the most militant portion of Dr. Schweitzer's international involvement.

In honor of his eightieth birthday celebration, letters and greetings poured in from around the world. The one that touched him most deeply in its tenderness and affection was from Albert Einstein. Einstein wrote on January 14, 1955:

I have scarcely ever known personally a single individual in whom goodness and the need for beauty are merged to such a degree of unity as in the case of Albert Schweitzer. This is especially gratifying in somebody who is blessed with robust health; he loves to dig in with his arms and hands to achieve the end to which his nature impels him. This robust health which demands immediate action has saved him from becoming, through his moral sensitivity, a victim of gloomy pessimism. He could thus preserve his joyous nature in spite of all the disappointments which our time brings to every sensitive individual.

He loves beauty not only in art proper, but also in purely intellectual fields, without being impressed by sophistry. A never disconcerted instinct preserves in him in everything a vital presence and directness.

Everywhere he avoided rigid tradition. He fights against it anywhere it is in any way hopeful for the individual. One can feel it clearly when, in his classical works on Bach he discloses the dross and mannerisms with which the professionals have obscured the creations of the beloved master and injured their simple straightforward effect.

It seems to me that the work in Lambaréné has been in no small part a flight from the tradition of our cultural circle, petrified and lifeless in a moral sense, a calamity which the simple individual faces as good as powerless.

He did not preach and did not warn and did not dream that his example would be an ideal and a comfort to innumerable people. He simply acted out of inner necessity.

There thus still lies hidden, everywhere in many people, an indestructably good core. Otherwise they would not have recognized him and his simple greatness.[10]

In his reply to Einstein, Dr. Schweitzer touched upon their mutual concern for peace and especially their advocacy of ceasing all atomic testing. Schweitzer wrote on February 20, 1955:

About the question of new tests with the most modern Atomic Bomb, I cannot understand that the U.N. cannot make up its mind to bring the matter to a discussion. I am getting letters asking that you and I and some others should raise our voices to demand such an action of the U.N. But we have raised our voices enough. We cannot dictate anything to the U.N. It is an autonomous body and has to find in itself the incentive and feeling of responsibility to try to prevent a threatening disaster. From the distance I cannot judge what prevents them to rise to the occasion. And if the attempt proved fruitless it would at least have been undertaken and it would have revealed where the opposition is.

I spent some time in Europe during the second part of 1954. My principle task was to work out the speech for Oslo on the problem of peace. As I had therefore to occupy myself with the history of the thought for peace, I made the to me surprising discovery that Kant in his writing "Towards Eternal Peace" is concerned only about the legal side of the problem and not with its ethical side. The ethical side stands in the foreground by Erasmus of Rotterdam. The more one occupies oneself with Erasmus, the more one likes him in spite of his faults. He certainly is one of the most important champions for culture which is built on the humanitarian idea.[11]

This letter was the last Schweitzer wrote to Albert Einstein. The physicist died on April 18, 1955. In response to his passing, Schweitzer wrote a personal note of condolence to Einstein's niece:

June 18, 1955

Dear Miss Einstein,

The death of your honored uncle has moved me deeply. We got to know each other at a time in Berlin and felt right away drawn to each other. At first it was difficult for me to overcome the shyness which the great physicist inspired. Later on we met at Oxford. We did not get together very often. Also, we did not write to each other frequently. But we both knew that we understood each other and that we had the same ideals. We took part, from a distance in each other's life. There existed an inner bond between us. We always knew of each other and we heard from each other through other people. I was deeply moved that your uncle had, in writing and in speaking, mentioned me so kindly and that he stressed the similarity of our lives and our conception of the world . . .

It is noteworthy that in the memoria which have been dedicated to him there was mentioned not only the great scholar, but the man and his humanity. He had obviously also as a man his significance in our time, as a representative of a deep humanitarian culture, in a time when it is most important to preserve this ideal for mankind.

I consider the friendship with your uncle one of the most beautiful things in my life.

With best thoughts,
Your devoted Albert Schweitzer

Recalling some of Einstein's thoughts, it can be seen that Schweitzer had been correct in assessing the similarity of ideas that bound the two men together. A frequently quoted passage of Einstein's reflects their common denominators. Einstein wrote:

"Strange is our situation here upon earth. Each of us comes for a short visit, not knowing why, yet sometimes seeming to divine a purpose. From the standpoint of daily life, however, there is one thing we do know: that man is here for the sake of other men . . . for the countless unknown souls with whose fate we are connected by a bond of sympathy. Many times a day I realize how much my own outer and inner life is built upon the labors of my fellow men, both living and dead, and how earnestly I must exert myself in order to give in return as much as I have received and am still receiving."[12]

Death and sorrow began to haunt Schweitzer. He was losing those he loved. Helene came to Africa in the fall of 1956 with him and stayed until March 1957. Weak, sickly, and enervated, the years of illness had taken their toll as she approached her eightieth year. Returning to Switzerland, she died quietly on May 30, 1957. A few weeks later Dr. Schweitzer

arrived there by boat. At the end of the year he carried
Helene's ashes back for burial outside his window at the
Lambaréné hospital—the place for which she had made so
many sacrifices during her lifetime. He then returned to
Europe the following year to close the Black Forest residence
and move their belongings to the Günsbach house. On this
trip, in 1958, he received the Sonning Prize of 10,000 Danish
crowns and the Joseph-Lemaire Prize. He returned late in the
year to Lambaréné, having said his farewell to Europe. The
world did not know that this was to be his final visit to his
native continent. After closing the house at Königsfeld, Black
Forest, the old doctor visited Alsace, and went up from
Günsbach to Kaysersberg on a sentimental journey into his
past, recalling, "Here I was born. Now I came down into the
valley to a small mountain lake. How often we walked here
with my mother after the four-hour journey from Günsbach,
to sit here with her. When she came down from the high
mountains around the end of the valley, she would say, 'Here,
children, I am completely at home. Here among the rocks,
among the woods. I came here as a child. Let me breathe the
fragrance of the fir tree . . . Do not speak. After I am no
longer on the earth, come here and think of me.' I do think of
you, Mother. I love as you did this refuge from the world, this
niche.

"Now I have left the mountains and the castles and the
woods. I stand before the church and see the swallows once
more. The swallows are gathering for the journey south. We
will set out together. But a time will come when I will not
see you when you gather for this journey, and you will set out
for the south without me, for I will have gone on a longer
journey from one world to another. Hurry with your going,
so that cold and death from starvation do not surprise you
here! Farewell until we meet in Africa under the southern
sky."[13]

Dr. Schweitzer had by this time in his life become a favorite
subject for sculptors, and many busts of his features had been
fashioned by different artists. The cast of his neck, chin and

forehead, along with his strong, lined facial features and the unruly mop of his hair and shaggy mustache were attractive to artists. The American sculptor Louis Meyer went to Günsbach with the hope of sculpting Dr. Schweitzer's strong hands. He arrived at Schweitzer's home late one day, only to be turned away by Mme. Emmy and others there, faithful guardians of his privacy, who, in keeping him from strangers, often overprotected him. He was always anxious to meet those who came to see him. They explained politely but firmly that Dr. Schweitzer had already seen forty people that day, and that his strength had been overtaxed. Unhappily, Louis Meyer wandered through the city, and eventually coming upon the village church, with its door open, went in and sat down. A few minutes later, Dr. Schweitzer entered to practice at the organ, and seeing the dejected stranger sitting there brooding, sat down beside him and inquired what was troubling him. Distressed at his story, Dr. Schweitzer insisted that Mr. Meyer should come and stay at his home.

Later when the sculptured hands were exhibited, an admirer of them wrote to Louis Meyer, and a correspondence ensued which resulted eventually in their meeting and falling in love. They wished to be married by Dr. Schweitzer and he was able to meet them at a small chapel on the Rhine where the ceremony was performed.[14] Although twenty-six years older than his bride, the octogenarian Meyer was thus happily married through this odd, chance association with Dr. Schweitzer.

In 1955, Schweitzer had memorable meetings with Bertrand Russell about an issue consuming the passion of them both: opposition to nuclear warfare and the testing of nuclear weapons. Neither man issued a statement about their discussions, but each constantly expressed the highest regard for the other on every possible occasion afterward. Later, when a London newspaper criticized Schweitzer, Bertrand Russell came to his defense. Pablo Casals also was a very old friend, and the two men met in 1948 at a concert in Zürich. The visit after the concert by the famed cellist cemented a friendship they had built through frequent correspondence.[15] In the 1960s Casals confided to close friends in Puerto Rico that he had two regrets: one was his inability to visit Spain, his homeland, again, and the other was his inability to see and talk with Albert Schweitzer. Louis Cueto Coll thought he might be able to arrange such a meeting, and wrote to Schweitzer. Confessing his own desires to meet again also, Dr. Schweitzer pointed out that it was no longer possible for him to return to Europe, and that the climate of Lambaréné would undoubtedly be too severe for a man of Casals' age. Thus, the meeting never occurred.

Schweitzer once recalled the time that he had chided Casals, the militant and outspoken social idealist, for his strong controversial public utterances. Schweitzer had told Casals that it was better to create than to protest. "No," replied Casals, "there are times when the only creative thing we can do is to protest; we must refuse to accept or acknowledge what is evil or wicked." Later, after Schweitzer had joined the struggle against nuclear warfare and testing, Casals recalling the conversation, added, "I am glad my old friend is protesting too against nuclear weapon tests."[16]

Schweitzer's friendships with the intellectual and aesthetic leadership of the world continued to expand during his later years. The noted Greek writer, Nikos Kazantzakis, had been profoundly impressed by the writings of Schweitzer and had proposed him as a nominee for the Nobel Prize in Literature on a number of occasions, (which incidentally was never awarded to Schweitzer). In 1957, Kazantzakis visited Hong Kong, and was given a smallpox inoculation from which complications developed, as he flew by the polar route at high altitudes from Tokyo to Copenhagen. Intense air pressure apparently forced the vaccination to puncture and a fatal infection set in. After hospitalization in Copenhagen, he was advised to go to the University Clinic at Freiburg. Rhena Eckert-Schweitzer met him there and offered assistance. Schweitzer, in nearby Strasbourg for a lecture, came to visit his old friend at the clinic on several occasions. Kinion Friar, the translator and biographer of Kazantzakis wrote, "He was unable to resist the subsequent ravages of influenza (actually, septicemia), and died at 10:20 on the evening of October 26. His last days had been made happy by the visits of the man he most admired in the living world, Albert Schweitzer."[17]

After the war, Dr. Schweitzer heard from Martin Buber, the eminent Hebrew scholar and Israeli settler, who like Schweitzer recognized he was a European refugee. The two men therefore had something additional in common besides their mutual interests in the course of world civilization and the philosophy of religion. Both were existential thinkers, and both were world citizens. A long correspondence over many years followed. After the death of both within a relatively brief time, Rhena granted permission to the Buber estate to reprint the correspondence of these two men.

It has often been said that Schweitzer was not a sentimental man, and that statement is true. Yet he was a very humane, companionable person who responded sensitively to others, and reached out to them in many ways. In his later years, his closest friend outside of Alsace and Lambaréné, was probably Erica Anderson, who became his photographer, but more than that, an interpreter of his work and confidante. For many years it became part of the pattern of Schweitzer's life that every Friday afternoon he would write to Erica. In addition, Dr. Schweitzer for many years had made private notes for his use only in small blue notebooks. These contained random thoughts and subjective reactions, not meant for public gaze any more than his letters to Erica. From these notebooks alone, there are aspects of Schweitzer's life not yet revealed to the world at large.

In addition, he completed or worked on manuscripts which were never published in his life. These he kept in linen bags along with his old Strasbourg sermons. Some have now been published in Europe, and one in the United States by Harper & Row, called *Reverence for Life*. He had completed the biblical portions of a volume he called *The Kingdom of God*.

246 SCHWEITZER

This volume dealt with the ancient Hebrew's concept of and quest for the Heavenly Kingdom on earth. Schweitzer did not intend to end with the chapters he wrote, dealing with the Old Testament prophets, and Jesus and Paul. He had quite complete notes for a continuation of his study into the Roman Empire of the post-Gospel era, and fragmented notes on its application to later eras.

Schweitzer was greatly concerned with the quest for a "Good Society," which he found first formulated in the biblical concept of the Kingdom of God. At Lambaréné he never had the time, research facilities, or energy to complete his study. Under the able and astute editorial guidance of the Swiss theologian, Ulrich Neuenschwander, the completed portion has been published in Europe, was translated into English by the A. & C. Black Company in England, and appears in America as a Seabury title. However, the editorial decision to stop short of including the postbiblical notes, which were not completed, may preclude public study of a most important aspect of Schweitzer's thought on a Good Society with which he wrestled in his final years. The extensive notes of the relevant Gifford Lectures, also never published, are in his daughter's hands. In addition, the manuscript for his volume, *Chinese Thought and Its Development*, remain unpublished. Schweitzer's concern with all Asian thought has already been alluded to, and he was conscious that Chinese thought and its development were as important as the material in his study of *Indian Thought and Its Development*.

Schweitzer, as noted, lost many close friends through death in his final years. Yet in his theological and philosophical writings, Schweitzer seldom referred to concerns about God or immortality. One searches his works in vain for such reflections, but his humanity surpassed his theology, and it was with humanism in life that he was ultimately involved. Nonetheless, he told Erica Anderson, "You see, when I go to Europe, my first duty is to those I don't find any more. Gradually, there are more of those graves I visit than those I still find. Gradually, gradually, there are fewer and fewer of those who shared my youth with me." But he added to her, "It always seems to me, when I visit their graves, that they know it." This is the sentimentality of a man whom his closest friends often called unsentimental. Still, he never sought to justify a concept of immortality objectively in his theological writings. Only as an elderly, frail person, thinking about and missing old friends, did his longing for communication with those who had passed away emerge. And he felt they were still with him as long as he thought of them.[18]

The main building of the Leper Village, built with the money won from the Nobel Peace prize, housing its clinic and pharmacy, was named the Greta Langerfelt House in memory of the baroness, another good friend, who died on February 27, 1953. In his last letter to her, Schweitzer had spoken of the progress made in clearing the site and the beginnings of the buildings. She responded enthusiastically and suggested the money just raised in Sweden for the hospital should be used for this village. Dr. Schweitzer never forgot her kindness, encouragement and friendship during those dreary days of 1920, when he suffered his great depression and was rescued from it while in Sweden.[19]

Another whose kindness he never forgot until the day he died was, again, Erica Anderson. She had first come to Lambaréné in the spring of 1951, and had returned to the hospital approximately two dozen times. Already an established photographer, her motion picture on Grandma Moses was widely acclaimed and won honors as a documentary at the Cannes Festival. Her two films made in Schweitzer's final years tell the story of the hospital and the philosophy behind it more vividly than any other accounts in any medium. Her books of photographs and comments interpreted his message and life for many. But above and beyond her contribution as an interpreter, were her personal contributions to the life of Lambaréné and to the doctor himself. She worked while there: writing hundreds of letters, serving as a greeter and hostess, running errands, working in the dining room, acting as interpreter, and joining construction gangs.

She made possible his final trips to Europe, by working out itineraries, adjusting schedules, writing ahead for the necessary accommodations. In the 1950s, Schweitzer was too well known in Europe to be able to travel by public transportation, he had no private transportation, and would not fly. Erica, who was by birth an Austrian, knew Europe, possessed a car, and drove him wherever it was necessary to go. Back in the United States she established the Albert Schweitzer Friendship House in Great Barrington, Massachusetts, for the interpretation of Schweitzer's life and philosophy. Here, in the Berkshire Mountains, so much like those of Alsace, students may come to discuss, study and consider the many-faceted contributions of Albert Schweitzer.

Thus, Schweitzer saw his friends come and go. And he was well aware that his own life was moving on.

The Modern Schweitzer Hospital

The Schweitzer Hospital that developed after the war, was really Schweitzer's third hospital. True, there had been a continuity, and it would be difficult to date the time of change or growth except for the actual move to a new site. Dr. Schweitzer had established the original hospital at the Protestant Mission of Lambaréné (Andende) in 1913. In 1927 he had removed it two miles upstream to establish the independent Schweitzer-Bresslau Hospital. This larger, well-staffed hospital continued into the period of the Second World War. By the end of that war, the hospital's staff had become depleted. However, with a new impetus from the attention and aid given the hospital by medical, educational and philanthropic agencies, a new phase of the hospital's growth had begun. Dr. Schweitzer, now well along in years had become more of an administrator than a practicing physician. He was also now able to be selective in choosing his staff; he was no longer forced to rely solely on friends from Alsace and Switzerland. A steady influx of skilled people applied for the opportunity to serve with him in Africa. He had to screen candidates, evaluate their potential and check references and experience for physicians, surgeons or nurses. The Schweitzer Hospital had grown from a provincial institution to a major medical center.

With new opportunities for applicants came new responsibilities and requirements. Gone were the days of the one-man operation at Lambaréné. The hospital had evolved, as an institution, into one that was more than what Emerson would have called "the lengthened shadow of a great man." And as Dr. Schweitzer moved through his seventies and eighties up to his ninetieth year, the hospital continued to grow and render its free services, under his watchful eye and with its enlarged staff.

Now, in the 1950s at Lambaréné, there was a competent medical group which held regular staff meetings, voting on matters of general policy which were then cleared with Dr. Schweitzer. His chief of staff from 1959 to 1964, Rolf Müller, was an able, intelligent and energetic surgeon. Virtually every doctor and specialist who had gone to Lambaréné to work has paid tribute to the high quality of his leadership. He and his colleagues did confer, and, on occasion, would defer to Dr. Schweitzer's judgment. In any hospital the medical staff must always deal with an administrator, according to well-defined rules. Schweitzer's legendary memory and his encyclopedic knowledge made him an extremely valuable consultant for any case out of the ordinary that the general staff confronted. The untold thousands of Africans he had treated under so many different kinds of conditions, and the many thousands of successful operations he had performed, gave staff doctors every assurance that his knowledge was invaluable. Accordingly, though no longer taking his turn in surgery or in the pharmacy, Schweitzer, even at ninety, was a participant in an outstanding team of physicians and surgeons.

In addition to his consulting of the medical staff, Schweitzer administered a sprawling hospital of over seventy-five buildings, serving seven hundred patients a day, which with family attendants required nine tons of food weekly. To keep an operation of this size functioning efficiently required all of Schweitzer's amazing energy, foresight and executive ability.

"The very large number of people served daily at this hospital indicated it cannot be closed, even with my own death," the doctor said. While there is a government hospital also operating in the area now—on the island—it is clear that it could not handle one-sixth of the patients cared for by the Schweitzer Hospital. Accordingly, Dr. Schweitzer continued to build for the future. "I want to have the buildings in good condition, so that in the first two years after I am gone, the question of the physical plant will not create problems for those who will be the administrators," he explained. As he had throughout his life, Schweitzer continued to look ahead.

The Schweitzer Hospital had grown from simple beginnings in a fowl house served by a single doctor and his nurse-wife, assisted by a native orderly. Gradually buildings, a new site, nurses and other staff including a team of physicians had come into being. It had begun in the days when the medicine of the white man was a mystery, and there had been real competition for Schweitzer with fetishmen and witch doctors. It had struggled with taboos and tribal customs, and out of this vast agglomeration there evolved a hospital uniquely fitting the African situation. It clearly retained seeming cultural anachronisms in the course of its growth, but at the same time they made sense in a culture of people who still lived in transition, the commingling of the old and new were part of Africa's life.

Many persons without an educational background in African culture and development, flying into Lambaréné and by-passing the culture out of which the hospital grew, may not understand the reasons for individual hibachi fireplace cooking, for example. It seems inefficient, but it was necessary to overcome the natives' fear of poisoned food. The need for family attendants and tribal quarters in the rural portion of a country still controlled by tribal patterns of thought, also may not be understood. They too were necessary if the African was to feel at home at the hospital and accept it.

In consequence, the Schweitzer Hospital is unlike any other in the United States or in Europe. Growing out of the flexible working philosophy of Dr. Schweitzer as he blended his knowledge of medical needs with the culture of the African, it is also unique among African hospitals. It is unlike a hospital created on paper by doctors, architects and medical societies, invited to establish a new modern hospital facility. The justification of the unique Schweitzer Hospital is that, plain and simply, it has worked. This has been proven by the large number of patients who prefer its rustic setting and informality to the more formal hospitals recently erected in the area. Sick people, facing personal insecurities and uncertainties, need the comfortable familiarity of a hospital that relates to their own background. This the Schweitzer Hospital in Africa provided.

Many who have visited the hospital have described it as a village for healing, a jungle clinic, a health camp, or an African medical center. Some say the name "hospital" is a misnomer as it does not meet the requirements of a modern metropolitan facility. Dr. Richard Friedmann, a long-time physician on the hospital staff, pointed out, "We don't practice here as they do at Mt. Sinai Hospital. But New York methods will not work here just as our methods are not practical there." As in any other reputable hospital, as Dr. Rolf Müller, formerly chief of staff, pointed out, "Money goes first for modern medicine and equipment." For this reason, a façade of modern construction is not found at the hospital. This condition amazes some visitors, in part, because the Schweitzer Hospital is probably the world's most famous hospital.[1] People expect it to be typical of the other great, but metropolitan, hospitals. Its very uniqueness, however, has much to do with its fame: i.e., the third Schweitzer Hospital can only be understood in terms of its cultural setting. (With Dr. Schweitzer's death in September 1965, a fourth hospital has come into existence. The new Albert Schweitzer Hospital, continuing Schweitzer's own legal provisions to carry on his work, with his daughter and a trusted doctor in charge, will be based on the legacy he created in more than half a century.)

The Schweitzer Hospital, still standing on the rising point of Adolinanongo, "Looking out over the Peoples," home of the legendary Sun King, N'Kombe, spreads out over a wide area. The hill has many tall trees—palm, orange, breadfruit, kapok, mango and banana. Grapefruit and pineapple grow abundantly as well as a rich variety of other fruits, vegetables and flowers. The area's tangled and dense underbrush is still a constant enemy advancing against buildings and paths.

Spread throughout the wide area covered by the hospital grounds lie seventy-five buildings in several well-defined areas. The central buildings stand on the slope rising up from the landing on the river where all goods are unloaded, and where most patients disembark. They include the long low building in which Dr. Schweitzer had and several senior staff members have their rooms which open onto a long veranda running the length of the building. The laundry and the post office are also located in this building.

Across the way in the central hospital compound lies the hospital kitchen, and beyond that is the central dining room for the staff. Behind it are the new buildings for the nurses, female patients and visitors, and various storerooms and worksheds. Downstream lie the buildings where the doctors and European patients are housed, and below them is the surgery and the pharmacy with consultation rooms. The tribal wards are separate buildings farther down the river, and there are also some located above the surgery area. Continuing upward in that direction from the central compound, there is a footpath which goes past several small villages of thatched huts to the Protestant Mission where the hospital originated. Along that path, after a short distance, is the Leper Village. Dr. Schweitzer built a road connecting the hospital area with the new Trans-Gabon Highway, and he bought a truck in 1959, and shortly thereafter, a jeep to travel it.

Up the road between the compound area and the Leper Village, there is an old cemetery under ancient trees now covered by a thick overgrowth. This is not the hospital cemetery with crude wooden crosses for the dead, but a Moslem memorial area on which ancient stones stand sentinel. On some, there is the familiar crescent of the Moslem, and the eroded lettering of the inscriptions appears to be Arabic when it can be read at all. Dr. Schweitzer believed that in this cemetery there were some original graves of victims of a smallpox or yellow-fever epidemic that occurred over a century ago. His theory was that a Moslem trading caravan was passing through this stricken area, and that the epidemic took its toll

among the caravan. Most of the graves, however, marked recent Moslem burials because the Gabonese would not allow
public burial of Moslems on Lambaréné Island where their
colony was. Schweitzer therefore permitted them to bury their
dead at the hospital.

Such a Moslem cemetery at the Schweitzer Hospital is a
reminder that the Islamic presence in Gabon is older than the
Christian. The first major caravan traders, as well as the bearers of outside culture to the Africans, were Moslems from
north of the Sahara. Since medieval times they had traveled
tropical Africa not only as traders and bankers, scribes and
learned men, but as priests and proselytizers of their mono-
theistic, highly ethical religion.

Along with these Moslem stones in the cemetery, there is
one with a cross on it which stands apart. It too has a story
connected with it. Nearly half a century ago, Dr. Schweitzer
met an old derelict on the wharves of Port Gentil, who told
tales of Count de Brazza; he was identified by others as the
one-time cook of the famed explorer. Now crippled, blind and
penniless, he touched Dr. Schweitzer as he thought of the
former glamor and drama of this man's life and the wretched-
ness of his present condition. Schweitzer took the old cook
back to Lambaréné, where he lived out his final days in peace.
In this ancient cemetery which had endured the passing of
generations and the changing of cultures, Dr. Schweitzer buried the old man, and erected the cross, identifying him as the
cook to Count de Brazza, the man who had helped open up
the Ogowe basin.

Another link of the hospital's with the past, unmarked by
a burial stone, is the memory of Robert Hamil Nassau, M.D.,
S.T.D., the dedicated founder of Presbyterian missions on the
upper Ogowe River. He was an explorer who had attended
West Point with the hope that the government would com-
mission him to head an exploration party to chart and map
equatorial Africa. He was disappointed when such a policy
was not accepted. Therefore, he turned to preparations to go
to Africa as a missionary, becoming a physician as well. The

climactic years of his life were spent in the Lambaréné area and the mission stations remained his memorial. Dr. Schweitzer liked to tell Americans the story of his inspired life.[2]

Four permanent staff members in these final years were Drs. Rolf Müller and Richard Friedmann, the Swiss physician, Dr. Walter Munz of Arbon who became the first chief of staff following Schweitzer's death, and the American physician, Dr. Fergus Pope.

The Schweitzer Hospital remains an unusual institution. In Africa, as elsewhere, civilization has become more centralized, highly organized and as a result, more depersonalized. But Schweitzer and his hospital continued to offer familiar native comforts and a home to people he frequently described as bearing "the mark of pain." He created this spirit and atmosphere, and it prevails today.

Not only patients and their families, but visiting doctors as well, bear witness to the value of the hospital. One American physician's reaction is that of Dana L. Farnsworth, M.D., the Director of Health Services at Harvard University. He wrote:

All over the world people in "underdeveloped countries" are struggling for a better way of life. Specialists in public health are concerned with the eradication of preventable diseases as well as with the more immediate forms of relief from pain and suffering. It is in the attempted solution of these hundreds of other similar problems that confront us from day to day that Dr. Schweitzer's life pattern has become significant to practitioners of medicine. The medical profession may have erred in paying too little attention to the social and cultural factors involved in any program designed to raise the level of health in a given community. And, finally, physicians have tended to think more in terms of disease and pathology than in those of health and the social customs that tend to impair the effectiveness and happiness of people. Whatever may be one's view on such controversial matters, Dr. Schweitzer's practice of taking into consideration the needs and wishes of the natives in the area surrounding his hospital at Lambaréné is of great relevance. He has not tried to remold their habits and cus-

toms according to European concepts. Instead, he has tried to help
them on their own terms.[3]

Dr. Paul Dudley White, Boston heart specialist, and among
the foremost American physicians, is another firm supporter
of the hospital. Dr. White twice visited Schweitzer in Lambaréné and in addition sent a third medical team to help at
the hospital following the death of Dr. Schweitzer. In 1960 he
went with a team of heart specialists to do research on cardio-
vascular disease among the natives. In 1963 he went again,
and when Dr. White returned from Gabon on September 6,
1963, he reported the various innovations that were taking
place at the hospital. He commented that he had challenged
Dr. Schweitzer to do more in the field of preventive medicine.
Dr. White said, "Just plain public-health work such as clearing
the swamps and ridding the region of malaria-infected mos-
quitoes would cut Dr. Schweitzer's work in half." He added
that he would like to do more to interest others in helping out
in the Lambaréné area, ".which probably has more disease
than anywhere else in the world. The hospital is very overcrowded and patients come regularly and so fast it is difficult
to count them, and 'just dump themselves on the hospital,' "
Dr. White explained. He added that, in his opinion, "The
Schweitzer Hospital has a better staff than other hospitals
in Africa," and paid particular tribute to the white registered
nurses and medical staff. He noted, however, that the staff
was not able, understandably, to endure the climate for long,
and thus experienced a large turnover.

On medical matters, Dr. White reported that he found the
same high incidence of high blood pressure in Gabon that he
had previously found among American Negroes. "There is no
coronary disease, however, in Gabon, but as their society becomes more prosperous, coronaries will also prosper as they
have in this country. There must be a happy mean between
our overnutrition and soft life, and their malnutrition and
hard life," he said.

Dr. White recommended that specialists and international
agencies, including more American foundations, should move

in to undertake the larger research and public-health projects.

"Dr. Schweitzer went there with a mission to help the natives and to do something for the world. What he has done is remarkable. His hospital stands by itself, and should move others to take new forward steps," Dr. White said.

Asked if he considered the Schweitzer Hospital a good one, he replied, "It obviously is. Its record over the years is outstanding."[4]

The hospital's record is indeed outstanding, considered from the statistical side alone. The tag-and-numbering system devised in the earliest years of the hospital, continue to be the basis of recording the entrance of patients. From this record, between 1924 and 1965, the period of Dr. Schweitzer's management, there were 19,872 surgical patients and a total of over 125,000 new patients admitted during these years. Since the system of enumeration used the same tag number for return patients, the total number of patients must have been at least 150,000 during this time, conservatively speaking. The average number of new patients admitted to the hospital each month during Dr. Schweitzer's last year was 423. In that year there were 120 deaths at the hospital, but 406 births, and over 2000 births recorded between 1936 and 1965.[5]

While Dr. Schweitzer clearly was helped during most of his administration by other surgeons, physicians and nurses, this successful record was due in great part to his management of the hospital and his personal magnetism with which he attracted both donors and patients.

The Leper Village is the best example of specialization at the Schweitzer Hospital. It was a village set apart, built completely with the funds awarded from the Nobel Peace prize. The Leper Village accommodated two hundred patients. At the time of Schweitzer's death, it housed one hundred and sixty adults and twenty children. Throughout the 1960s until his death, the doctor in charge of the Leper Village was the Japanese physician, Dr. Isao Takahashi.[6] With the help of his European and African nurses, he carried on a remarkably successful program.

The Japanese doctor, a charming, energetic and able leader, explained his role by saying to American visitors, "I am chief palaver judge as well as physician and foreman of the cleaning-up details. Your American drugs now cure leprosy," Dr. Takahashi would say, "but the African does not understand he is cured. He recalls the long history of retarded cases that broke out at a later time, and infected others. Accordingly, African superstition says a leper is accursed, and one who deals with him will be cursed. Therefore, even after cure, many lepers must stay here because they will not be accepted back in the villages. Dr. Schweitzer wants us to make clear that they will always have a home here, and even if they go out, they can return at any time they need to."

Looking at the lepers, who live here in peace if with resignation, one cannot help but recognize the psychological value of Schweitzer's program which provided a home, with dignity and freedom, for these unfortunates. An even greater blessing is the fact that the miracle of science could help them. But, in the end, it was the love and compassion of the old doctor who wished to make a home for these once neglected folk that brought them ease and comfort.

Progress of all kinds did continue at Lambaréné. In addition to the other units already noted, the other facilities deserve mention. There is a section of the hospital grounds area set aside as a place for the elderly to live. Second, there is a new building, set aside in 1969, for Biafran children, refugees of the recent Nigerian war. Five years after Schweitzer's death, the hospital continues to grow and expand its services to meet new needs—a pattern of development very much in keeping with the doctor's own vision of his hospital.

As in his life, the hospital continues to represent Schweitzer's ethics of Reverence for Life in action. The evolution of the hospital was in this direction. Beginning with the thought of reparations for the wrong done the black man, Schweitzer moved on to see the hospital as the means by which he could carry on the practice and make a demonstration of Reverence for Life. On this basis alone can the accomplishments and complexity of Lambaréné be judged.

21

The Man Within

The chronological order of most of Albert Schweitzer's activities and the details of most of his life and accomplishments have now been sketched. The accounts of his deeds could be enlarged. His works continue to be read and studied, quoted and paraphrased: what emerges is a portrait of one of the most widely respected men of our time. Yet something more is needed to understand Schweitzer: an effort to find the man within, to discover the deep personal ideals and philosophy which motivated him.

Schweitzer in his lifetime opposed this attempt. "My life is my argument," he would say so frequently. Dr. A. A. Roback once told George Marshall that he was sure Dr. Schweitzer would not like his letters quoted. Staff members always urged correspondents not to publish his letters. Thus his friends always held quotations from his letters to a minimum. As have his biographers. But their restraint up to now has impeded the clearest possible presentation of Schweitzer's thought and reactions, for it is personal correspondence that most often reveals the unconscious or subconscious thoughts of a man. Dr. Schweitzer, in requesting minimal exposure of his correspondence, has thus unwittingly forced upon the public an image of himself as a somewhat austere, aloof—almost cold— personality. Through his letters, however, he emerges as a warm and sensitive man, a generally decisive yet sometimes hesitant thinker, cautiously finding his way through life.

Long ago he wrote:

To this fact, that we are each a secret to the other, we have to reconcile ourselves. To know one another cannot mean to know everything about each other; . . . A man must not try to force his way into a personality of another. To analyze another . . . is a rude commencement, for there is a modesty of the soul which we must recognize, just as we do that of the body. The soul too has its clothing of which we must not deprive it, and no one has a right to say to another: "Because we belong to each other as we do, I have a right to know your thoughts." Not even a mother may treat her child in that way.[1]

Yet there is nonetheless a need to come to grips with the mind of a man of the magnitude of Schweitzer, to probe and observe it from the time of his first decisions to that of his major, ultimate one, his renunciation of Europe.

Albert Schweitzer, the individualist, the religious liberal, the man who stood by himself, thus offered no direct encouragement to others to reach his mind, except through his writings and through his external life itself which revealed the application and depth of his thought. He was, in fact, as the words above imply, a lonely man—surrounded by people, and yet estranged from much of life. In his ninetieth year, a women's magazine carried a full-page quotation of Dr. Schweitzer including the phrase, "I am a king in friendship but a pauper in time." This was in great part true; he was a busy man. But, in addition, it must be added that there were few people with whom he was fully at ease.

The reticence of Schweitzer about his innermost self, then, is a challenge to the person who wishes to understand him. One can strip away the outer layers of an onion and find, as Peer Gynt did in Ibsen's play, that there is nothing remaining at the center, or one can find a solid core at the end of such a process; so with people. The process itself is difficult to manage without totally denuding a man's soul. The greatest truth may well be that a man's strengths and weaknesses, his innermost dreams and deepest frustrations, are known only to himself, and can never be fully comprehended by others. Of Schweitzer, while this must be true, as it is of all men, one can nonetheless observe his mind through its many windows that he himself opened, and thus at least catch glimpses of his true, deepest nature, that of a brilliant human being who contributed in so many ways to modern culture. Henry Clark, the author of *Ethical Mysticism of Schweitzer*, wrote that as a student he met Schweitzer in Oslo, and asked at which school and under what professors he should study "to get the best possible education in your thought." Clark wrote that Schweitzer responded, "Read my books! No one can express the ideas of a man so well as he has expressed himself in his writings!"[2]

In his autobiographical memoirs, it is true that Schweitzer provided some measure of information about his thoughts and accomplishments. But such discussions are few and scattered among his many works. The reader of them can only roughly estimate the emotional aspects of his experiences. It is for this reason that it is absolutely necessary to reveal the man behind the intellectual accounts, the human being who emerges in letters, personal relationships and artistic expression.

Schweitzer has often been compared to Bach, whom Schweitzer identified in the title of his masterful study as "the poet-musician." Certainly there is this dual quality about Schweitzer himself. He was a well-balanced man of aesthetic taste and accomplishment, a sophisticate who responded to the smallest emotional overtones and nuances of life. Thus, Schweitzer must first perhaps be comprehended as a deeply emotional person as well as an intellectual. He himself indicated that his greatest personal identification was always with Goethe. This statement offers at least one key to his mind. He wrote, "Goethe is the personality with which I have been most deeply concerned . . . What attracts me in him is that he is a man of action at the same time that he is a poet, a thinker, and in certain domains a savant and a man of research. And what binds us together in the deepest depths of our being is his philosophy of nature."[3]

Robert Haney, when senior tutor of Adams House, Harvard University said in an address on the occasion of Schweitzer's ninetieth birthday before the Friends of Albert Schweitzer in Boston:

The connections between the two men are strikingly close. They share much the same temperament, the same ideals, and, often, the same frustrations. The writings of Goethe have profoundly influenced Schweitzer. The ideas that concerned the sage of Weimar throughout his life and that even recur in his works find in Schweitzer a sympathetic friend. Schweitzer's life and thought may be profitably interpreted as a counterpoint to Goethe's themes, a melody of indescribable beauty in itself, but owing its pattern to an earlier time. We can never know how much Schweitzer owes to Goethe's works; Schweitzer himself does not know. But if we attend to the harmonies that exist between the very real doctor of Lambaréné and Goethe's semi-autobiographical characters in *Wilhelm Meister* and *Faust*, we shall begin to glimpse how much Goethe has meant to Schweitzer as teacher, exemplar, comforter and mirror.[4]

But the above statement illustrates some of the important influences upon the introspective, pensive mind of Albert Schweitzer.

No one has yet fully explored the depths of what can in all honesty be called his tortured soul. Some have seen him simply as lonely. Others have observed his pessimism. In the *Epilogue* to his autobiographical account, and in passages appearing in his *Philosophy of Civilization, Indian Thought and Its Development, Memoirs of Childhood and Youth* and his Goethe lectures, the theme of despondency, estrangement and pessimism do indeed stand out. Candidly and clearly these attitudes are revealed: "Two perceptions cast their shadow over my existence. One consists in the realization that the world is inexplicably mysterious and full of suffering; the other is the fact that I have been born into a period of spiritual decadence for mankind."[5] In the *Epilogue*, he continued, "With the spirit of the age I am in complete disagreement." Here, in reading his serious, personal philosophical reflections, one is touched by the deep anguish with which he reacted to life. One discovers a truly tortured person, unable to come to terms with what seemed to him to be the definite, gradual decline of culture, humanity and civilization as a whole.

The particular existentialism of his cousin, Jean-Paul Sartre, offered no answer for him. He noted that modern schools of thought arose which created doubts "as to whether thinking (i.e., rationalism) would ever be capable of answering current questions about the world and our relation to it in such a way that we could give a meaning and a content to our lives." Once, George Marshall offered him the book *Existentialism and Religious Liberalism* to read. Schweitzer found humorous the thought of calling Sartre a "religious man." He explained, "He calls me Uncle Albert, and we are related through our fathers; we have corresponded for years; and when he was a little youngster I used to dandle him on my knee, but he is not a religious thinker. Camus is, but not Sartre. To him it is also a world of despair, but there is a difference between him and me. In my own life I find a purpose; he knows none in a religious sense."[6]

Yet, as can be seen from this statement, Schweitzer was not anti-existential. The thought of Camus appealed to him, "after all we are both Africans as well as Frenchmen," he once said. Like Camus, Schweitzer was a critic of modern civilization, who saw its shortcomings, but in the end his response was intellectual, rational, rather than either theological or existential.

He had come to feel "that the catastrophe of civilization started with the catastrophe of a world-view,"[7] and thus turned his attention to this issue. In doing so, he was led in time to reject the very bases of the Christian religion as well as those of the philosophical systems of Europe. Consequently, he began early to speak for himself, rather than to identify with the mainstream of current ethical and religious thought. He rejected and denied much that was taught, indeed what most others were being taught. He was thus tortured mentally by the knowledge that in his philosophical and spiritual attitudes, he stood alone. He found the needed community with others only through the type of humanitarian service he rendered. His reason for going to Africa was, therefore, more than an act of humanistic witness; it was a personal necessity.

He found, as an adult, that the belief he had held since childhood in the importance of rational thought was usually given lip service by others, but seldom followed. To him, it seemed civilization was failing precisely because of the absence of clear thinking.[8] And Schweitzer, as a determined intellectual, could not accept this failure lightly. . . . Society needed both library and laboratory.

To him, careful, deep thought provided the essential, necessary means for solving problems and correcting shortcomings or failures. But in the world around him he saw conformity and the lack of individual reflection. He saw people govern their lives, their deliberate actions, and their outlooks by what he felt were irrational, or anti-rational, impulses. Herd man, civilized man, he believed, was coming closer and closer to irrationality in both behavior and thought. It was a relief, therefore, for him to look back on the age of the Enlightenment, or the classical eras, when he felt men were governed by the mind and exalted reason. Schweitzer, who was perhaps the last of the Enlightenment minds, although born over a century later, was true to the principles of reason, naturalism and thought. These elements combined to form not only the bases of his religion but the substance of his culture. The ethical imperative to love he derived from Jesus of Nazareth, but he found the motivations of Stoicism more helpful than that of Christianity. Thus, his was a broadly influenced dissent from modern unexamined civilization, all in an effort to recreate what he felt were the necessary conditions for a rational society and a creative culture.

He was concerned with the great issue of relating man's thought to the life he lives and that same thought to the universe in which he lives. He wrote, "All thinking must renounce the attempt to explain the universe. What is glorious in it is united with what is full of horror. What is full of meaning is united with what is senseless. The spirit of the universe is at once creative and destructive—it creates what it destroys and destroys what it creates, and therefore it remains to us a riddle. And we must inevitably resign ourselves to this." In this renunciation of an affirmative world-view, Schweitzer was now embarked on the most daring new avenue of thought in his time. No Western thinker, he himself said, ever really dared to do this before, with the possible exception of Spinoza. The universe and its order had been accepted by all schools of modern thought right up through the existentialists. Only Spinoza and Schweitzer dissented, and of these two, only Schweitzer offered a comprehensive alternative to the prevailing view. To all the others, the universe had been regarded as benevolent and good; moral and rational; stable and consistent. A universal consistency and an order had been assumed, a good design. Western thought has held over and over that ours is a moral universe, that only man is immoral; that it is a rational world, that only man is nonrational. This has been described, argued and justified in a hundred ways by prominent thinkers. Judaeo-Christianity, science, rationalism, mysticism, democracy and autocracy, art and literature —disciplines and individual schools of thought all have said this.[9]

But this was not true of Albert Schweitzer. Following his own reasoning, he was forced to the logical conclusion that the universe was morally, rationally and objectively neutral. It did not take sides; it was simply there. It remained for man to take sides, to make life meaningful, and consistent. Man both could and must do this. He alone was capable of morality. Schweitzer opened the door through which the existentialists later passed, but unlike many of them, he found the ethic too compelling to allow him to stop without arriving at some meaning or purpose. And meaning and purpose he found in the will to live, in greeting and rejoicing in every aspect of creation. Here was the positive value he found in all forms of life itself. It is doubtful if this simple position could be taken by anyone with less than a universal mind, and a profound grasp of many fields of knowledge. Only a thinker of the stature of Schweitzer was able to convincingly cut his way through the accumulated knowledge of his culture to come to this most basic conclusion from a rational, analytical development of ethics. He had spent countless years wrestling with this great issue. He stood by his conclusions: "I acknowledge my great debt to the Stoics. To my mind it is the greatest formal philosophy in human history. To the extent that I can be identified with any school, I should be proud to be related to the Stoics."[10] He was perhaps one of the first scholars to see that Stoicism led to existentialism.

Schweitzer in his thought drew from the intellectual systems and ideologies of the Eastern world as well as those of the Western world. It is for this reason that the present writers have suggested that along with the two volumes of the *Philosophy of Civilization*, one should also read *Indian Thought and Its Development*, to fully understand Schweitzer's ideas. In this volume, one finds a further amplification of his philosophy, initially developed in the first two volumes of his thought, but which needed aspects of Eastern philosophy to clarify it.

Eastern thought, Schweitzer found, complemented his understanding of the world-view of Western thought. In the East, the world-view of man is relatively passive; indeed one must renounce the world to accept life. However, the Eastern world-view, fails to offer the motivations for accepting life as it is. It moves from passivity to negation, and becomes a life-destructive philosophy rather than a life-affirming philosophy. It is at this point that Schweitzer parted company with the Eastern thought of Hinduism and Buddhism and returned to the Stoics and to Jesus for his ethical imperative. The Eastern systems are world-and-life negating, and became for Schweitzer an ethical dead end. But it was important to him that he end with a negation of the old progress theory (and its naïve optimism) and pursue life affirmation growing out of a rational ethical system, rather than from merely a belief in the supernatural. This he found in his naturalism, which became clarified in the ethical norm of *Reverence for Life*, itself a rational ethic. In following this belief, he made a significant contribution to all philosophical and ethical systems.

Like Schweitzer, Pierre Teilhard de Chardin felt a need to break from the European mainstream of thought that dominated art, drama, and Christianity. He wrote in a letter in 1923:

> . . . I feel, more strongly than ever, the need of freeing our religion from everything about it that is specifically Mediterranean. I do not believe—note well—that the majority of Oriental thought patterns are anything but outmoded and obsolescent, fated to disappear along with the human type to which they are native. But I do say that by taking these forms, decayed though they be, into account, we discover such a wealth of potentialities in philosophy, in mysticism and in the study of human conduct that it becomes scarcely possible to be satisfied with an image of a mankind entirely and definitely enveloped in the narrow network of precepts . . . in which some people think they have displayed the whole amplitude of Christianity.[11]

Schweitzer's dissent in philosophy and ethics tied in rather closely with his dissent against nationalism, colonialism and militarism. It also explains his dissent against the established orthodoxy of Western religions. Thought rather than faith became primary for him. It seriously began for him during the days of his World War I internment, and it was then that he began to ask what was happening to civilization.

He turned not only to the study of Spengler for his lessons, but to Schopenhauer, Nietzsche (and his call for a superman to govern society) and to Kant, the study of whose works had led him to a doctor of philosophy degree years before. He also acknowledged Fichte's influence later. His studies of the Enlightenment, of course, were, in addition, fruitful. However, the concern about life affirmation and world negation he discovered most prominently in the work of Schopenhauer and Nietzsche. Schopenhauer, he found, did not take a pessimistic world-view in the passive manner of the Eastern students, but did, rather, seem to be guilty of moral or intellectual suicide. He did not hold the answer for Schweitzer. He advocated the bliss of Nirvana as providing the will to live, but not a confrontation with real life itself. Nietzsche, on the other hand, although deriving some of his thought from Schopenhauer, ultimately rejected him and his philosophy. Schweitzer concluded that "Nietzsche is at bottom no more unethical than Schopenhauer. He is misled by the ethical element which there is in life affirmation. He gives the status of ethics to life affirmation as such. Thereby he falls into the absurdities which follow from an exclusive affirmation of life, just as Schopenhauer falls into those of an exclusive denial of life."[12]

From this conclusion followed the development of Schweitzer's own thoughts set forth in his writings, in which he sought to avoid the absurdities he found in European philosophy, and to correct the negation and withdrawal he could not accept in the Oriental philosophies. Philosophical inquiry was always viewed by Schweitzer as a means to the pragmatic end of assisting mankind in finding its place and role in the universe, to help it create the good life. It was the hope of achieving these goals, which transcended, even through dissenting thought, his pessimism. He wrote in *The Philosophy of Civilization:* "Civilization can only revive when there shall come into being in a number of individuals a new tone of mind independent of the one prevalent among the crowd and in opposition to it, a tone of mind which will gradually win influence over the collective one, and in the end determine its character."

In this same vein and toward these same goals Martin Buber also worked alone. Like Schweitzer, he had set his face against the crowd. It is true that there were others that, like he, subscribed to the spiritual rather than merely geographical destiny of Zionism, but none were as articulate or outspoken as Buber. The mysticism that had been so much a part of vision and activity of his life flowed into his speeches and books. And while some wanted a narrow definition of Zionism, Buber wished to expand and enlarge its ethical dimensions. He continued to believe that Zionism was for all peoples—that it offered a blessing to the Arabs as well as to the Jews, a spiritual realm as large as mankind itself. He wrote:

Our voice calls the Jewish people . . . to be always loyal to the Spirit and not revert to dogma. That will not be easy for our nation; nor do we wish to leave them to their own devices—that is something their true and rightful leaders have never done. But when those leaders inquired what way had to be taken, they did not look for counsel to the disposition of the people, but only to the Spirit who has revealed to them and in them. And it must always be so. Our desire is to obey the Spirit so that he may become real through us. As long as we are of the Spirit, we have the seed of true life within us."[13]

The bond between Buber and Schweitzer joined together two men who refused to accept the parochial limitations of religion. They went beyond doctrinal boundaries in search of the will and truth of God that would reveal the need for harmony among all men. Both men learned much from each other in the course of their friendship.

Schweitzer also learned a lesson from the life of Renan, whose personal tragedy affected Schweitzer greatly while he was at work on *The Quest of the Historical Jesus*. Ernest Renan, the nineteenth-century French rationalist, was one of the first scholars to make full use of the historical criticism of the Gospels. His study of this material led directly to his rejection of the Gospels as historically accurate or reliable. Schweitzer, in carrying on his study, discovered that this conclusion arrived at early in life by Renan, stood in the way of the further creative scholarship he might have accomplished in his life. For it had effectively paralyzed Renan's thought, forcing him to become a constant defender of revolutionary positions strongly taken as a young man. Renan's concerns were different from Schweitzer's: the doctor was much more involved with history during the life of Jesus than in dwelling on the errors of that history that appeared in recorded accounts. Schweitzer did see himself in a somewhat analogous position to that of Renan in his rejecting established dogma, but he realized that thought itself could not be allowed to become a straitjacket. Thought, for Schweitzer, had its greatest fulfillment in action. Like Renan, he was estranged from the larger community of the Church, but unlike Renan, he did not become trapped by this situation or the theological positions he took. He told Norman Cousins, "I think I can understand how Renan's work affected him when he didn't allow it to redefine his life for him. This is what I mean when I say I came to Lambaréné because I wanted to make my life my argument. I didn't want my ideas to become an end in themselves."[14]

Thus, thought was required by Schweitzer to constantly define life, and to redefine life as it changed. The two, thought and life, mind and action, thinking and doing, could never, to him, be severed. Their interrelation and interaction were always necessary. For Schweitzer to challenge thought was to challenge society, and vice versa. Once arrived at his position of rebellion in both life and thought, Schweitzer remained an undaunted individualist. At no point during the remainder of his life did he return to the mainstream in either philosophical thought or life-style.

In helping to explain some of the doctor's decisions, the profound influence Goethe had upon him must be noted again. Schweitzer had first begun his study of Goethe at Strasbourg, where he occupied the same room in which Goethe had once lived. Reading in his philosophy courses, it puzzled him that Goethe had stood aloof from the new forces of German idealistic philosophy represented by Kant, Fichte and Hegel, among others. Goethe's mature philosophy, however, his kindness, and his unshakable sense of justice, bound Schweitzer to him. Almost by chance, Schweitzer said he had read the description of Goethe's *Harzreise*. The doctor wrote, "It impressed me wonderfully that this man whom we regard as an Olympian should have set out in the midst of the rains and mists of November to visit a preacher's son who was plunged in deep spiritual distress, in order to bring him some spiritual assistance . . . So I learned to love Goethe, and when it happened that I had to undertake some work in my own life for the sake of some man or other that needed help, I said to myself, 'That is your Harzreise.' "[15]

Goethe became even more personally meaningful to him in other ways. The mind of Schweitzer—penetrating, all encompassing, constantly wrestling with great issues—functioned best when it could personalize intellectual concerns. It was through people that such concerns came alive and acquired vitality for him. Goethe had asked the question in the *Sorrows of Werther*, "Must those things that make a man happy necessarily become the source of his misery?" Schweitzer's entire life offered an affirmative answer to this question. It was true of Schweitzer as a pensive, introspective boy; as a student, who in a moment of ecstasy, felt life was too good and he must find some way of compensating through service to others for the richness of his existence. The renunciation of Europe that helped bring him to Africa as a mature man also was a partially affirmative answer to that same question. For it represented a search for the fulfillment of the essential misery needed in life. Further, the joys of accomplishment in scholarship led to Schweitzer's estrangement from the Christian Church he dearly loved. Finally, his love for his wife, Helene, faithful to the end, however fulfilling or unfulfilling, brought with it years of misery as they were separated by his mission and her broken health.

When Schweitzer considered and made his decision to go to Africa, as a physician, it was the semiautobiographical accounts of Goethe's Wilhelm Meister that helped him clarify his thoughts. Schweitzer recalled,

Goethe was the comforter who found the words for me while others, even those who best understood me, found fault with my decision to study medicine, for which, they said, I was really not fitted, and while they tormented me with objections, telling me this was quixotic, I was able to reflect that this adventure would not perhaps have been entirely quixotic to him, the great man— who permits his Wilhelm Meister to become at the last a surgeon, in order that he may be able to serve, although he is completely unprepared for it.[16]

Again the identification with Goethe was helpful.

Schweitzer, in his constant battle to clear the jungle, thought of Faust clearing land for his community. Schweitzer wrote, "Whenever I was in complete despair, I thought of Goethe, who had imagined his Faust, in the end, busily regaining land from the sea where man might live and find nourishment."

In Schweitzer's work in New Testament studies, other scholars have recalled his fascination with Faust. Faust too wrestled for example with the problem of the translation of the Gospel according to John:

> 'Tis writ, "In the beginning was the Word."
> I pause, to wonder what is here inferred.
> The Word I cannot set supremely high:
> A new translation I will try.
> I read, if by the spirit I am taught,
> This sense: "In the beginning was the Thought."
> This opening I need to weigh again,
> Or sense may suffer from a hasty pen.
> Does Thought create, and work, and rule the hour?
> 'Twere best: "In the beginning was the Power."
> Yet, while the pen is urged with willing fingers,
> A sense of doubt and hesitancy lingers.
> The spirit comes to guide me in my need,
> I write, "In the beginning was the Deed."[17]

Schweitzer throughout his life offered himself the deeds of his life: "I am only a person living his religion," he said; and again, many times, "My life, my argument." The Christian belief was not enough for Schweitzer, and the deed became basic to his whole approach to human existence.

The anguish of Schweitzer is also visible through analogy to Faust. One recalls Faust's frustration at the fact that his view of the sea is blocked by a neighboring hut. Finally he complains to Mephistopheles, who burns the hut, killing its elderly occupants, while Lynceus, the watchman in the castle tower, looks on from his observation post. At a sight too gruesome to behold, he cries in torment:

Must ye eyes—such things discerning—
Must I, so far-sighted be?
Down the little chapel crashes,
Burdened under branches fall.
Winding upward, pointed flashes
Seize upon the tree-tops tall.
To their roots the trunks, ignited,
Hollow, purple-red, glow on.

. . . .

Gone what once the eye delighted,
With the centuries is gone.[18]

Incessant struggle against the elements, disease, apathy, ignorance, slovenliness and selfishness, lead the strong and the active to courses of action which in the inner recesses of their hearts they pay for. For when one has a strong conscience, sensitivity, high principles and a discriminating mind, one must suffer with others. This was Schweitzer's lot. There was no element of ruthless brutality in Schweitzer, but for some reason, he identified with the crime of Mephistopheles, as he felt must all civilized men. He wrote: "I cannot avoid reflecting that, in order to preserve life, I have to destroy other life."[19]

Man allows wars to happen through silence. He permits the ravages of disease simply by not making available sufficient funds for cure and research. He sponsors contamination of the atmosphere through atomic testing. He upsets the balance of nature on every hand through a callous and careless use of land. Schweitzer, from his lookout post in Lambaréné, also had the tortured eyes of Lynceus, a soul horrified to behold so much, without means of sounding the saving alarm. His voice was also an anguished cry. "My own fate has been such that I have vitally experienced in the very fiber of my being the fortunes of our age and concern about our humanity."[20]

In the end, Schweitzer, a man of integrity, carried a deep personal sense of guilt, not for his own shortcomings, but for those of the modern era. He was part of it, for as he said so often, "We belong to one another"; all men are members of a global community who carry the wounds and injuries of life.

If this guilt had thoroughly preoccupied Schweitzer's mind, it would have killed him as a relatively young man. Few men could bear, as he did, such a deep personal sense of anguish and survive.

But compensation for Schweitzer was found in his involvement in concrete programs. In dealing with people and their problems, a tolerable acceptance of life became possible for him. He was by nature gregarious—a lover of his fellow man, who enjoyed the simple joy of companionship and the opportunity for good conversation and for laughter.

His sense of humor was spirited and offered another form of salvation for him. He could laugh at himself and with others about himself. He could tell a good story. He reported, for example, that once he was traveling on a train in America when two girls came up to him and asked: "Dr. Einstein, will you give us your autograph?" "I did not want to disappoint them," he said, "so I signed their autograph book, 'Albert Einstein, by his friend Albert Schweitzer.'" He loved such stories of mistaken identity. Once, during the period when Max Schmeling was European Heavyweight Boxing Champion, Schweitzer, in Europe, was surrounded by some small boys eagerly collecting autographs. As he signed their books, he asked one child, "Is my autograph so valuable?" The boy responded, "Oh, yes! With two of your autographs I could trade for one of Max Schmeling." Another humorous anecdote about Schweitzer concerns a popular plaster bust of him, cast in 1929, when he was in the prime of manhood. His cheeks were full; his chin protruded, his bushy hair and large mustache stood out. An incident of confusion later created by this bust was a source of great amusement to Schweitzer. A hotel in Strasbourg exhibited it, he recalled, and on one occasion, the Council of Europe met there. One of the delegates stopped the meeting and asked the manager to remove the offensive bust. The manager asked the delegate what was offensive about it. "We don't like Stalin," was his reply. One of Schweitzer's nephews also had a copy of this bust in his parlor. This was his elder brother's son, Paul-Pierre Schweitzer, Minister of Finance in the French Republic before becoming chairman of the International Monetary Fund. A French Communist came to visit him once, and whispered, "We're glad to see you're one of us," nodding approvingly at the bust.

The humorous anecdotes about Schweitzer are endless. When once asked about his unfinished manuscripts, Dr. Schweitzer replied, "Don't talk to me about my unfinished manuscripts. A chicken only makes a noise when it has laid an egg. Only after I have published a book will it be right to talk about it. Fortunately there are chickens at Lambaréné, or I wouldn't have learned this good lesson."[21] Norman Cousins has reported many delightful conversations with the doctor which show the workings of Schweitzer's mind.

His broad sympathy was shown in his continuing membership in his old family church, even while he was reaching out to the Church of the most liberal Protestant dissent, the Unitarians, for a significant relationship with those who, like him, had separated themselves from the mainstream of Christian institutionalism. He said laughingly once, "In Europe I am supported by liberal Catholics, but in America by liberal Protestants." He was in fact a thorough humanist, and his universalist religious beliefs preceded the modern ecumenical movement by decades. In his *Memoirs of Childhood and Youth,* he recalled the little village church in Günsbach used by both Protestants and Catholics, and noted:

One thing more have I taken with me into life from this little church, that was Protestant and Catholic at the same time, I mean religious tolerance. These Catholic-Protestant churches, which had their origin in the irresponsible edict of a ruler, are for me something more than an historical phenomenon. They are a symbol to show that the differences which separate churches today are things which are destined ultimately to disappear. When I still was merely a child, I felt it to be something beautiful that in our village, Catholics and Protestants worshipped in the same building, and my heart fills with joy today whenever I set foot inside it. I should like all the churches in Alsace which are still used by both confessions to remain so, as a prophecy of, and an exhortation to, a future of religious unity, upon which we must ever keep our thoughts fixed if we are really and truly Christians.[22]

As one delves into the thought of Schweitzer, one finds over and over that it is inextricably bound to deed, the *acts* of his life. It not only prompted the actions by which he lived, but it formed a stream of consciousness which led to the further development of his thought itself. Tortured, introspective, creative, estranged, Schweitzer had a mind that was ruthless in its demanding logic. And the fruits of his intellectual struggles had far-reaching influence.

Dr. Richard Friedmann spent his sabbatical leave from Lambaréné in the United States in 1962. During this period, he stayed for two weeks in Berkeley, California, with Paul Tillich, the noted Protestant theologian. In the course of their discussions, Friedmann asked Tillich how it was that he never found mention of Schweitzer in his books. Tillich responded that everything he wrote presupposed the theological position and influence of Schweitzer. "But shouldn't you publicly acknowledge this?" Friedmann persisted.

Tillich thought a moment and then replied, that it seemed to be

"a fact of life that the most important things are taken for granted. What is most important to life, for instance? We talk about food and water, but that which is most important, which we would not survive for a few minutes without, air, we hardly ever refer to. We take for granted the air we breathe, as we do the great germinal thinkers who have become basic to our entire systems of thought."[23]

22

The World Citizen

In the late 1950s and early 1960s, the last years of his life, Albert Schweitzer emerged as truly a world citizen. He had seen the last of Europe and would spend the rest of his days in Africa. He told visitors to Lambaréné in 1962 that the Africans were his people and would not understand if he left and died on foreign soil. He had given his life to the hospital and here he wished to die. But this did not mean that he had lost all interest in Europe or Western civilization. To the contrary, his concerns about these spheres were growing.

While the hospital had moved forward as a more active, better equipped and more complex institution during the postwar period, Schweitzer's own interests expanded, and he involved himself in the new problems created by the precarious conditions of the world scene. The more he saw of European culture, however, the more he appreciated the Africans' simple ways. Some years before he had been asked what he did in Lambaréné for the advancement of culture. Dr. Schweitzer, whose disdain for Western culture was already well known, replied, "I supply slop basins to the residents of the neighborhood of Lambaréné!" The specifics of this cryptic answer became clear in those years when one visited Lambaréné and noted the use of the head for bearing burdens. Traditionally, baskets form the base for a "head bundle," but in Lambaréné, the most popular means of carrying goods on the head was the large, flat, enamel water basins, stolen from the hospital and easily identifiable by the initials "ASB" which, for years, were printed in black on all equipment of the Schweitzer Hospital. (The "B" represented Bresslau in the hospital's name during Mrs. Schweitzer's lifetime.)[1]

Another story from Europe, told and retold, reveals his disdain for appearances. Schweitzer was to be guest of honor at a reception during one of his visits to Europe. Upon arrival at the designated house, he was haughtily directed to the servant's entrance by the doorman. Without a word, Schweitzer obliged and made his way through the back of the house to the embarrassment of his hostess, while the guests coming to meet him were being formally announced at the front door. To have met Schweitzer was to know how completely in character the incident was.[2]

Many persons meeting him during the 1950s and 1960s were deeply touched by his unusual simplicity. An American woman wrote: "How moving it is to find a man rather than a public figure. That, for me, was a religious experience, to have my hope confirmed that he had continued to do his work modestly." That fame and acclaim had not altered his humility was indeed an exhilarating and moving discovery.

The casual simplicity of his manner, dress and behavior and that of the natives were seen vividly at Lambaréné. For many, the Sunday morning worship service was an amazing and wholly unique religious experience. John Gunther, the late author and reporter, noted among other things, that this hospital was the only mission he visited in Africa which was without a chapel. (It must be remembered that this hospital was not a mission enterprise and that Dr. Schweitzer's mission beginnings had faded far into the background.) On Sunday, when the bell for chapel would ring, a throng would move to the "avenue of suffering" as it had been called, outside of the pharmacy, where every morning and afternoon, except Sunday, patients lined up to be seen by the doctors and nurses. Here, an outdoor service is held. African adults, with children and suckling infants, sit on the ground, in the doorways, on the porches and steps, looking expectantly toward the outdoor rostrum where a sermon in French is preached.

One Sunday service observed by George Marshall was typical. Standing beside the preacher were two interpreters: one Galoan and one Fang. The preacher (a medical doctor) would read a statement without much emotional expression. He would stop, and one of the interpreters would step forward and give the message in his native tongue. He did so with great enthusiasm, much swinging of his arms and gesturing to emphasize the statement's highlights, all of which was amazing to see for he offered far more in his interpretation of the message than had been present in the original words of the speaker. Then, the second interpreter stepped forward and his method of communication was different. He sang or intoned the sermon, chanting at times in a loud singsong voice. When he had finished, the preacher would read his next thought in the same phlegmatic tone of voice. The native interpretations would then start again. This particular service observed was at the Schweitzer Hospital during the doctor's lifetime, but the doctor himself was not present at it. He was to be found elsewhere that morning, as so often was the case, inspecting cement poured the previous day. The forest reverberated to the closing hymn sung in French by the African congregation.

Quite a different experience was provided by the evening devotional service conducted by the doctor in the dining room each night. Many of these services were seen as well by George Marshall. This service was entirely given by Schweitzer, and it had an appropriate sacred air about it. Schweitzer's message often reflected his own roots in the past and summed up the purposes for which he lived.

Following the evening meal, it was always dark outside because night comes early at the equator. The white dinner tablecloth was lit by kerosene lamps with their homemade dark green shades in an even row down the center of the table. Above and behind, all was in shadow. The meal finished, uniformed members of the staff, as though by a prearranged signal, arose and quietly laid out well-worn hymnbooks on the table.

The low murmur of voices ceased. Everyone would look toward the center of the table where Dr. Schweitzer with one massive hand, picked up a hymnbook and thumbed through the pages. He stopped at a page, called out a number in German, and then rising ponderously and slowly, would walk quietly around the table to a piano in the room. One had the sense that he was meditating as he walked. He sat at the piano and slowly began to improvise. He played for a minute or so and then struck the chord of the hymn. Remaining seated, the dinner company instantly became a congregation and joined in singing the words which were printed in German. Both melody and lyrics were familiar to all.

From the earliest notes, one became aware that this was not the famous piano with organ pedals and zinc lining presented to Schweitzer by the Paris Bach Society so many decades before and to which so many people often refer. That organ-piano had been returned to Europe in 1962 for badly needed repairs; it had been worn out by the high humidity of the wet season and the rigorousness of the tropical climate. It now reposes in Schweitzer's home at Günsbach. Here in the dining room Schweitzer used an old ship's piano brought up from Cape Lopez many years ago.

At the conclusion of the hymn, Dr. Schweitzer would walk slowly around the table to his place, seat himself deliberately, open a well-thumbed Bible to a page where he had placed a bookmark, clear his throat, announce the Bible passage and begin reading it in both German and French. He finished the passage, announced a prayer, flipped the pages back to another bookmark at Matthew: 7, and read the Lord's Prayer. Closing the worn Bible, he would glance around the table at the hushed expectant faces wreathed in lamplight and would begin a discussion of the passage just read. With the thoughts of the readings in their minds, the hospital staff would retire for the night, walking back to their cabins by lamplight.

Schweitzer explained to Norman Cousins in 1955, "As a young man, my main ambition was to be a good minister . . . I completed my studies; then, after a while I started to teach. I became the principal of the seminary. All this while I had been studying and thinking about the life of Jesus and the meaning of Jesus. And the more I studied and thought, the more convinced I became that Christian theology had become overcomplicated. In the early centuries after Christ, the beautiful simplicities relating to Jesus became somewhat obscured by the conflicting interpretations and the incredibly involved dogma growing out of the theological debates. . . ."[3]

Schweitzer continued an interest in the quest for religious truth all of his life. For example, he wrote the manuscript of *The Kingdom of God and Primitive Christianity* in 1950–1951, although it was not published until released by his daughter in 1968, three years after his death. This study basically substantiates and simplifies much of the material that appears in *The Quest of the Historical Jesus* and is his mature summary and reflection on the subject and his thoughts about it.

Perhaps the most significant passage in this entire book is a footnote on page 128 in which Schweitzer wrote that in a passage found on pages 378 and 379 of *The Quest of the Historical Jesus:* "I still believed that in the pre-Messianic tribulation a load of guilt that encumbered the world and was delaying the coming of the Kingdom could be expiated by believers, and that Jesus, therefore, in accordance with the Servant passages, regarded his vicarious sacrifice as an atonement. *As the result of further study of late Jewish eschatology* and the thought of Jesus on his passion, *I find that I can no longer endorse this view.*"[4]*

This passage which states that Schweitzer no longer believed that Jesus had a concept of his atonement marks a significant change in Schweitzer's outlook, eschatology and religious orthodoxy.

The doctor's interests in the 1950s and 1960s now touched many fields and ranged far beyond the scope of his early accomplishments. He had joined with his old friend, Einstein, and others in protesting nuclear warfare. "The protest against the H-bomb," he wrote on April 14, 1954, to the London *Daily Herald*, "should be started by the scientists. If they all

* Author's italics.

raised their voices, each one feeling himself impelled to tell the terrible truth, they would be listened to, for then humanity would understand that the issues were grave. . . . But the scientists must speak up. Only they have the authority to state that we can no longer take upon ourselves the responsibility for these experiments, only they can say it. There you have my opinion. I give it to you with anguish in my heart, anguish which holds me from day to day."[5]

When Schweitzer received the Nobel Prize for Peace he sent to Oslo a series of three radio addresses which were broadcast on April 28, 29 and 30, 1958. In these three addresses, reported in full at that time in the New York *Times* and the *Saturday Review* and published in book form under the title, *Peace or Atomic War?*, Schweitzer called upon scientists, statesmen and all other concerned peoples to be moral, to not be responsible for stunting the growth of future generations. Speaking as a physician he said, "Only those who have never been present at the birth of a deformed baby, never witnessed the despair of its mother, dare to maintain that the risk in going on with nuclear tests is one which must be taken under existing circumstances." He quoted the renowned French biologist and geneticist Jean Rostand, who called the continuation of nuclear testing *"le crime dans l'avenir"* (the crime projected into the future).

His third address called for a summit conference to deal with the elimination of the testing of atomic weapons. He concluded by saying, "The summit conference must not fail: mankind will not again tolerate failure. The renunciation of nuclear weapons is vital to peace."[6]

Later, in August 1963, Dr. Schweitzer wrote President Kennedy expressing his jubilation about the fulfillment of his dream for a successful nuclear arms conference. Now Schweitzer was one of the most active crusaders on behalf of peace, and few men in our time have equalled him in making their voices heard in every corner of the world as a proponent of peace.

It seemed strange that this man, who had avoided—or at

least remained aloof from—all public controversy of a political nature, had changed so rapidly and so radically.

Dr. Homer Jack, later the Director of Social Responsibilities for the Unitarian Universalist Association, served for many years as Executive Director of the American Committee on Africa, and the SANE* organization, and had visited Dr. Schweitzer in Africa four times since the end of World War II through 1962, as well as in Günsbach on two occasions. He stated that Dr. Schweitzer's attitude of political commitment had developed considerably during this period, as Schweitzer's piety and personal ethics had grown into full social consciousness and the willingness to accept and to become involved in the world's controversies. By 1960, Schweitzer was inextricably involved with social problems and faced the consequences of his public statements without fear. According to Jack, Schweitzer's phenomenal growth of social consciousness was one of the most remarkable examples of human progress he had ever seen in a man of any age. Schweitzer did grow remarkably as a person during this period, long after he had passed the normal age of retirement. It is interesting to see how and why this development took place.

Dr. Schweitzer had achieved early recognition as a theologian, musician and philosopher and then as a physician. In this latter capacity, he had begun to read more and more scientific works. He had become conversant in the fields of chemistry, biology and physics. He was a friend of another great European expatriate, as has been noted, Albert Einstein. With the passing of the years, Dr. Schweitzer had in sum come to think of himself as a philosopher, scientist or doctor rather than as a minister or theologian.

A portrait of Charles Darwin hung on the wall of his room, rather than a likeness of Kant, Goethe, Zwingli or Luther. Contact with medical researchers and the great foundations, the steady, time-consuming reading of scientific papers and journals all led to his closer identification with the world of

* The National Committee for a Sane Nuclear Policy.

science. Science makes a tangible contribution in a world of
disease and despair. This was a fact to Schweitzer and he
could not help but affirm it in both his thoughts and actions.
He still retained the humanitarian sensitivity of his religious
and philosophical background. He simply combined it with his
knowledge of science. What emerged was a viewpoint which
held that science must be humanized and deal with the practical problems of people living, suffering and dying in an increasingly pressured world.

When, shortly after the explosion of the first atomic bombs
on Hiroshima and Nagasaki, Dr. Einstein wrote him a letter
of concern, Schweitzer realized that, as a scientist, he must
now speak out. For science was not only constructive; it could
be, as the bombs demonstrated, destructive and deforming.
Civilization hung in the balance. War had become a means
of mass murder and now, with the nuclear bomb in harness,
humanity was moving farther along the road of extinction.
The first reports of nuclear burns and damage to cell and
tissue were shocking. As both a scientist and humanitarian,
he was compelled to enter the arena of public controversy.
A strong stand on a controversial public issue would perhaps
alienate some of the people whose financial support he received, but conscience would not allow him to remain silent.

He preceded any announcements, as always, by reading and
studying. He needed more than passing knowledge of the
issues to speak and work effectively. He began reading intensely the books, newspapers and periodicals of the world.
He also began corresponding with key thinkers in the world
of science and public opinion. Not only Einstein, but Martin
Buber, Père Dominique Pire, Bertrand Russell, J. Robert Oppenheimer, Linus Pauling, Dag Hammerskjold, Adlai Stevenson, Aneurin Bevan, Norman Cousins and a host of other
editors, writers, scientists and ministers became his correspondents. Leaders of the United World Federalists, of the
National Committee for a Sane Nuclear Policy, and of church
peace groups not only wrote, but came to visit Lambaréné.
Cousins, the editor of *Saturday Review*, came there in 1955

with the zeal of an evangelist for peace, and undoubtedly helped to motivate Schweitzer to further public involvement.

The excitement of the 1960s in Lambaréné was due in great part to the intense and active discussions concerning nuclear warfare, the issue which preoccupied Schweitzer's mind. Distinguished visitors of all kinds now came to Lambaréné to see and talk with him: politicians, diplomats, United Nations staff members, writers, peace-movement representatives, social scientists of various different disciplines—all interested in the larger concerns of creating a peaceful world. The visitors came to see Schweitzer as students to learn; as promoters to enlist; as politicians to exploit; as journalists to profit; as thinkers to probe; and as skeptics to be convinced. Some left feeling uplifted, and others dejected. But Schweitzer could not be all things to all people.

The common query by staff members to the Lambaréné visitor was, "What paper do you represent?" One of the staff confided that Schweitzer was always glad when Americans came because he liked to have the opportunity to talk about their government's attitude on nuclear war and bomb testing.

Most visitors were invited to join Dr. Schweitzer in his room after supper. There, by the light of a kerosene lamp, with the cluttered desk, and the dancing shadows behind it, with the mysterious noises of the river and jungle echoing through the open, screened windows, memorable discussions took place. Dr. Schweitzer was always interested in the main activities and interests of his guests, but after a brief talk about them, his mind always returned to the compelling concerns which filled him with anguish, the state of the world and nuclear warfare. He was apt to ask for his visitor's views on the international situation. Then he almost always expressed his own: great pessimism became of the lack of clearly articulated public opinion needed to arouse political leaders and stop the slow drift toward war. Unless there was a strong effort to prevent it, Schweitzer was sure that international affairs would deteriorate again into war. Only creative and positive action could save peace for the world. As he explained to George Marshall in 1962:

I have studied this matter. I have studied many civilizations and nations and the lesson is clear. Wars are not the result of organized intensive campaigns to create them, but are the result of a slow drifting laissez faire, so imperceptible that before anybody realizes it, war is forced upon them. However, there is no escaping the fact that today the nature of warfare and civilization has changed so much that it can no longer be absorbed by mankind. Of course, I know there are exceptions to every rule, and there have been nations that forced a war of conquest, but, as a rule, as you study history, neither side wanted most of the wars fought.[7]

His eyes would gleam and his intense personal feelings on the subject were revealed when he spoke about world events. The tangled mass of white hair fell over his brow as he shook his head emphatically and expressed his views. Public opinion must be awakened. Apathy must be overcome. The lethargy of our times must not be allowed to continue, or in a single generation civilization would be destroyed.

If one suggested to Schweitzer, as did George Marshall, that such spiritual arousal was the function of the churches, he was immediately told that the churches had had two thousand years to come to terms with the ethics of Jesus, those of brotherhood and peace, but had utterly failed. There was little hope to be found in the traditional churches, Schweitzer felt, and none whatsoever in those supported by the state. He told Marshall that it was with great sorrow that he had come to this conclusion.

Marshall quoted Schweitzer as adding:

"Once I thought three things could control public opinion, but I now discount the churches, except for the slight impact, like pebbles tossed in the ocean, made in limited areas by a few small churches. There are the Quakers who are an historic peace Church, and other people appreciate or take heart from their forthright stand. Then there are the Unitarians who form the historic Church of martyrs, composed of people who try to practice what Jesus preached. Their emphasis is on the ethical teachings of Jesus who stood for peace. But such small groups of church people as these are not able to influence public opinion any more than a pebble raises the level of the ocean. They do not have enough members between them," he explained.

"What are the two possible means of influencing public opinion? First come the government and parliamentary officials, the elected leaders who articulate policy and justify it. They have the means of creating public opinion, both favorable and unfavorable. The second is the press. The newspapers which are read by the masses, and the related mass media of our time, radio and television, have the power of influencing public opinion. A fearless political leadership and a courageous press could alert the populace to action. Unfortunately, they are too timid.

"The political leaders lead by following; they give no direction, but try to gauge public opinion and make their own ideas agree with it. Hence, you see in the United States and Western Europe that public opinion polls tell those who aspire to office what the people think and then the politicians outdo themselves to avoid conflicting with public opinion.

"The second source of leadership, the press, is haunted by the specter of closing, or having to merge as circulation drops, as have many metropolitan newspapers. Why do papers lose circulation? The management believes it is because people will not purchase a paper that does not agree with their own point of view, and the papers are forced to try and say exactly what the people believe. Therefore, the news media no longer molds public opinion, but follows it."

Into this vacuum, created by a lack of direction, a few must do what they can, Schweitzer told Marshall, hoping that in time, they will make a difference. There was no time for humanity to wait. Accordingly, Dr. Schweitzer called himself a pessimist.

But then, it was with great joy that he greeted the news of the success of the Geneva Conference in 1962–63 when the test ban treaty between the representatives of the United

States, Russia and other nuclear powers, was formulated and agreed upon. For the first time, it seemed to Schweitzer, the gloom of official double talk seemed to have been penetrated, and hope for mankind began to appear a realistic attitude. Both the Soviet Chairman and the American President assured the world of their personal support of the treaty. Several times previously, Dr. Schweitzer had expressed hope that President John F. Kennedy, a young leader, with his broad grasp of world affairs, unbounded energy, and fresh vitality would fulfill his promise of leadership. Now the doctor was jubilant and felt confirmed in his faith in the man.

On August 6, 1963, he wrote President Kennedy that "the treaty gives me hope that war with atomic weapons between East and West can be avoided." The treaty, he wrote, "was one of the greatest events, perhaps the greatest, in the history of the world." He went on, "When I heard of the treaty, I thought of my old friend, Dr. Einstein, with whom I joined in the fight against atomic weapons. He died at Princeton in despair. And I, thanks to your foresight and courage, am able to observe that the world has taken the first step on the road leading to peace."[8] The White House released this letter from Hyannisport, President Kennedy's summer home, in late August 1963, following the meeting of the Advisory Committee on Science which "unanimously endorsed the nuclear test ban treaty." The White House press release, after quoting Dr. Schweitzer's letter, went on to say, "The Committee believes that the continued unrestricted development and exploitation of military technology by both the Soviet Union and the United States would, in time, lead to a net decrease in real security." Evelyn Lincoln, secretary to President Kennedy, wrote that Schweitzer's letter created great excitement in the President's office "and he was extremely grateful to him for his views."[9]

Schweitzer, as a world citizen, was now involved in affairs and activities which affected people in many countries. Some reacted negatively to his participation, and some looked upon his activities in support of the control of nuclear weapons as "meddling," or "playing into the hands of Communists." Such critics were dismissed perfunctorily by Schweitzer.

Others turned to criticism of his hospital, and he answered them by asking: "How can those who know nothing about Africa tell me how to run an African hospital?" On his ninetieth birthday in 1965 he stated, "Africans themselves showed me the way. At first I wanted to build a hospital like those in Europe. But Africans—two simple laborers—convinced me that here the conditions are different. . . ."[10] Old friends who admired him, like Dr. Paul Dudley White, suggested that he should now move into public health projects and institutionalize research projects, but Schweitzer replied that he was now too old. Those who came after him must be the ones to make changes.

Friends such as Dr. Homer Jack, strongly supportive of Schweitzer's philosophy, ethics and personal witness, tried to prod him into more definite political stands on behalf of African independence, but the old doctor would shake his head, suggesting that if white men refrained from putting political pressure on the Africans, they would settle their own problems.[11]

Informed critics of Schweitzer in the United States were few. John Gunther and Connor Cruise O'Brien reported on weaknesses in both his complex personality and his operation of the hospital. And there was one particularly serious American critic of Dr. Schweitzer, the Afro-American scholar, civil rights leader, and writer, Dr. W. E. Burghard Du Bois. He wrote that Schweitzer represented the reactionary influences that undermined the African. From Dr. Du Bois, *The Crisis*, journal of the National Association for the Advancement of Colored People, adopted the term, "The Last of the Great White Fathers," and this epithet disturbed the minds of those who had hoped to find in Schweitzer a man thoroughly above reproach. Dr. A. A. Roback asked Du Bois to write a critique on "The Black Man and Albert Schweitzer." This article was published by Roback in *The Albert Schweitzer Jubilee Book*. Du Bois discussed Schweitzer's concept of the reparations the white man owed the black, and agreed that this position certainly was valid, but he challenged the idea that this repayment could be carried out within the system of colonialism as Schweitzer tried to do. There is, Du Bois said, a contradiction between the white man's culture and crimes on the one hand, and the healing doctor's efforts on the other that confused the African because of the contradiction. The further paradox, Dr. Du Bois suggested, was that Schweitzer also was confused, and did not understand that he assisted in perpetuating colonialism by making life tolerable under it. He quoted Schweitzer's own words as summing up what he called "the tragedy" of this situation. Schweitzer had written, "The tragic fact is that the interests of the colonies and those of civilization do not always run parallel but are often in direct opposition to each other." Du Bois then suggested that Schweitzer would have done better to have concerned himself with saving the souls of white men rather than the bodies of black men. Yet he did admit a personal appreciation of Schweitzer: "Albert Schweitzer was neither deceived nor enlightened. He saw the pain and degradation of this bit of God's earth as something he could alleviate; for many years he gave his life to it."[12]

23

Last Years and Controversy

Controversy surrounded Lambaréné during Schweitzer's last years. He was puzzled and dismayed at the virulence of continued personal attacks on him and the hospital. He had never expected that everyone would agree with him, on any number of issues for that matter, but he was surprised by the bitterness of some of his critics. He had always been a dissenter, an individualist going his own way. His pre-eminence in the fields of theology, philosophy and music had indeed come because he went beyond supposedly sacred frontiers. In the same vein, his medical center was not a prototype of the standard hospital operation, but rather a unique development resulting from what he found would best work under the circumstances at Lambaréné. His *Philosophy of Civilization* was a sociological critique of culture. His works on Jesus and Paul were challenges to the historic position of Christian doctrine. His stand against nuclear warfare marked him as a rebel in political matters, and his political individualism defied simple classification in the doctrinaire political climate of the independence movements in Africa. On all fronts, there were two groups of people confronting Dr. Schweitzer: those strongly for him and those against him.

People came to Lambaréné with varying points of view and reflected what they felt about Schweitzer in what they later wrote.

University teachers, theologians, philosophers, and medical men visited and found in Dr. Schweitzer an intellectual with whom they could talk, and they gratefully took away a deepened insight on a variety of issues from such discussions. These were men who enjoyed with the doctor the exchange

of thoughts, whatever their differences of opinion. And
Schweitzer enjoyed the opportunity such meetings provided
for repartee and intelligent conversation. Students came to
Lambaréné to learn from Schweitzer. In his last two years,
many young members of the American Peace Corps made the
trip up the Ogowe or overland to visit the hospital. Boy Scouts
from France journeyed from their homes to Lambaréné. In
1962, senior French Boy Scouts worked industriously at the
hospital all summer at heavy construction work, pouring
cement, building forms, and laying foundations. Young
teachers from Austria and Switzerland also came to Lambaréné to work during their school vacations. Then, there were
the laundresses, cooks, caretakers and nurses who over the
years, went there to work: the forerunners of a peace corps,
for Dr. Schweitzer inspired many young men and women to
do good works in Africa long before there was a formal program in which they could give of themselves. Even writers,
some pro-, some anti-Schweitzer, would join the construction
gangs, and their reports were enriched as a result of their
participation. The motives of all Schweitzer's visitors varied,
but the doctor welcomed them all.

One visitor, Dr. Paul Dudley White, said upon his return
from Lambaréné in 1963, "Dr. Schweitzer wears a sort of hair
shirt, but then we in this country wear soft shirts, and he
makes allowances for us." The noted heart specialist was making both a judgment of Dr. Schweitzer and a suggestion of
the need for a greater understanding of the man in all his
depth. Inasmuch as Dr. Schweitzer emerges from any profile
of him as an individualist and a non-conformist, carrying on
his life and pursuits without regard for the opinions of others,
this "hair shirt" concept is helpful.

The man on the summit occupies both a lofty and lonely
perch, and it was so with Schweitzer. In spite of his many
friends, the doctor, in his world of ideas and with his irresistible urge to apply ethical principles to culture, often stood
alone—loved, but not understood. His special type of loneli-

ness—that shared by many other notable men and women—
took several forms as has been shown.

He was a man torn between two countries and then later
two continents, who in the end rose above geographical confinement in his emergence as a world citizen. He was educated
in the universities of Germany and France, wrote his books
in both their languages, and received the greatest intellectual
honors of both countries, but never really found a true, comfortable home in either. Indeed, he refused to be bound by
nationalism or narrow loyalty. His was a total commitment to
all humanity and to a universal culture and ethic he wished
for all the world.

A few years ago, a European journal conducted a poll
among distinguished scholars which rated him third among
Western civilization's triumvirate of geniuses. The only two
ranked ahead of him were Leonardo da Vinci and, interest-
ingly, Goethe.

Dr. Schweitzer had gone to Africa in 1913 to "bury himself," but soon found he could not do that. Nonetheless, if
Schweitzer did have a home, it was in Africa. At the time he
arrived there, he was the only medical doctor in a thousand-
square-mile area between the Congo and the Gold Coast, in
malaria-infested West Equatorial Africa, serving a few miles
south of the equator in the world's most uncomfortable tropical climate. It was from this area in West Africa that most of
the slaves sold into bondage in the New World had been
shipped. Libreville, in the Gulf of Guinea, was named after
those liberated slaves returned by the English and French
men-of-war. Unfortunately, their campaign was a losing battle
against slave traders in the early nineteenth century. Schweitzer knew this local history, and it reinforced his commitments
to devote himself and it to Africa and the reparations he felt
the white man owed the black.

When Schweitzer was invited by Dr. Dana M. Greeley to
return to the United States in 1963 under the sponsorship of
several national and international organizations, he replied,
"Others must go and talk. I am now an old man who has

lived most of my life in Africa. My Africans would not understand it if I should not be with them at the end." Dr. Schweitzer had cast his lot with Africa as a place to both live and die. Here Helene was buried and he wished to lie beside her. In his thoughts, he was now of Africa. Europe held nothing more for him.

Africans responded to him strongly, and they found ways to show the importance of him and his hospital to them. When the Republic of Gabon was established, it created an order of merit, the *"Etoile du Gabon"*—"The Star of Gabon"—to be awarded to a small number of outstanding citizens who had made conspicuous contributions to the cultural life of the nation. Schweitzer was among those few honored by this singular award.

One of the English biographers of Schweitzer, Magnus Ratter, wrote in the pages of *The Observer*, London, on April 26, 1964:

"Stefan Zweig's words are memorable; having prepared material for a biography, he said, after a long interview, that Schweitzer's personality was too impressive." The impressiveness of Schweitzer noted by Stefan Zweig has been shared by many others.

In consequence of this study of his life, noting the man's strengths, weaknesses, consistencies, and disparities, we too are led to concur that Schweitzer is "too impressive," that his humanity is overwhelming. Bertrand Russell said, speaking of Schweitzer, that he "is one of those who has challenged the reverences of our day." We have shown Schweitzer to be a dissenter in many ways. But he was more than this, for his whole life was a great affirmation of positions taken requiring integrity and courage. Schweitzer stands among the most stalwart liberals of our time or any time, and it is fair to say that this is the image he created for himself.

It may be true, as Schweitzer implied, that the issue of his religious liberalism was responsible for much of the criticism he received. If this is so, his friends regret this fact. Obviously, many people attacked him for other reasons as well: for his stand on nuclear warfare, his opposition to war, his constant call for a more ethical civilization, his stubborn insistence that a man could be an individual in the modern world in spite of all the pressures upon him to conform.

Following an increase in what was felt to be unjustified criticisms of Schweitzer's activities and thought, a study packet of material on his life was prepared which became the basis for an earlier book by George Marshall, *An Understanding of Albert Schweitzer*.[1] A copy of the material was sent to Dr. Schweitzer, who responded as follows:

> Dr. Albert Schweitzer
> Lambaréné
> République, Gabonaise
>
> February 15, 1965

Reverend George N. Marshall
25 Beacon Street
Boston, Massachusetts, U.S.A.
Dear Friend:

I thank you for the presentation of my life and work, and above all for what you have written about me. I am astonished that you have been able to give so accomplished an account of my work and thinking. You also take care to tell the readers how best to help my hospital. You, yourself, have directed many gifts to us during this period.

I found very interesting the review of everything that has been written against me that you have also published. I, myself, have no overall understanding of these criticisms. How is it possible that people who do not know Africa give me directions about the equipment and the operation of my African hospital?

I have had the great fortune that people have given me the means for founding this hospital and to continue it. I have never bothered with the criticism of my hospital. I did what I considered to be correct, on the basis of my knowledge of Africa.

I owe you a great debt for the chronological biography. Now, at last, I am acquainted with the facts of my life!*

* See appendix.

Please excuse that I have not replied in time to your letter of October 29, 1964. I am, unfortunately, unable to write the article for you which you would like to have. I do not yet have the proper perspective of the political events of recent times. Goldwater has ceased to be a political problem. —The role of the U.S.A. in Vietnam is a great problem. What political role is China going to play? Will it succeed in gaining a foothold in Africa as it plans?

Please excuse my poor handwriting. For the last four years I have been suffering with writer's cramp. To me, writing is a great effort, and there are times when I write practically nothing. At my age, I cannot bring myself to resort to the typewriter or to the dictating of letters. Therefore, have forbearance.

With best thanks for your friendliness toward me,

I remain your devoted
Albert Schweitzer

To our knowledge, this letter was his last piece of social comment and his final defense. It is hard to believe that so many people who did not know the situation in Africa could lecture a man who had spent a lifetime there. But criticism never stopped him. He continued on his way, concerned for his people and dealing with problems, both local and international, as they arose.

Before a hushed audience on the occasion of his ninetieth-birthday breakfast (January 14, 1965), Dr. Schweitzer briefly summarized his career in these words: "At first I wanted to build a hospital like those in Europe, but two simple African laborers convinced me that conditions here were different. Therefore, I have built an African hospital for Africans."

Many years before his ninetieth year he had reflected on his past and written, "When I first came to Africa, I prepared to make three sacrifices: to abandon the organ, to renounce academic activities, and to lose my financial independence. But, like Abraham, I was spared the sacrifices."

Here in the jungle he had his music. Even though the old zinc-lined piano with the organ pedals had been sent to Europe for repairs in 1962 and was now at his Günsbach home, other pianos had been sent. And the electronic age had reached even remote Lambaréné, offering a Radio Gabon station.

He remained in touch with the academic community through the students, teachers and scholars from all over the world who congregated at the hospital.

And money was received regularly from book royalties, organ recordings and the many generous persons interested in his work. In fact, in February 1965, he wrote his old friend Dr. A. A. Roback of Cambridge, Massachusetts,

"It grieves me to hear that you have lost money in publishing works about me. If you will let me know how much you have lost, I shall repay you, for my wants are few, and I have more money than I need."

Thus it is true that Schweitzer did not have to sacrifice many of the things in life that were important to him. But he remained a humble if proud man. In 1949, Schweitzer repeated to Fulton Oursler words he had written in the 1920s:

"I must forgive lies directed against me because so many times my own conduct has been blotted by lies. I must forgive the lovelessness, the hatred, the slander, the fraud, the arrogance which I encounter, since I myself have so often lacked love, and have hated, slandered, defrauded, and been arrogant, and I must forgive without noise or fuss. In general, I do not succeed in forgiving fully; I do not even get as far as being always just. But he who tries to live by this principle, simple and hard as it is, will know the real adventures and triumphs of the soul."[2]

Most of all, he valued personal privacy, both his own and that of others.

"I think, therefore, that no one should compel himself to show to others more of his inner life than he feels it natural to show. We can do no more than let others judge for themselves what we inwardly and really are, and do the same ourselves with them. The one essential thing is that we strive to have light within ourselves."[3]

Perhaps because of this attitude, he understood the difficulty of properly comprehending the nature of others.

"We wander through life together in a semi-darkness in which none of us can distinguish exactly the features of his neighbor; only from time to time, through some experience that we have of our companion, or through some remark that he passes, he stands for a moment close to us, as though illumined by a flash of lightning. Then we see him as he really is."[4]

And, most tellingly, of mankind and civilization as a whole, he wrote:

"We believed once in the victory of truth; but we do not now. We believed in our fellow men; but we do not now. We believed in goodness; but we do not now. We were zealous for justice; but we are not so now. We trusted in the power of kindness and peaceableness; we do not now. We were capable of enthusiasm; but we are not so now. To get through the shoals and storms of life more easily we have lightened our craft, throwing overboard what we thought could be spared. But it was really our stock of food and drink of which we deprived ourselves; our craft is now easier to manage, but we ourselves are in decline."[5]

It is in the mood of this passage that he firmly stated "With the spirit of the age I am in complete disagreement."[6] Yet he held fast to his own integrity. He wrote on another occasion: "The great secret of success is to go through life as a man who never gets used up. That is possible for him who never argues and strives with men and facts, but in all experience retires into himself, and looks for the ultimate cause of things in himself."[7]

What these statements of his own reveal then is that he was a complex, thoughtful man, a man of immense depth, stirring controversy by his unwillingness to accept generally accepted truths, the common trivia of life, although he often did not participate directly in many of the controversies that surrounded him. He stood always as a dissenter, a free man, a non-conformist. He was one of the few independent thinkers who spoke and acted for himself, without a thought of what the world "expected" of him.[8] He was, indeed, almost unconscious of the world's expectations of him, and thus he went his solitary way.

Schweitzer lived his life with an individualistic perspective unusual in a world which is built primarily upon masses of people—organizations, institutions, powerful blocs and cliques.[9] Schweitzer told Bernard Redmont, an American radio commentator in Paris, "It's not enough merely to exist. It's not enough to say 'I'm earning enough to live and support my family. I do my work well. I'm a good father. I'm a good husband. I'm a good churchgoer.' That's all very well, but you must do something more. Seek always to do some good somewhere. Every man has to seek in his own way to make his own self more noble . . . You must give something to your fellowman. Even if it's a little thing, do something for those who have need of a man's help, something for which you get no pay but the privilege of doing it."[10]

Dr. Schweitzer told him, "Remember, you don't live in a world all your own. Your brothers are here too." These thoughts represent a personal philosophy that can fairly be said to have been fulfilled throughout his life. It has been called the "one-to-one philosophy," the principle of shouldering a part of other men's burdens ourselves. It was this philosophy which led him, as a young curate, to attempt the rehabilitation of vagrants and prisoners. It was this desire to help others that had drawn him to Africa. He recalled to Fulton Oursler how easy it was for people to say, "I would like to do some good, but I am so busy with my own responsibilities to my family and work that I don't have time. . . . Our greatest mistake, as individuals, is that we walk through life with closed eyes and do not notice our chances. As soon as we open our eyes . . . we see many who need help, not in the big things but in little things. Wherever a man turns he can find someone who needs help."[11] Schweitzer recalled that one day he was traveling through Germany on a train. In his compartment were two men, an older man and a young one, strangers to each other. Commenting that it would be dark when they reached the next city, the old man, worried and fretful, exclaimed, "I don't know what I shall do when I get there. My only son is in the hospital, critically ill. I had a telegram to come at once. I must see him before he dies. But I am from the country and I'm afraid I shall get lost in the city." The young man replied, "I know the city well. I will get off with you and take you to the hospital to see your son. Then I will catch the later train."

"As they left the train together they walked like brothers," Dr. Schweitzer added. To him, the key to life lay in concern for fellow human beings, which led in turn to humanitarian service.[12]

In the spring of 1964 Bertrand Russell wrote to a London newspaper, "It is not a very great discovery that Dr. Schweitzer's single-handed effort to help people blighted by disease may be superseded by modern medical facilities. It is obvious, however, that technical progress always carries with it the price of impersonal machinery, which is devoid of the humanity that a dedicated individual provides through his own action and example."[13] Schweitzer's lifetime service did indeed provide the kind of humanistic effort to which Lord Russell was referring. Schweitzer demonstrated the value of individual effort in a world that was increasingly minimizing the role of the individual.

Allied with his humanistic, individualistic philosophy of life was another aspect of his character, his purposeful self-sufficiency. He did not leave tasks for others. Rather, he did the job that needed to be done at a given time and was willing to let another take the credit. That the job was done was to him the important point. Thus he would repair an organ he wished to play, climbing a loft to tune the instrument on which he was to give a concert that night. He became, as has been said, not only a doctor for his Lambaréné hospital, but also its surgeon, pharmacist, quartermaster, purchasing agent, architect, construction foreman, builder, lumberman, hand laborer, cement mixer, gardener and plumber. A major aspect of the amazing achievement at Lambaréné was the fact of how much of it was conceived, built and carried forward by one man's hand, will and intellect. It has been said that he took on too much responsibility, but if this is true it was because he simply could not avoid any work that he saw needed doing.

Reverence was of course always a part of his credo. In his last year, two staff members were bitten by a dog and an epidemic of rabies broke out at the hospital. Dr. Schweitzer made the difficult decision that all dogs and cats must be sacrificed to halt the spread of the disease. Reverence for Life, ironically, required this of him. His decision lost the life of even his own beloved dog, Tchu-Tchu. But this could not be helped; the dictates of his conscience and philosophy always came first.

Finally, a sense of thanksgiving was a source of Albert Schweitzer's power which he himself has documented, yet which is not properly recognized as playing such an important role in his life. Obviously, a person with his many abilities and accomplishments must have had a special motivation which urged him forward. And this motivation was an overwhelming sense of appreciation and gratitude for the bounty of life, the richness of his personal relationships.

Schweitzer, in his *Memoirs of Childhood and Youth,* wrote:

I am stirred by the thought of the number of people whom I have to thank for what they gave me or what they were to me. At the same time, I am haunted by an oppressive consciousness of the little gratitude I really showed them when I was young. How many of them have said farewell to life without my having made clear to them what it meant to me to receive from them so much kindness and so much care! Many a time have I, with a feeling of shame, said quietly to myself over a grave the words which my mouth ought to have spoken to the departed, while he was still in the flesh.[14]

He went on to say that "we ought all to make an effort to act on our first thoughts and let our unspoken gratitude find expression. . . . A great deal of water is flowing underground which never comes up as a spring . . . we ourselves must try to be the water which does find its way up; we must become a spring at which men can quench their thirst for gratitude." He added that often one's inner light goes out, or flickers, and then is relit only by a spark from the outside, from contact with another person: "Thus each of us has cause to think with deep gratitude of those who have lighted the flames within us."[15]

Thus, as Schweitzer looked at life, he found a deep need to repay life for its goodness and to recognize that his accomplishments came through efforts other than his alone. His entire life became an act of thanksgiving for all the privileges and opportunities which were his and as repayment for the insight he had been blessed with to enable him to contribute to the advancement of truth in religion and ethics. And, it bears repeating that far ahead of his time he felt the need to make reparations for the wrongs done by the white man to the black. This desire for atonement was another lifelong motivating force.

Many people came to know in Schweitzer what Erica Anderson called his "gift of friendship." People, great and small, known and unknown, from many walks of life, visited Lambaréné in his final years. Among them were some prominent figures in show business, such as American television stars Jack Paar and Hugh O'Brian; Mrs. Otto (Marion M.) Preminger from Hollywood and London actress Susan Hampshire, who told Dr. Schweitzer she had "come to find out for herself" what the hospital was like. Another well-known visitor was Olga Deterding, the Dutch oil heiress, who worked in the kitchen. Indeed, many workers and nurses of the hospital were at first occasional visitors who then stayed on. The English nurse, Joan Clent, was bicycling through Africa when she stopped by and ended up staying for years. She became the senior nurse in the leper village, and Susan Hampshire worked with her while there. Mrs. Hanna Oberman, who spent years as a hospital helper, was the widow of the Rotterdam pastor who was publicly executed by the Nazis as a prominent hostage. Other people from all over Europe and the United States spent short or long times at the hospital. Some became well-known names to those who wrote to Dr. Schweitzer, such as Clara Urquhart of London and Lotta Gerhold of Vienna, for they answered many letters for Schweitzer and helped interpret his work.

Typical of many visitors was Albert Jenkins, a United States State Department official, who came to Lambaréné in 1958 while on his way to a diplomatic conference in the Congo and took a side trip to the hospital. He confided about Schweitzer "When he learned at the luncheon table in Lambaréné that my doctor friend and I had to leave in fifteen minutes to catch our plane, despite our protests he immediately went for his hat and said he would accompany us in the little one-lung putt-putt motorboat we had hired to come the two miles upriver. My conversation with him was so interesting that it did not occur to me even to take his picture, although I had a camera hanging around my neck all the while until we were at the airport almost ready to leave. I then asked his head nurse who was with us whether he would object to my taking his picture. She said 'of course not. He is the most accommodating of men.' I thought she looked a little funny in saying that, however, and I hesitated. Then she added, 'but he has so obviously enjoyed talking with you. If you would now forget to take his picture he would remember and love you forever—he is so tired of being Niagara Falls.' Naturally I did not then take his picture. (I will confess to you that from the inside of the plane and largely with my children in mind, I did take one color slide of him and his head nurse, but at such a distance it cannot be called a good picture.)"[16]

The *Life* magazine article covering his ninetieth birthday (the issue of February 19, 1965), ended with its author, Hugh Moffett, writing of the *Life* team's departure. "Dr. Schweitzer and a few associates came to the dock to see us off . . . He stood long by the shore . . . I watched his figure grow smaller and smaller . . . an acquaintance asked the question so often put to visitors.

" 'Well, are you for him or against him?'

"My answer surprised both of us a little:

" 'Oh, I'm for him, of course. He's a friend of mine!' "

This may be the final verdict, as it was for Henri Monfrini, the Swiss ambassador to the Ivory Coast. He previously served as the United Nations Advisor on Technical Assistance to Underdeveloped Countries in Africa. His office was for two years in Libreville, the capital of Gabon. He agreed with the modern emphasis that new progressive steps were necessary to aid the developing countries to make their forward thrust into the technological age, and he was conversant with the attitude that all old efforts in Africa were out of date. This naturally was the avant-garde attitude toward colonialism, missions, and toward such individual enterprises as the Schweitzer Hospital. He made his first visit there with great reservations. After several inspection trips, long conversations with Dr. Schweitzer and his staff, and with Gabon officials, and with patients, he came to the conclusion that the Schweitzer Hospital set the pattern for technical assistance in the future because it had come to terms with African culture.[17] In discussing his own personal experiences in Lambaréné, Monfrini added, "The most remarkable factor about Schweitzer is his ability to make a friend of you. No matter what your reservations or defenses, it almost never fails that everyone ends up feeling that he has found a new friend in him."[18]

Among Schweitzer's older friends was Joseph, his first orderly. In 1960 he had returned to Lambaréné, his working days over. Those who visited the hospital in the 1960s remember him. He would come up to a visitor and say, "Parlez-vous Français, English?" and talk in the language in which the visitor replied. He used to say: "I am Joseph, Dr. Schweitzer's first assistant. I am the same age as le Grand Docteur." Whether or not they were born in the same year is uncertain, but they died in the same year, Joseph a few months after the doctor, and his grave is in the cemetery at the hospital, a reminder of the heritage of workers who were there over the years, and of the older people who found a home there.

Time was running its course for Schweitzer. But the old doctor remained concerned about the direction the world would take in the future. In the summer of 1965, he felt the global political situation was becoming more critical. The Vietnam conflict had come to upset him greatly. The world's failure to take additional steps to control nuclear weapons raised other fears for the future. The Middle Eastern situation was another which Schweitzer felt could lead to a world-wide war. Finally, the continuing poor relationships between the United States, Russia and China, the three great powers, made it clear that the world situation was seriously deteriorating. Schweitzer feared that all the progress of the past two decades might be for nought. "Perhaps I should make another world-wide radio appeal, as I did in Oslo," he told his confidants. To Rhena, his daughter, he began talking about the need for the time, energy and strength to prepare another appeal. "I should make one more effort," he would say. "If only I can have the time, and am not too tired." If there was a personal tragedy for Schweitzer in the last months of his life, it was in this final frustration of his inability to strike another blow for peace.

On August 12, 1965, Dr. Schweitzer went to the shores of the Ogowe River as the far-off chant of the leper oarsman announced the arrival of guests. Long-time European colleagues of Dr. Schweitzer from Switzerland and Alsace had come to visit and were welcomed as close friends. The old friends present included Mme. Emmy Martin of Günsbach, M. Charles Michel of Strasbourg, and Fritz Dinner, among others. Some of the guests were members of the association which, according to French legal documents executed in the year 1931, became the owner of the Schweitzer Hospital, effective on October 13, 1933. The group, called the *Association de l'Hôpital du Dr. Albert Schweitzer* of Strasbourg, France, was charged with continuation of the hospital in the event of Dr. Schweitzer's incapacity. Happy with the arrival of the members of the association, Dr. Schweitzer's spirits

seemed revived. His fatigue that summer had been noticeable, and it was a pleasure for his staff to note his renewed
energy. Unfortunately, it was short-lived.[19]

On Monday, August 23, 1965, Schweitzer read the Bible
and played the hymn following supper for the last time. Instead of the usual biblical dissertation, he quietly returned
to his seat, and in a calm low voice said he wished to review
his hopes for the continuation of the hospital, and to give
instructions for its maintenance in the event of his death.
Fritz Dinner reported that he was impressed by the doctor's
clear, firm voice. However, after the discussion, Dr.
Schweitzer seemed immediately fatigued, and the next day
ceased his regular attendance at meals. Thursday and Friday,
August 26 and 27, he called for the jeep, and was driven
around the hospital grounds, inspecting, or at least viewing
every building. "One could observe that his eyes wandered
over the hospital and its buildings as if he took them in, like
the last view of his life's work, or—who can tell—as though
taking leave," Fritz Dinner wrote. The following week
Schweitzer spent in bed. He died quietly on Saturday night,
September 4, 1965, at 10:30 P.M.[20]

Simplicity had always marked interment at Lambaréné.
Burial always took place immediately with brief prayers, and
without pomp. Simple pine coffins were used, and graves
marked by unadorned crosses. There was no variation from
this pattern followed for Dr. Schweitzer's burial, for he had
left strict instructions on the matter. He had ordered the
cross to match those used for Mlle. Hausknecht, and his wife,
Helene, and he had supervised the construction of the bare
coffin in which he was to be buried.[21]

The service was conducted by the new Chief of the Medical Staff, Dr. Walter Munz, who read the Psalm and offered
the prayer. M. Bongo,* Vice-President of Gabon, the personal representative of the President of the country, gave a
eulogy for the nation. Burial took place Sunday afternoon as

* Later second President of the Republic.

doctors, nurses, students and patients attended. Placed in the coffin with Schweitzer was his battered old hat and a small bag of rice that he always carried with him for feeding the chickens—a slight concession to sentiment.

The President of the Republic of Gabon urged Schweitzer's daughter, Rhena, and Dr. Munz not to tear down the old buildings, but to keep the village atmosphere of the hospital which had made everybody feel so much at home. This atmosphere, he remarked, had shown Schweitzer's complete understanding of his people.[22] The hospital of Schweitzer should go on as it began, in the spirit and with the form given it by *le Grand Docteur*. And the common people of Africa, to whom Schweitzer devoted the balance of his life, remembered him.

Months later, large groups of Africans continued to come on Sunday afternoons, gathering at the burial site. Many traveled great distances, and groups of up to one hundred came in flotillas of pirogues from up or down the river to the hospital. A staff member described one such occasion: "With lighted candles they walked up the hill and held a moving service at the grave. Others, on hearing the monotonous sounds of the tom-tom, came to join the dancing and to express their own grief." In chant, song and dirge, they expressed their joy that their beloved Doctor had been buried on their soil. They were persons of all ages and conditions: the strong and the active; cripples and lepers; mothers with babies on their backs. They brought flowers for the grave or presents for the hospital, purchased out of their meager resources. At the grave they read from the Bible, sang, spoke and prayed. Later, farther up the hill, they would dance until dark to the rhythmic music of the drums, often wearing symbolic tribal masks.

One of the volunteer workers at the hospital once asked an elder of one of the groups what was being said in the prayers. He replied, "We thank God that he sent Dr. Schweitzer to us and that he was our good shepherd who gave his life for us, stayed with us, was buried in our soil and under our palm trees."

More than the Nobel Peace prize or any other award, this was the kind of tribute Albert Schweitzer would have rejoiced at receiving.

Footnotes and Chapter References

Prologue

1. Marshall, George N., *An Understanding of Albert Schweitzer*, New York, 1966, Philosophical Library, pp. 5–10.

Chapter 1   Childhood and Youth: Toward the Light

1. Schweitzer, Albert, *Memoirs of Childhood and Youth*, New York, Macmillan, 1961 edition, p. 27 (hereinafter cited as *Memoirs*).
2. *Op. cit.*, pp. 29–30.   3. *Ibid.*, p. 29.   4. *Op. cit.*, p. 28.
5. Buber, Martin, *Between Man and Man*, New York, Macmillan paperback, 1965, p. 23. Introduction by Maurice Friedman and an Afterword by the author. Translated by Ronald Gregor Smith and Maurice Friedman.
6. *Memoirs*, p. 8.   7. *Op. cit.*, p. 48.   8. *Op. cit.*, pp. 45–46.
9. *Memoirs*, pp. 54–55.   10. *Op. cit.*, p. 56.   11. *Op. cit.*, p. 65 ff.
12. Cuénot, Claude, *Teilhard de Chardin*, Baltimore, Helicon Press, 1965 edition, p. 50 (*La messe sur le monde*).
13. *Ibid.*, p. 420.

Chapter 2   Early Commitments

1. *Memoirs*, p. 7.   2. *Op. cit.*, p. 32.   3. *Op. cit.*, p. 13.
4. *Op. cit.*, p. 40.   5. *Op. cit.*, p. 41.   6. *Ibid.*, p. 41.
7. *Op. cit.*, p. 38 ff.   8. *Op. cit.*, p. 42 ff.   9. *Op. cit.*, pp. 42–48.
10. *Op. cit.*, pp. 43–44.

Chapter 3   The Scholar Emerges

1. Schweitzer, Albert, *Out of My Life and Thought*, New York, Holt, 1949 edition, p. 15 ff. (hereinafter cited as *Life*).
2. *Op. cit.*, p. 16.
3. *Madame Curie*, a biography by Eve Curie, translated by Vincent Sheean, New York, Doubleday, Doran, 1937, p. 258 ff.
4. *Life*, p. 16.   5. *Op. cit.*, pp. 16–19.   6. *Op. cit.*, pp. 21–22.
7. Kiernan, Thomas (ed.), *A Treasury of Albert Schweitzer*, New York, Citadel Press, 1965, p. 331.
8. *Op. cit.*, pp. 330–31.   9. *Life*, p. 25.   10. *Op. cit.*, p. 26.
11. *Op. cit.*, pp. 25, 26.   12. *Op. cit.*, pp. 15–16.

Chapter 4   Organist and Organ Builder

1. Münch, Charles, A Tribute to Albert Schweitzer, *Music in the Life of Albert Schweitzer*, Charles R. Joy (ed.), Boston, Beacon Press, p. 9.
2. *Life*, Chapter 7, pp. 60–69.   3. *Op. cit.*, p. 61.
4. Quoted in Clark, Henry, *The Ethical Mysticism of Albert Schweitzer*, Boston, Beacon Press, p. 44.
5. *Life*, p. 130 ff.   6. *Op. cit.*, Chapter 8, pp. 70–83.
7. *Music in the Life of Albert Schweitzer*, pp. 220–21.
8. *Op. cit.*, pp. 156–57.   9. *Life*, p. 144.   10. *Op. cit.*, p. 167.
11. *Op. cit.*, p. 79.

Chapter 5   The Academic Life

1. Beek, M. A. and Sperna Weiland, J., *Martin Buber: Personalist and Prophet*, Newman Press, Glen Rock, N.J., 1968, pp. 88, 93.
2. *Op. cit.*, p. 87.
3. Wilder, Amos, "Albert Schweitzer and the New Testament" reproduced in the symposium, *In Albert Schweitzer's Realms*, A. A. Roback (ed.), Cambridge, Sci-Art Publishers, 1962, p. 351.
4. *Life*, p. 30.   5. *Op. cit.*, pp. 51–52.
6. Schweitzer, Albert, *Quest of the Historical Jesus*, New York, Macmillan, 1961 edition, p. 4. (hereinafter cited as *Quest*).
7. *Op. cit.*, p. 6.   8. *Life*, p. 9.   9. *Op. cit.*, pp. 54–55.
10. *Op. cit.*, pp. 6–7.   11. *Op. cit.*, pp. 7–8.
12. Schweitzer, Albert, *Kingdom of God and Primitive Christianity*, New York, Seabury Press, 1968, pp. 68–130.
13. *Life*, pp. 156–57.   14. *Op. cit.*, pp. 42, 43.

Chapter 6   Second Decisions: Africa and Mission Service

1. *Life*, p. 85.   2. *Op. cit.*, p. 86.   3. *Op. cit.*, p. 85.
4. Cuénot, Claude, *Teilhard de Chardin, op. cit.*, p. 27 (at the beginning of his priesthood).
5. Cousins, Norman, *Dr. Schweitzer of Lambaréné*, New York, Harper, 1960, pp. 190–91 (hereinafter cited as *Cousins*).
6. *Memoirs*, p. 14.   7. *Cousins*, p. 190.   8. *Ibid.*, p. 190.
9. *Op. cit.*, p. 191.   10. *Life*, pp. 87–88.
11. *Reverence for Life*, Sermons of Albert Schweitzer, translated by Reginald H. Fuller, New York, Harper & Row, 1969, pp. 56–57.
12. *Ibid.*, pp. 56–67.   13. *Life*, p. 84.   14. *Op. cit.*, pp. 89, 91.
15. *Op. cit.*, p. 89.   16. *Op. cit.*, pp. 89, 90.   17. *Cousins*, p. 192.
18. *Ibid.*, p. 192.
19. From "A Gift of Presence" by Jean Mouroux in *The Religious Experience* (ed.) by George Brantl, New York, George Braziller, 1964, Vol. II, p. 988.

20. *Ibid.*
21. *Reverence for Life*, Sermons of Albert Schweitzer, *op. cit.*, p. 85.

Chapter 7　Breaking from Europe

1. *Life*, p. 91.　　2. *Op. cit.*, p. 219.
3. Schweitzer, Albert, *The Philosophy of Civilization*, translated by C. Y. Campion, New York, Macmillan, 1932, p. 36.
4. *Op. cit.*, p. 15.　　5. *Op. cit.*, p. 12.　　6. *Op. cit.*, p. 38.
7. *Op. cit.*, p. 20.　　8. *Life*, p. 240.
9. Bonhoeffer, Dietrich, *Letters, Lectures and Notes from Collected Works*; Volume One, 1928–1935: *No Rusty Swords*, ed. and introduced by Edwin H. Robertson, trans. by John Bowden; William Collins Sons & Company, Limited, 1965, London, p. 124.
10. Schweitzer, Albert, *The Kingdom of God and Primitive Christianity*, edited by Ulrich Neuenschwander, translated by L. A. Garrard, New York, Seabury Press, 1969 edition, p. 183.
11. Beek, M. A. and Sperna Weiland, J. *Martin Buber op. cit.*, p. 5 (letter to Stefan Zweig).
12. *Op. cit.*, p. 98.　　13. *Life*, p. 89.　　14. *Op. cit.*, p. 98.
15. *Op. cit.*, pp. 106–7.　　16. *Op. cit.*, p. 104.　　17. *Ibid.*
18. *Op. cit.*, p. 106.　　19. *Op. cit.*, p. 107.　　20. *Op. cit.*, p. 102.
21. Schweitzer, Albert, *Psychiatric Study of Jesus*, Boston, Beacon Press, 1948, Beacon paperback, 1958; see *Life*, pp. 108–10 also.
22. *Life*, p. 108.　　23. *Op. cit.*, p. 114.　　24. *Op. cit.*, p. 112.
25. *Ibid.*

Chapter 8　The Renegade Missionary

1. *Life*, pp. 96–97.　　2. *Op. cit.*, p. 97.　　3. *Op. cit.*, p. 95.　　4. *Ibid.*
5. *Op. cit.*, p. 96.　　6. *Ibid.*　　7. *Op. cit.*, p. 94.　　8. *Op. cit.*, p. 97.
9. *Ibid.*　　10. *Ibid.*　　11. *Op. cit.*, pp. 112–13.　　12. *Op. cit.*, p. 114.
13. *Op. cit.*, pp. 112–13.　　14. *Op. cit.*, p. 113.
15. *Op. cit.*, pp. 113–14.　　16. *Op. cit.*, p. 113.　　17. *Op. cit.*, p. 86.
18. *Op. cit.*, p. 113.　　19. *Ibid.*　　20. *Op. cit.*, pp. 112–13.
21. *Op. cit.*, p. 114.　　22. *Ibid.*　　23. *Op. cit.*, pp. 114–16.
24. *Op. cit.*, p. 116.　　25. *Op. cit.*, p. 138.

Chapter 9　Arrival in Africa

1. Schweitzer, Albert, *On the Edge of the Primeval Forest* (*More from the Primeval Forest*) New York, Macmillan, 1961, pp. 7–8 (hereinafter cited as *Edge*)
2. *Ibid.*　　3. *Op. cit.*, p. 8.　　4. *Ibid.*　　5. *Ibid.*　　6. *Ibid.*
7. *Ibid.*　　8. *Ibid.*　　9. *Op. cit.*, p. 9.　　10. *Ibid.*
11. *Op. cit.*, pp. 9–10.　　12. *Op. cit.*, pp. 10–12.　　13. *Op. cit.*, p. 10.
14. *Ibid.*　　15. *Op. cit.*, p. 11.　　16. *Op. cit.*, pp. 11–12.

17. *Op. cit.*, p. 11.   18. *Op. cit.*, p. 14.   19. *Op. cit.*, pp. 15–16.
20. *Ibid.*   21. *Op. cit.*, p. 15.   22. *Op. cit.*, pp. 16–17.
23. *Op. cit.*, p. 15.   24. *Op. cit.*, p. 16.

Chapter 10   The First Mission Hospital

1. *Edge*, p. 17.   2. *Op. cit.*, pp. 17–18.   3. *Op. cit.*, pp. 18–20.
4. *Op. cit.*, pp. 3–6.   5. *Ibid.*   6. *Op. cit.*, p. 27.
7. Joy and Arnold, *The Africa of Albert Schweitzer*, New York, Harper Bros.,
   1948, and Boston, Beacon Press, 1948, p. 7. (Pages are unnumbered and
   our annotations begin by counting the Introduction, "Prisoner of
   Lambaréné," as page 1.) See also Schweitzer, *The Hospital at Lambaréné
   During the War Years 1939–1945*, New York, Albert Schweitzer Fellowship, 1947, p. 8.
8. *Edge*, p. 27.   9. *Op. cit.*, p. 20.   10. *Ibid.*   11. *Ibid.*
12. *Op. cit.*, p. 21.   13. *Ibid.*   14. *Op. cit.*, p. 24.
15. *Op. cit.*, p. 38.

Chapter 11   Doctor in the Jungle

1. *Edge*, pp. 36, 60.   2. *Op. cit.*, p. 105.   3. *Op. cit.*, p. 62.
4. *Op. cit.*, p. 22.   5. *Op. cit.*, pp. 49, 51.   6. *Life*, pp. 139–41.
7. *Edge*, p. 44.   8. *Op. cit.*, p. 63.   9. *Ibid.*   10. *Op. cit.*, p. 24.
11. *Op. cit.*, pp. 23–24.   12. *Ibid.*   13. *Op. cit.*, Chapter 7, pp. 75–91.
14. *Op. cit.*, pp. 27–28.   15. *Op. cit.*, pp. 28–29.   16. *Op. cit.*, p. 29.
17. *Op. cit.*, pp. 29–30.   18. *Op. cit.*, pp. 41–42.   19. *Op. cit.*, p. 22.
20. *Life*, pp. 142–43.   21. *Edge*, pp. 4, 47.
22. *The Africa of Albert Schweitzer*. Last page.
23. *Edge*, p. 22.
24. Ratter, Magnus, *Albert Schweitzer, Life and Message*, Boston, Beacon
    Press, 1950, p. 79.

Chapter 12   At Home in Africa

1. Schweitzer, Albert, *African Notebook*, New York, Holt, 1939, p. 45 ff.;
   (hereinafter cited as *Notebook*)
2. *Op. cit.*, pp. 48–49.   3. *Op. cit.*, p. 50.   4. *Op. cit.*, p. 56.
5. *Op. cit.*, p. 58.   6. *Op. cit.*, p. 62.   7. *Op. cit.*, pp. 63–64.
8. *Op. cit.*, p. 64.   9. *Op. cit.*, p. 65.   10. *Op. cit.*, p. 131 ff.
11. *Edge*, pp. 33–34.
12. *Op. cit.*, pp. 124–25; also see Turnbull, Colin M., *The Lonely African*,
    New York, Simon & Schuster, 1962, Chapter 3, pp. 83, 221, 230 ff.
13. *Ibid.*   14. *Op. cit.*, pp. 79 ff.; 105 ff.   15. *Life*, p. 143.
16. *Edge*, p. 31.

Chapter 13   Prisoner of War

1. *Life*, pp. 144–45.   2. *Ibid.*   3. *Ibid.*   4. *Edge*, p. 93.
5. *Op. cit.*, p. 92.   6. *Op. cit.*, pp. 155–58.   7. *Life*, p. 145.
8. *Ibid.*   9. *Edge*, pp. 93–95.   10. *Life*, p. 145.
11. *Edge*, pp. 113–16.   12. *Life*, p. 148.   13. *Life*, p. 145.
14. *Op. cit.*, p. 98.   15. *Life*, pp. 146–61.   16. *Op. cit.*, pp. 146–47.
17. *Op. cit.*, p. 148 ff.
18. *Op. cit.*, p. 29. (see also Mrs. Charles E. B. Russell, *The Path to Recon-struction*, New York, Holt (Boston, Beacon Press, 1946), p. 9.
19. *Life*, pp. 148–55; 197–201.
20. *Ibid.* (see bibliography for works cited)
21. *Op. cit.*, pp. 156–57.   22. *Op. cit.*, p. 163.   23. *Op. cit.*, p. 164.
24. *Op. cit.*, p. 165 ff.   25. *Op. cit.*, pp. 168–69.
26. *Op. cit.*, p. 166.   27. *Op. cit.*, see p. 156.   28. *Op. cit.*, p. 173.
29. *Op. cit.*, p. 176.   30. *Memoirs*, p. 59, *Life*, pp. 178–79.   31. *Ibid.*
32. *Op. cit.*, p. 179.   33. *Op. cit.*, pp. 179–80; 184.
34. *Op. cit.*, pp. 184–85.   35. *Op. cit.*, p. 186.   36. *Op. cit.*, p. 185.
37. *Op. cit.*, p. 202.   38. *Op. cit.*, pp. 202–3.
39. See Anderson, Erica, *The Schweitzer Album*, New York, 1965, Harper & Row, pp. 24–29, esp. 29.
40. Seaver, George, *Albert Schweitzer: The Man and His Mind*, New York, 1947, Harper Bros., p. 83.
41. This passage is quoted by Seaver from Oskar Kraus, *Albert Schweitzer, His Work and Philosophy*, (*sein Werk und seine Weltanschauung*), 1929, Berlin, Pan-Verlag, p. 68.

Chapter 14   The Return to Lambaréné

1. *Life*, pp. 189, 195–96; see also *Edge*, p. 121.
2. A bibliography of American editions of Schweitzer's works; publishers and dates of available editions will be found in the Appendix.
3. *Life*, p. 203.   4. *Op. cit.*, p. 195.   5. *Op. cit.*, p. 179 ff.
6. *Edge*, pp. 121–22; see also *Life*, p. 204.   7. *Edge*, p. 125.
8. *Op. cit.*, pp. 125–27.   9. *Op. cit.*, p. 128.
10. *Ibid.*   11. *Op. cit.*, p. 129.   12. *Ibid.*   13. *Op. cit.*, pp. 129 ff.
14. *Op. cit.*, p. 137.   15. *Op. cit.*, pp. 139–40.   16. *Op. cit.*, p. 141.
17. As told by Rhena Schweitzer who read the Noel Gillespie journals sent, after his death, to the Schweitzer Archives in Günsbach, Alsace, France.
18. *Edge*, p. 145.   19. *Op. cit.*, p. 161 ff.   20. *Op. cit.*, p. 164.
21. *Op. cit.*, p. 161 ff.   22. *Op. cit.*, p. 185.
23. *Op. cit.*, p. 188 ff.; see also *Life*, pp. 206–7.   24. *Op. cit.*, p. 2.
25. *Op. cit.*, Chapter 18, pp. 190–91; 192–202; see also *Life*, pp. 208–11.

Chapter 15   Between the World Wars

1. *Life*, p. 207.   2. *Ibid.*   3. *Edge*, p. 199.
4. Horn, Alfred A., *Trader Horn*, New York, Simon & Schuster, 1927, also,
   Notebook, pp. 1–35.
5. *Edge*, p. 142.   6. *Op. cit.*, p. 165.   7. *Op. cit.*, p. 143.
8. *Op. cit.*, pp. 191–92.   9. *Op. cit.*   10. *Ratter.*
11. *Op. cit.*, pp. 204, 279.
12. *Op. cit.*, pp. 195–96; Østergaard-Christiansen, p. 58.
13. Østergaard-Christiansen, *At Work With Albert Schweitzer*, Boston,
    Beacon Press, 1962; pp. 66–75.
14. Marshall, *op. cit.*, p. 128 ff.   15. *Edge*, p. 134.

Chapter 16   Albert Schweitzer's Ethics

1. *Edge*, p. 123.   2. *Life*, pp. 156–57.
3. *Teilhard de Chardin Album*, "Spiritual Power of Matter" p. 60.
4. Schweitzer, Albert, *The Philosophy of Civilization* (2 Vols.), Vol. I—
   Decay and Restoration of Civilization, Vol. II—*Civilization and Ethics*,
   New York, Macmillan, paperback ed., 1960, pp. 310–11.
5. Van Paassen, Pierre, *That Day Alone*, New York, Dial Press, 1941, pp.
   372–77.
6. Buber, *op. cit.*, p. 8.
7. Seaver, Appendix I, pp. 317–28, reprint article "Civilization and Colonization," also, see *Edge*, pp. 75–95; 113–18.
8. *Edge*, p. 105.   9. *Ibid.*, pp. 115–16.
10. Schweitzer, Albert, *Indian Thought and Its Development*, Boston, Beacon
    Press, paperback ed., 1960, pp. 83–84.
11. *Life*, p. 233.   12. *Ibid.*   13. *Op. cit.*, p. 234.

Chapter 17   The Challenge of Europe

1. Marshall, p. 104.   2. Schweitzer, *Phil. Civ.* pp. 29–39.
3. *The Christian Century*, published by the Christian Century Foundation,
   407 So. Dearborn, Chicago, Ill., November 21, 1934.
4. Schweitzer, Albert, *Goethe: Five Studies*, Charles Joy editor, Boston, Beacon Press, 1961, pp. 95–100.
5. *Ibid.*
6. Stated in personal conferences between Marshall and Schweitzer in July
   1962. Marshall later sent a copy of his notes to Schweitzer and received
   back a confirmation on November 2, 1962. Schweitzer turned the copy
   over to Frau Lotte Gerhold of Vienna who sat in the conferences as a
   translator, and she confirmed Marshall's notes as corroborating her own,
   with one historical exception (a reference to Charles V) in a letter dated
   March 22, 1963.

7. See Hochhuth, Rolf, *The Deputy*, New York, Grove Press, 1964. Preface, p. 7. (unnumbered)
8. *Men of Dialogue: Martin Buber and Albrecht Goes*, edited by E. William Rollins and Harry Zohn, preface by Martin Friedman, New York: Funk & Wagnalls, 1969, from the address by Martin Buber to German Book Trade (1953), "Genuine Dialogue and the Possibilities of Peace," p. 21.
9. See footnote 6 above.   10. *Chardin Album*, p. 115.
11. *Life*, (Postscript by Everett Skillings) p. 254.   12. *Life*, pp. 251–52.
13. Roback, A. A., *The Albert Schweitzer Jubilee Book*, Cambridge, Mass., Sci-Art Publishers, 1945, p. 26.
14. *Life*, pp. 249–50.   15. *Op. cit.*, p. 188 ff.   16. *Ibid.*

Chapter 18   *War Comes Again*

1. Schweitzer, Albert, *The Hospital at Lambaréné During the War Years 1939–1945*, New York, January 1947, Special Bulletin, The Albert Schweitzer Fellowship, 866 United Nations Plaza. (This 19-page report of Dr. Schweitzer to the supporting agencies is the definitive account of the war years. It has been the source of accounts included in other works such as Skilling's "Postscript" to the 1949 edition of *Out of My Life and Thought*.)
2. *Op. cit.*, p. 5.   3. *Op. cit.*, pp. 4–5.   4. *Ibid.*
5. *Op. cit.*, pp. 5–6.
6. *Op. cit.*, pp. 6–8. See also *Life* (Postscript), p. 260.
7. *Ibid.*   8. *Life*, pp. 269–70.
9. Verification from Dr. Richard Freidmann, long-time resident doctor at Lambaréné and a citizen of Gabon.
10. Schweitzer, *War Years*, p. 17; also *Life*, p. 265.
11. *Op. cit.*, pp. 17–19.   12. Verification by Rhena Eckert-Schweitzer.
13. See Gunther, John, *Inside Africa*, New York, 1955, Harper Bros., for general postwar development of African independence movements. Of special interest is the account of his visit to Lambaréné, chapter 35, "A Visit to Dr. Albert Schweitzer." Also see *The Courier of the Albert Schweitzer Fellowship*, New York, January 1955, for Schweitzer's report "Eight Years in Lambaréné Hospital by Dr. Albert Schweitzer to Friends of the Hospital in all Lands, from 1946 to 1954" (22 pages).
14. Østergaard-Christiansen, pp. 36–37.   15. *Edge*, p. 182.
16. Marshall, who was in Gabon right after the government was seated, heard these accounts repeated by nearly all the Europeans and Americans there. Any hospital staff member of 1960–62 will corroborate.
17. See concluding essay in Joy and Arnold, *The Africa of Albert Schweitzer* entitled "Our Task in Colonial Africa" by Albert Schweitzer.

Chapter 19   *The Postwar World*

1. Letter loaned to Marshall by Magnus Ratter.
2. The Einstein letters were traced by John Denues of Saugatuck, Connecticut, who spent the summer of 1965 in Lambaréné and heard Schweitzer

refer to correspondence with Einstein. That fall Denues, a high school senior, went to Princeton, New Jersey, and traced down the letters which are herewith quoted. Permission to reprint is granted by the Trustee of the Einstein Estate. (Unfortunately Einstein letters to Schweitzer are still being sorted out from the trunks and metal food containers in which Schweitzer dumped his answered mail.)

3. See letters and magazine articles.
4. See Noel Gillespie letter, dated July 12, 1950, describing their visit. Found in A. A. Roback *Realms*, p. 303.
5. From an address of recollections by Mr. Arnold at a ninetieth birthday commemoration and reception for Mrs. Rhena Eckert-Schweitzer, 25 Beacon Street, Boston, (Eliot Chapel) on January 14, 1965.
6. See Emory Ross description in *Saturday Review*, September 1965.
7. *Ibid.*
8. Interview with Dr. Mellon in Haiti in March 1968. There have been a number of magazine articles concerning Mellon's Schweitzer Hospital in Haiti, and a book, *Dr. Mellon of Haiti*, by Peter Michelmore, New York, Dodd, Mead, 1964. (Dr. Mellon suggested some inaccuracies are contained therein.)
9. See Joy, *Albert Schweitzer, An Anthology*, 1947, 1956 & 1965, New York, Harper & Row, and Boston, Beacon, for list of awards and prizes, enumerated in "Biographical Data" specifically see pp. 342–45.
10. See footnote 2 above.   11. *Ibid.*   12. *Cousins*, p. 113.
13. Anderson, Erica, *The Schweitzer Album*, New York, 1965, Harper & Row, p. 20.
14. *Op. cit.*, p. 22. Also draws upon recollections of Rhena Eckert-Schweitzer on occasion of dedication of Louis Meyer Bas-Relief, presented to Unitarian Universalist Association by Friends of Albert Schweitzer, Miriam Rogers, Chairman, in June 1966.
15. Anderson, *op. cit.*, see pp. 118–23 for Schweitzer and European friends.
16. Privately printed and circulated manuscript by Louis Cueto Coll, Santurce, Puerto Rico (1902 McLeary St.).
17. Quotation is from Kinion Friar, *Introduction*, *The Odyssey, A Modern Sequel*, by Nikos Kazantzakis, New York, Simon & Schuster, p. XXIV. (Account from Rhena Eckert-Schweitzer)
18. Anderson, p. 67.
19. See *The Courier of the Albert Schweitzer Fellowship* (January 1955) pp. 6–8.

Chapter 20   The Modern Schweitzer Hospital

1. Christiansen, p. 20.
2. In a library you may find Dr. Nassau's book, *My Ogowe*, long out of print and classed now as a rare book.
3. Dr. Dana Farnsworth in Roback *Realms*, p. 280 ff.
4. Wire-service interviews appearing in the Boston *Globe*, September 6, 1963 and Boston *Sunday Herald*, September 8, 1963.

5. See Appendix for tables.
6. Dr. Takahashi returned to Japan in 1966 in poor health.

Chapter 21   The Man Within

1. *Memoirs*, p. 69.   2. Clark, *op. cit.*, preface.   3. Joy, *Goethe*, p. 3.
4. Unpublished manuscript by Robert Haney, Adams House, Harvard University.
5. *Life*, p. 219.
6. See Sartre, Jean-Paul, *The Words*, New York, Braziller, 1964, p. 2 for Sartre's description of family relationship. Also see Marshall, p. 20.
7. *Life*, p. 149. [This translation has substituted "this attitude" for "world-view" (Weltanschauung).]
8. *Life*, pp. 219, 230.   9. *Ibid.*   10. Cousins, p. 119.
11. *Teilhard de Chardin*, p. 137 (letter of May 27, 1923).
12. See particularly George Seaver, *Albert Schweitzer Christian Revolutionary*, New York, Harper 1944. The three books by George Seaver listed in the bibliography, plus Henry Clark's study, help clarify his sources for his *Philosophy of Civilization*, but his own work of this title is essential for a grasp of his conclusions.
13. Buber, Martin, *op. cit.*, p. 6.   14. Cousins, p. 195.
15. Schweitzer, *Goethe: Five Studies*, p. 6.
16. *Op. cit.*, pp. 6–19.   17. *Goethe*.   18. *Goethe*.   19. *Life*, p. 233.
20. *Goethe*, p. 29.
21. Jack, Homer, "Laughter in Lambaréné," in the *Unitarian Universalist Register-Leader*, January 1965, p. 4.
22. *Memoirs*, pp. 46–49.   23. Related in personal recollections.

Chapter 22   The World Citizen

1. Repeated frequently at Lambaréné by staff members. Retold in various memoirs of visits to Lambaréné.
2. *Ibid.*   3. Cousins, pp. 190–91.   4. *Kingdom of God*, p. 128 fn.
5. Marshall, p. 93.
6. Schweitzer, Albert, *Peace or Atomic War?* New York, Holt, 1958.
7. Frau Lotte Gerhold's notes confirmed Marshall's of these conferences. See above, letter of March 22, 1963 (chapter 17, fn. 6).
8. This quote is from the Washington *Post*—Los Angeles *Times* story of Carroll Kilpatrick appearing in the Boston *Globe*, September 1, 1963.
9. Letter of February 9, 1968.
10. Marshall, p. 166. (This volume—*An Understanding of Albert Schweitzer*—is a study of the area of criticisms.)
11. See Homer Jack's collection of essays and evaluations of Schweitzer: *To Dr. Albert Schweitzer on his 80th Birthday* (a Festschrift), Evanston, Illinois, 1955, Friends of Albert Schweitzer. A truly memorable collection of personalities acquainted with Schweitzer contributed.

12. Du Bois, W. E. B., "The Black Man and Albert Schweitzer" in A. A. Roback *Jubilee Book*, pp. 121–27.

Chapter 23   Last Years and Controversy

1. Marshall, George N., *An Understanding of Albert Schweitzer*, New York, Philosophical Library Inc., 1966.
2. *Reader's Digest*, October 1949. Quoted by Fulton Oursler in article on Schweitzer. It appears elsewhere in books by and about Schweitzer.
3. *Memoirs*, p. 70.   4. *Op. cit.*, pp. 68–69.   5. *Op. cit.*, p. 74.
6. *Life*, Epilogue p. 219.   7. *Memoirs*, p. 76.   8. *Op. cit.*, p. 66.
9. *Life*, pp. 84–85.
10. *This Week Magazine*, New York, "Words to Live By," November 29, 1959.
11. *Reader's Digest*. October 1949, *op. cit.*
12. *Ibid.*
13. Bertrand Russell's letter to the editor was in response to an April 19, 1964 article on Schweitzer, and appeared shortly thereafter.
14. *Memoirs*, p. 65.   15. *Op. cit.*, pp. 66–68.   16. Letter.
17. Monfrini, Henri, *Schweitzer Demain*, Lausanne, Payot, 1966.
18. *Ibid.*
19. Marshall, Appendix A for account of last days by M. Charles Michel, Mme. Emmy Martin and Mlle. Mathilde Kottmann, p. 174.
20. *Ibid.*   21. *Op. cit.*, pp. 10–11.
22. Marshall, Appendix B, pp. 175–77.
23. Letter of Ali Silver dated May 12, 1965.

Bibliography

"Obviously, no book about Schweitzer can substitute for those written by him. When the Doctor was in Oslo in 1954 to receive the Nobel Peace prize, I had the good fortune to meet him and ask him the question, 'Where should I go and under what particular professors should I study in order to get the best possible education in your thought?' His reply to my question . . . 'Read my books! No one can express the ideas of a man so well as he has expressed them himself. . . .'"

Henry Clark
(Preface, Ethical Mysticism of Schweitzer)

This is a working bibliography of works referred to or used as reference in this volume. All are in the English language, and though many were either simultaneously, or earlier, published in England, the editions given are the American. (Standard original German editions of Schweitzer's writings are also given.) Many paperback editions are currently being published and it is not possible to give an up-to-date listing of such. In those instances where we have used the paperback editions, there were no available clothbound editions still in print. The page references given are in every case those of the specific editions used; hence the date and publisher are a key to our references.

The "working bibliography" method that follows consists of listing (1) those books by Albert Schweitzer; (2) collections based on his own words; (3) studies of Schweitzer by others; (4) related works referred to in the text; and (5) recordings and motion pictures. This is followed by (6) the periodical bibliography, which is a listing of the periodicals, journals and news stories referred to in the text and in the notes.

Books by Albert Schweitzer

Schweitzer, *African Notebook*, 1939, New York, Holt. (*Afrikanische Geschichten*, 1938, Leipzig: Felix Meiner.)

Schweitzer, *Christianity and the Religions of the World*, 1939, New

York, Holt. (*Das Christentum und die Weltreligionen*, 1924, Bern: Paul Haupt.)

Schweitzer, *Eight Years in Lambaréné Hospital from 1946 to 1954*, Albert Schweitzer Fellowship, New York, January 1955. (22 pages)

Schweitzer, *The Hospital at Lambaréné During the War Years 1939–1945*, New York, January 1947, Albert Schweitzer Fellowship. (19 pages)

Schweitzer, *Indian Thought and Its Development*, 1960, Boston, Beacon Paperback ed. (*Die Weltanschauung der Indischen Denker. Mystik und Ethik*, 1935 München: Beck.)

Schweitzer, *J. S. Bach*, 1962, Boston, Bruce Humphries (2 volumes paperback). (J. S. Bach, 1908, Leipzig: Breitkopf und Hartel.)

Schweitzer, (with Charles-Marie Widor), *Johann Sebastian Bach—Complete Organ Works*, copyright renewed 1940, New York, G. Schirmer, Inc. Five volumes presenting "a critico-Practical Edition" of the orchestrations with a valuable "Preface containing General Observations and the manner of performing . . . and Suggestions for the Interpretation of the compositions contained in each volume." To understand and appreciate the insight and musical interpretation of Dr. Schweitzer, the reading of these prefaces is a rewarding experience. The orchestrations are standard works for organ performances. (*J. S. Bachs Orgelwerke*, Kritisch-praktische Ausgabe. Zusammen mit Charles-Marie Widor, 1912–1914.)

Schweitzer, (with Edouard Nies-Berger), *Johann Sebastian Bach—Complete Organ Works*, Volume VI, 1954, New York, G. Schirmer, Inc. This work with the collaboration of Dr. Nies-Berger continues the projected series which had been dormant since the death of Charles-Marie Widor, with a new volume. Volumes VII and VIII by Nies-Berger and Schweitzer published in 1967.

Schweitzer, *Kingdom of God and Primitive Christianity*, 1966, New York, Seabury Press. (*Reich Gottes und Christentum*, 1966, München, C. H. Beck.)

Schweitzer, *Memoirs of Childhood and Youth*, 1963, New York, Macmillan paperback ed. (*Aus Meiner Kindheit und Jugendzeit*, 1923, München: C. H. Beck.)

Schweitzer, *Mystery of the Kingdom of God*, 1960, New York, Macmillan. (*Das Abendmahlsproblem*, 1901, Tubingen: Mohr.)

Schweitzer, *The Mysticism of Paul the Apostle*, 1960, New York, Macmillan. (*Die Mystik des Apostels Paulus*, 1930, Tubingen: Mohr.)

Schweitzer, *On the Edge of the Primeval Forest* and *More from the*

Primeval Forest, 1931 (reissued 1961), New York, Macmillan. (*Zwischen Wasser und Urwald,* Bern: Paul Haupt; München: C. H. Beck; *Mitteilungen aus Lambaréné,* Drei Hefte 1925, 1926, 1928, Bern: P. Haupt; München: C. H. Beck.)

Schweitzer, *Out of My Life and Thought,* 1949, New York, Holt, with a "Postscript 1932–49" by Everett Skillings. (*Aus meinem Leben und Denken,* 1932, Leipzig: Felix Meiner.)

Schweitzer, *Paul and His Interpreters,* 1948, New York, Macmillan. (*Geschichte der paulinischen Forschung von der Reformation bis auf die Gegenwart,* 1912, Tubingen: Mohr)

Schweitzer, *Peace or Atomic War?,* 1961, New York, Holt.

Schweitzer, *The Philosophy of Civilization,* two volumes in one: I *The Decay and Restoration of Civilization* (*Kulturphilosophie I: Verfall und Wiederaufbau der Kultur,* 1923, München: C. H. Beck); II *Civilization and Ethics,* 1960, New York, Macmillan paperback ed. (*Kulturphilosophie II: Kultur und Ethik,* 1923, München: C. H. Beck.)

Schweitzer, *The Psychiatric Study of Jesus,* 1943, Boston, Beacon (also in paperback) (*Die psychiatrische Beurteilung Jesu,* 1913, Tubingen: Mohr.)

Schweitzer, *The Quest of the Historical Jesus,* 1961, New York, Macmillan (1968 edition with a new Introduction by James M. Robinson) (*Von Reimarus zu Wrede,* 1906, Tubingen: J. C. B. Mohr; *Geschichte der Leben-Jesu-Forschung,* Neu bearbeitete und vermehrte Auflage des Werkes *Von Reimarus zu Wrede,* 1906, Tubingen: Mohr.)

Schweitzer, "The Religious Philosophy of Kant," 1965, in A *Treasury of Albert Schweitzer,* New York, Citadel. [*Die Religionphilosophie Kants,* 1899, Freiburg i/B.: J. C. B. Mohr (Paul Siebeck)]

Schweitzer, *Reverence for Life,* 1969, New York, Harper & Row. (*Strassburger Predigten,* 1966, München: C. H. Beck.)

Collections and Compilations Based on Dr. Schweitzer's Writings

Charles Joy, ed., *Albert Schweitzer: An Anthology,* 1947, New York, Harper; 1965, enlarged, Boston, Beacon paperback ed. (This anthology of thousands of quotations, topically presented, well indexed and with adequate references to English language editions, is a valuable major source for persons working from a limited library of Schweitzer books, or needing a quick reference for quotable material.)

Charles Joy, ed., Schweitzer; *Goethe: Five Studies*, 1961, Boston, Beacon paperback ed.

Charles Joy, *Music in the Life of Albert Schweitzer*, (with selections from his writings), preface by Charles Münch, 1951, New York, Harper; Boston, Beacon paperback ed.

Schweitzer, *Pilgrimage to Humanity*, 1961, New York, Philosophical Library (a brief anthology, sequentially arranged).

Studies about Schweitzer

Anderson, Erica, *Albert Schweitzer*, 1961, New York and Philadelpia, Chelton Company (in "Meet Your Great Contemporaries" series).

Anderson, Erica, *Albert Schweitzer, Gift of Friendship*, 1964, New York, Harper & Row.

Anderson, Erica, *The Schweitzer Album*,* 1965, New York, Harper & Row.

Anderson, Erica and Exman, Eugene, *The World of Albert Schweitzer*, 1955, New York, Harper.*

Babel, Henry, *Schweitzer tel qu'il fut*, 1966, by les éditions de la Baconniere à Boudry-Neuchâtel, Switzerland. (In French)

L. Østergaard-Christensen, *At Work with Albert Schweitzer*, 1962, Boston, Beacon Press.

Clark, Henry, *The Ethical Mysticism of Albert Schweitzer*, 1962, Boston, Beacon Press. Stress is on the ethical and religious basis of Dr. Schweitzer's mysticism, drawing mainly from his early writings.

Cousins, Norman (with Clara Urquhart), *Dr. Schweitzer of Lambaréné*, 1960, New York, Harper. (Also possesses an excellent photographic section.)

Franck, Frederick, *Days with Albert Schweitzer*, 1959, New York, Holt, Rinehart & Winston. (A helpful volume by the American artist-dentist who worked at the hospital.)

Jack, Homer, ed., *To Albert Schweitzer on His 80th Birthday*, 1955, Evanston, Illinois. A collection of excellent articles. Order through Dr. Homer Jack, c/o 25 Beacon Street, Boston, Mass. 02108.

Joy, Charles and Arnold, Melvin, *The Africa of Albert Schweitzer*, 1948, New York, Harper; 1948, Boston, Beacon Press. (Another excellent photographic-essay book.)

* A superb photographic-essay book.

Joy, Charles, *The Animal World of Albert Schweitzer*, 1951, Boston, Beacon.

Kraus, Oskar, *Albert Schweitzer, His Work and Philosophy*, New York, Macmillan (*sein Werk und seine Weltanschauung*, 1929, Berlin, Pan-Verlag.)

Langfeldt, Gabriel, *Albert Schweitzer, A Study of His Philosophy of Life*, 1960, New York, Braziller. (See critiques below.)

Marshall, George N., *An Understanding of Albert Schweitzer*, 1966, New York, Philosophical Library Inc.

Monfrini, Henri, *Schweitzer Demain*, 1966, Lausanne, Payot. (In French)

Montague, Joseph Franklin (M.D.), *The Why of Albert Schweitzer*, 1965, New York, Hawthorn Books Inc.

Mozley, E. N., *The Theology of Albert Schweitzer*, 1950, London, A. & C. Black.

Phillips, H. M., *Safari of Discovery*, "The Universe of Albert Schweitzer," 1958, New York, Twayne Publishers.

Ratter, Magnus, *Albert Schweitzer: Life and Message*, 1950, Boston, Beacon Press.

Regester, John D., *Albert Schweitzer*, 1931, New York, Abingdon Press.

Roback, A. A., ed., *Albert Schweitzer Jubilee Book*, 1955, Cambridge, Mass., Sci-Art Publisher.

Roback, A. A., ed., *In Albert Schweitzer's Realms*, 1962, Cambridge, Mass., Sci-Art Publisher.

Russell, Mrs. Charles E. B., *The Path to Reconstruction*, New York, Holt; Boston, Beacon Press. "A Brief Introduction to Schweitzer's Philosophy of Civilization."

Seaver, George, *Albert Schweitzer, A Vindication*, 1951, Boston, Beacon Press.

Seaver, George, *Albert Schweitzer, Christian Revolutionary*, 1944, New York, Harper.

Seaver, George, *Albert Schweitzer, The Man and His Mind*, 1947, New York, Harper.

Two commemorative volumes have been published, with notable essayists contributing, by The Friends of Albert Schweitzer, 71 Williston Road, Brookline (Boston), Mass.

Critiques on Schweitzer

Murry, J. Middleton, *The Challenge of Schweitzer*, 1948, London, Jason. Raising the question, "Is Schweitzer a Christian or not?"

and seemingly answering that he is not, in a doctrinal sense. In rebuttal, George Seaver wrote *Albert Schweitzer, A Vindication.*

Knight, Victor, *Verdict on Schweitzer*, 1964, New York, John Day Co. Raised and then purported to answer the question "Is Schweitzer a saint or a fraud?" and was generally regarded as making charges rather than giving a verdict. Marshall's *An Understanding of Albert Schweitzer* devotes a chapter to comments on this book, and covers the same period of Schweitzer's life. Gabriel Langfeldt's volume, *Albert Schweitzer, A Study of His Philosophy of Life*, is a Norwegian psychiatrist's examination of the questions raised by Murry and Knight. Langfeldt (Norwegian) and Monfrini and Babel (French) deal constructively with such criticisms in their languages.

Other Books Referred to in the Text

Beek, M. A. and Sperna Weiland, J., *Martin Buber, Personality and Prophet*, 1968, Glen Rock, N.J., Newman Press.

Bonhoeffer, Dietrich, *Gesammelte Schriften*, ed. by Eberhard Bethge, 1958–1961, München: Chrs. Kaiser Verlag.

Buber, Martin, *Between Man and Man*, 1965, New York, Macmillan paperback.

Cuénot, Claude, *Teilhard de Chardin*, 1965 edition, Baltimore, Helicon Press.

Curie, Eve, *Madame Curie*, 1937, New York, Doubleday, Doran. Translated by Vincent Sheean.

George, André (preface), *Teilhard de Chardin Album*, London: Collins, St. James Pl., (New York: Harper & Row, Inc., 1966), from *L'énergie humaine*, Paris: Sevil, 1962, by Teilhard de Chardin.

Gunther, John, *Inside Africa*, 1953, New York, Harper, Chapter 35, "A Visit to Dr. Albert Schweitzer."

Hochhuth, Rolf, *The Deputy*, 1964, New York, The Grove Press; Preface by Dr. Schweitzer.

Horn, Alfred A. (ed. Ethelrede Lewis), *Trader Horn*, 1927, New York, Simon & Schuster.

Kazantzakis, Nikos, *The Odyssey, A Modern Sequel*, 1958, New York, Simon & Schuster (for the Introduction by Kinion Friar).

Michelmore, Peter, *Dr. Mellon of Haiti*, 1964, New York, Dodd, Mead & Co.

Mouroux, Jean, "A Gift of Presence" in *The Religious Experience* (ed. by George Brantl) 1964, New York, Braziller.

Rollins, E. William and Zohn, Harry, eds., *Men of Dialogue: Martin*

Buber and Albrecht Goes, 1969, New York, Funk & Wagnalls.
Sartre, Jean-Paul, *The Words*, 1964, New York, Braziller.
Turnbull, Colin M., *The Lonely African*, 1962, New York, Simon &
    Schuster
Van Paassen, Pierre, *That Day Alone*, 1941, New York, Dial Press.

Recordings and Motion Pictures

Columbia Masterwork Records, SL-175, Albert Schweitzer, Organ:
    Bach, Mendelssohn. "Recorded at the Parish Church, Günsbach,
    Alsace." Three long-playing recordings of Dr. Schweitzer, 1952–
    53.
16-mm motion picture, sound, color, Albert Schweitzer, photographed
    and prepared by Erica Anderson. Available through film-rental
    agencies or directly from Erica Anderson, Albert Schweitzer
    Friendship House, Hurlburt Road, Great Barrington, Mass.
The Living Work of Albert Schweitzer, produced by Erica Anderson
    and Mrs. Rhena Eckert-Schweitzer, photographed by Erica Ander-
    son. Information as above, or from the Albert Schweitzer Fellow-
    ship, 866 United Nations Plaza, New York, N. Y. 10017.

Periodicals Referred to in Text or Used as Sources

Boston *Globe*, September 1, 1963 (for Carroll Kilpatrick's story from
    Hyannisport of Dr. Schweitzer's letter to President Kennedy).
Boston *Globe*, September 6, 1963.
Boston *Herald*, A.P. Newsfeatures, January 5, 1964.
Christian Century, November 21, 1934, published by Christian Cen-
    tury Foundation, 407 South Dearborn Street, Chicago, Illinois.
Contemporary Review, January 28, 1927.
Life magazine, February 19, 1965.
London *Daily Herald*, April 14, 1954.
New York *Times*, November 5, 1954 (Nobel Peace prize address).
The Observer, London, April 26, 1964; April 19, 1964.
Reader's Digest, October 1949.
Saturday Review, January 14, 1961; March 16, 1963; and May 18, 1957
    "A Declaration of Conscience" issue; September 25, 1965—
    (life assessment).
This Week Magazine, November 29, 1959.
The Unitarian Universalist Register-Leader, January 1965.

A Chronological Biography*

"I owe you a great debt for the chronological biography. Now, at last, I am acquainted with the facts of my life!"

Albert Schweitzer, February 15, 1965
(from a letter to George Marshall)

January 14, 1875—Born at Kaysersberg, Alsace.
1880–84—Student in the village school at Günsbach, Alsace, where his father was pastor.
1885–93—Student at the gymnasium at Mülhausen, Alsace.
October 1893—Studied organ with Widor in Paris.
November 1893—Began studies at the University of Strasbourg.
April 1894 to April 1895—Military service.

1895—Twentieth Year

1896—Resolved to devote life to the direct service of humanity beginning at the age of thirty.
1898—Published first book, a tribute to former organ teacher, Eugene Münch.
1898–99—Studied at the Sorbonne and also studied organ again with Widor.
April to July 1899—Studied philosophy and organ in Berlin.
July 1899—Received doctorate degree in philosophy at Strasbourg.
December 1899—Appointed to the staff of St. Nicholai's Church in Strasbourg.
December 1899—Book on Kant published.
July 1900—Obtained a licentiate degree in theology.
September 1900—Ordained at St. Nicholai as a regular curate.
May 1901—Provisional appointment at St. Thomas Theological School in Strasbourg.
1901—Book on the Last Supper published.

* Following earlier biographical tables prepared by Homer Jack, Charles Joy and A. A. Roback.

October 1903—Appointed principal of St. Thomas College in Strasbourg.

1905—*Thirtieth Year*

January 14, 1905—Informed friends of decision (to study medicine and go to Africa) and began study of medicine in Strasbourg.

1905—Biography of Bach published in Paris; on October 5 attended first lecture in medical school.

1906—Books on Jesus and on organ building and organ playing published.

1908—German edition of biography of Bach published.

1911—Book on Paul published; passed state medical examinations in October.

June 1912—Married Miss Helene Bresslau on June 18.

1912—First of six volumes of his edition of Bach's works published.

February 1913—Received degree of doctor of medicine, after having finished thesis and completed a year of internship.

March 26, 1913—Embarked at Bordeaux for the first sojourn in Africa, building hospital near Lambaréné, Gabon, French Equatorial Africa.

1913—Thesis on the psychiatric study of Jesus published and second edition of his book on Jesus also appeared.

1914—Interned at Lambaréné as an enemy alien (German national).

1915—*Fortieth Year*

September 1915—Concept of *Reverence for Life* conceived while journeying on Ogowe River.

September 1917—Taken to France with wife and interned.

July 1918—Returned to Alsace in an exchange of internees. His mother is killed. His health breaks down.

1919–21—Accepted pastorate at St. Nicholai in Strasbourg and also became a hospital physician.

January 14, 1919—Only child, Rhena, born.

1920—Honorary doctorate from theological faculty in Zürich.

1920–24—Gave lectures and organ concerts in many European countries, first in Sweden, where he realized Lambaréné was not lost to him.

1923—Two volumes of his *Philosophy of Civilization* are published.

April 1924—Second sojourn in Africa.

1926—Moved hospital to new site also near Lambaréné.

1925—*Fiftieth Year*

July 1927—In Europe for lectures and concerts.
August 28, 1928—Received Goethe Prize from the City of Frankfurt.
December 1929—Third sojourn in Africa.
1930—Second book on Paul published.
1931—*Out of My Life and Thought* published.
February 1932—In Europe for lectures, concerts and writing.
April 1933—Fourth sojourn in Africa.
October 13, 1933—Legal establishment of *Association de l'Hôpital du Dr. Schweitzer*
February 1934—In Europe and later gave Hibbert Lectures at Oxford and Gifford Lectures at Edinburgh.

1935—*Sixtieth Year*

1935—Book on Indian thought published.
February 1935—Fifth sojourn in Africa.
September 1935—In Europe to give concerts, deliver second course of Gifford Lectures and to make organ recordings.
February 1937—Sixth sojourn in Africa.
February 1939—Arrived in Europe and returned to Africa on next boat because of imminent outbreak of Second World War.
March 1939—Seventh sojourn in Africa.
1939–44—Retrenchment of hospital program due to World War II. Helene joined him in Lambaréné.

1945—*Seventieth Year*

August 10, 1947—Message to IARF, Berne, Switzerland entitled "Religious Freedom."
October 1948—In Europe for first time since beginning of Second World War.
July 1949—Trip to the United States.
October 1949—Eighth sojourn in Africa.
June 1951—In Europe to visit Mrs. Schweitzer and to give concerts and lectures.
1951—Elected to membership in French Academy.
December 1951—Ninth sojourn in Africa.
July 1952—In Europe to lecture and give recitals.
October 1952—Delivered lecture to the French Academy.
December 1952—Tenth sojourn in Africa.

1952–53—Three 12-inch long-playing records of Bach issued.

November 1953—Awarded the 1952 Nobel Peace prize.

June 1954—In Europe.

November 1954—Delivered speech in Oslo, Norway, on presentation of Nobel prize.

December 1954—Eleventh sojourn in Africa.

1955—Eightieth Year

January 14, 1955—Celebrated eightieth birthday.

October 19, 1955—Honorary Member of British Order of Merit by Queen Elizabeth.

October 22, 1955—Honorary Doctor of Laws from University of Cambridge.

November 11, 1955—Received order Pour le Mérite from West German Republic.

December 1955—Twelfth sojourn in Africa.

April 24, 1957—"Declaration of Conscience" issued in Oslo by Nobel Prize Committee.

May 30, 1957—Death of Mrs. Schweitzer in Switzerland.

December 4, 1957—Thirteenth sojourn in Africa begins; carried ashes of Mrs. Schweitzer for burial in Lambaréné at hospital. Since death of Mrs. Schweitzer, Dr. Schweitzer has remained in Lambaréné. "Others must go and talk now," he says, "my Africans would not understand if I left them at the end."

April 28, 29, and 30, 1958—Three radio appeals from Oslo, Norway: "Peace or Atomic War?"

November 5, 1961—Accepted membership in the Unitarian Universalist Church of the Larger Fellowship.

December 1961—Said there was no question of separating himself from the larger community of Christians or from the traditional churches of Alsace which he served as a minister.

August 1963—Wrote to President Kennedy, hailing test ban treaty.

July 1964—Dr. Schweitzer designated Dr. Walter Munz as doctor in charge, succeeding Dr. Rolf Müller.

1965—Ninetieth Year

January 14, 1965—Celebrated ninetieth birthday. Mayors of Kaysersberg and Lambaréné join together in Lambaréné celebration.

August 28, 1965—Dr. Schweitzer designated his daughter, Rhena, as administrator of hospital.

September 4, 1965—10:30 P.M., Dr. Schweitzer died.

ANALYSIS OF MEDICAL RECORDS AT HOSPITAL SCHWEITZER 1924-1966

YEAR	LETTER	NUMBER OF PATIENTS	NUMBER OF OPERATED-PATIENTS	AVERAGE MONTHLY IN-PATIENTS	AVERAGE MONTHLY GARDIENS	NUMBER OF DEATHS	NUMBER OF BIRTHS	AVERAGE MONTHLY DEATHS	AVERAGE MONTHLY BIRTHS	NUMBER OF LEPERS UNDER TREATMENT
1924	A	(1500)	5(1-5)	(70)						
1925	B	1682	52(6-57)	(100)						
1926	C	(2000)	111(58-168)	(140)						
1927	D	(2500)	114(169-282)	(140)						
1928	E	2408	110(283-392)	(140)						
1929	F	2313	122(393-514)	(140)						
1930	G	1984	128(515-642)	150		148		12		
1931	H	2191	214(642b-855)	154		74		6		
1932	J	2727	429(856-1284)	171		81		7		
1933	K	3407	522(1285-1806)	215	64	97		8		
1934	L	3428	526(1807-2332)	222	71	99		8		
1935	M	3233	403(2333-2734)	241	74	122		10		
1936	O	3382	389(2735-3113)	238	70	119	65	10	5	
1937	P	3693	508(3125-3632)	274	84	102	71	9	6	
1938	Q	4204	429(3633-4061)	243	92	116	90	10	7	
1939	R	3777	409(4062-4470a)	203	83	99	60	8	5	
1940	S	2315	198(4471-4668)	116	43	65	55	5	5	
1941	T	1976	185(4671-4855)	133	30	62	43	5	4	
1942	U	1863	112(4861-4972)	122	29	59	42	5	4	
1943	V	1804	41(4973-5013)	103	12	71	40	6	3	
1944	W	1770	116(5014-5139)	149	31	57	42	5	4	
1945	X	1594	104(5141-5244)	163	58	67	33	6	3	
1946	Y	2216	371(5246-5616)	178	52	92	35	8	3	
1947	Z	3490	606(5618-6223)	193	54	90	50	8	4	
1948	A	3468	523(6225-6747)	247	33	92	52	8	4	
1949	B	2688	378(6748-7125)	263	22	105	50	9	4	
1950	C	2551	467(7126-7589)	154	51	81	68	7	6	61+120=181
1951	D	3101	504(7590-7993b)	191	62	121	78	10	7	162+202=364
1952	E	2145	807(7594-8400)	170	22	97	67	8	6	272+70=342
1953	F	2028	368(8401-8768)	167	46	94	73	8	6	236+51=287
1954	G	2694	317(8769-9085)	195	77	88	77	7	6	243+43=286
1955	H	3090	559(9086-9545)	243	79	81	85	7	7	215+28=243
1956	J	3024	406(9546-9951)	266	72	59	99	5	8	172+36=208
1957	K	3663	488(9952-10439)	318	82	69	113	6	9	171+32=203
1958	L	4097	469(10440-10901)	301	86	94	188	8	16	177+33=210
1959	M	4342	485(10902-11383)	279	85	82	180	7	15	170+26=196
1960	N	4595	511(11384-12077)	327	63	72	197	6	16	156+29=185
1961	O	6240	801(12078-12878)	325	69	108	309	9	26	153+30=183
1962	P	5740	950(12879-13848)	347	102	94	340	8	28	140+21=161
1963	Q	5804	1062(13849-14817)	374	97	113	358	9	30	137+17=154
1964	R	5289	968(14818-15733)	357	112	114	325	10	27	120+14=134
1965	S	5901	1152(15734-19872)	423	136	120	406	10	34	115+18=133
1966	T	5227	1174(19873-21048)	396	68	133	414	11	35	103+16=119
totals:		137,121 (+6000)	18,593				3,805			3,588

CHART OF OPERATIONS, BIRTHS AND DEATHS — LAMBARENE — 1924-1965

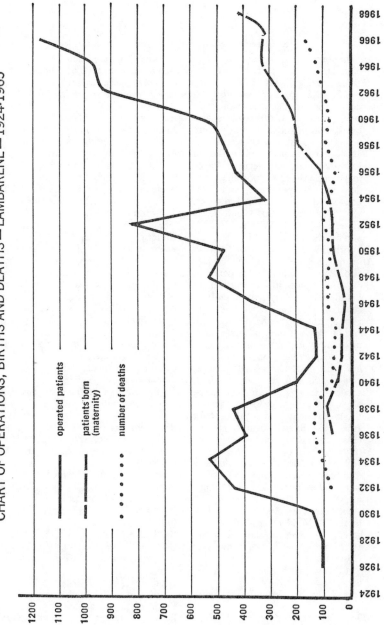

operated patients

patients born
(maternity)

number of deaths

Index